HE WHO OVERCOMES

*Discover the Keys to Overcome
Through a Surrendered Life*

ANGELA G. WALKER

HE WHO OVERCOMES: *Discover the Keys to Overcome through a Surrendered Life*

© Dr Angela G Walker 2023
First Edition

All rights reserved. This book or any portion of it may not be reproduced or used in any manner without the written permission of the author except for the use of brief quotations in a book review or what is allowed under fair use guidelines. The author appreciates the opportunity to share the material in this book and will grant most permission requests quickly.

Unless stated otherwise, scripture quotations are taken from the Holy Bible New International Version (NIV) Bible. Copyright © 1973, 1978, 1984 by International Bible Society.

Scripture marked 'NKJV' are taken from the New King James Version. Copyright © 1982 by Thomas Nelson, Inc.

Scripture marked 'NLT' are taken from the New Living Translation. Copyright © 1996, 2004, 2007 Tyndale House Publishers, Inc.

Scripture quotations marked 'TPT' are taken from The Passion Translation. Copyright © 2014 by BroadStreet Publishing.

Cover Artist & Graphics: Caroline Bishop

ISBN: 9798391973027

Acknowledgements

I would like to thank those who contributed towards the proof-reading and editing of this book, especially Rachel Gray, Steve Hale and Gill Hunt. Thank you so much for all your time and effort!

Also, I would like to thank Caroline Bishop for designing the cover, including the photo-shots, photo editing and graphic design work.

This book is a new version of my previous book *'His Warrior Bride'*. It includes new chapters along with some re-edited chapters from the former book.

HE WHO OVERCOMES

CONTENTS

Introduction 7
1 Understanding the Spiritual Realms 11
2 Walking in Kingdom Authority 21
3 Operating with the Sword of the Spirit 47
4 Recognising Your Spiritual Armour 71
5 Weapon of Fasting 95
6 Power In the Blood 111
7 Overcoming the Battle of the Mind 127
8 Godly Wisdom & Discernment 147
9 Pursuing the Fear of the Lord & Holiness 161
10 Accessing the Courts of Heaven 175
11 Promotion In the Wilderness 193
12 He Who Overcomes 211
Conclusion 229
Appendix A: Prayer 231
Appendix B: Spiritual Discernment 233
Appendix C: Books by the Author 235
Appendix D: About the Author 241

HE WHO OVERCOMES

Introduction

The Spirit of God was moving again in my life as He was preparing me for a new season. After three years serving as a medical missionary with Iris Global in Mozambique, God was redirecting my path. He revealed that my medical tools were no longer to be my main tools but side tools. He was leading me along an unfamiliar path.

To my surprise, He was calling me to serve in another war-torn nation, South Sudan. Unlike Mozambique, there were soldiers with guns parading the streets and barriers patrolled by army men guarding the entrances and exits to every town. It felt like I was living in a military camp. During my time in South Sudan, God spoke to me using spiritual military language, as if I was serving Him in His army. He revealed how the fruit of His Spirit is our spiritual armour and weapons. Our spiritual armour is not something we put on and then take off, but rather something we wear daily as part of our lifestyle.

After my time in South Sudan, the Lord called me to a season of 'assigned rest'. During this season, He was circumcising the different areas of my heart. I felt like I was being shaken as He loosened me from various forms of pride, control, fear, unbelief and insecurities. He was transforming my heart and calling me into a deeper place of union with Him, one of abiding in His Presence.

During this season of rest, I saw God's people in chains lying on the ground and unable to stand. These chains were stopping them from fulfilling His plans and purposes and becoming all they were created to be. These were His wounded warriors. However, once their chains were removed and hearts were healed, they arose as His bridal army. Each person developed their *spiritual* muscles from the fruit of the Spirit, from a place of intimacy in the secret place with Jesus. In this secret place, their wounds were healed as they submitted each area of their orphan hearts to Him. As they humbled themselves before God, they developed a deep awareness of their true identity and divine authority.

I saw King Jesus walking throughout this earth. His robe was huge and formed like a massive canopy that trailed behind Him. Under His robe gathered a bridal company - His end-time army. As He moved throughout the land, people either fled from His most glorious Presence or desperately ran to Him. Those who ran to Him came under His divine protection.

God is preparing a bridal army - those who choose His will above their own and follow Him wherever He goes, and are willing to lay down their lives, whatever the cost. They will overcome by the blood of the Lamb and the word of His (or their) testimony, as they yield their lives to Him, even unto death (Revelation 12:11). These are His sanctified vessels, His laid-down lovers, His worshipping warriors, and His living temples.

May He open the eyes of your heart to seek His face and to not settle for anything less than to see His Kingdom come and will be done. There is nothing to lose but everything to gain as we choose to pursue Him above everything else. May He draw you deeper into the chambers of His heart as you pursue His Presence. The power of love is stronger than life, for love conquers all!

(The words 'bride/bridal', 'son/sonship', 'he/warrior/army', are non-gender specific but refer to both genders in the context of the Body of Christ).

*They conquered him completely
through the blood of the Lamb,
and the powerful word of His testimony.
They triumphed because they
did not love and cling to their own lives,
even when faced with death*

Revelation 12:11 (TPT)

1

Understanding the Spiritual Realms

Our struggle is not against flesh and blood...but against the spiritual forces of evil in the heavenly realms

Ephesians 6:12

IT was during my gap year with Youth With A Mission when a veil was removed from my eyes. I became aware of the unseen realms and that they are more real than the things we see in the visible realm. Suddenly, it dawned on me there were spiritual battles going on in the invisible realms. This was the first time I discovered such a thing known as 'spiritual warfare'.

Paul said: *'Our battle isn't against flesh and blood... but against the spiritual forces of evil in the heavenly realms'* (Ephesians 6:12). As we learn to recognise and overcome the works of the enemy, then we will be in a position to help others overcome. We can only help others overcome what we have already overcome ourselves. We are in the world but not of the world. Jesus who descended also ascended, higher than *all the heavens* (Ephesians 4:10).

There appear to be three heavens, two kingdoms and two realms, so let's take a look at these.

Two Realms

The word *realm* is used when referring to a place and there are two main realms - the natural and supernatural (or spiritual). The *natural realm* refers to what is visible to the natural eyes including the earth and universe, whereas the *supernatural* or *spiritual realm* is what is unseen and invisible to the natural eyes and includes the heavenly realms and hell.

Hence, a *spiritual realm* may be seen as a place or sphere of supernatural activity in the heavens. Whereas the natural realm is temporal, the supernatural realm is eternal. *'So we fix our eyes not on what is seen, but on what is unseen. For what is seen is temporary but what is unseen is eternal'* (2 Corinthians 4:18).

As human beings we have a spirit and our spirit resides in our physical bodies. When we die, our spirit leaves our bodies and God decides where our spirit goes. God is Spirit (John 4:24) and He created us in His image, as spirit beings. Jesus is the Way, the Truth and the Life (John 14:6) and was sent by the Father, as His One and only Son, so that those who believe in Him may have eternal life (John 3:16).

Three Heavens

So the invisible realm consists of the heavens. The first sentence in the Bible says: *'In the beginning God created the heavens and the earth'* (Genesis 1:1). There is more than one heaven but just one earth. God created the whole universe by the words He spoke from His mouth. *'By faith we understand that the universe was formed at God's command, so that what is seen was not made out of what was visible'* (Hebrews 11:3).

It is interesting that the Greek word used in the original translation for 'heaven' in the *'Our Father'* prayer (Mathew 6:9) is actually plural and not singular. In other words, the sentence reads thus: *'Our Father, in the heavens, holy is Your name...'*. This refers to there being more than one heaven, just like the scriptures refer to the 'heavens', 'heavenly realms' and the 'highest heaven'.

Paul makes reference to there being a *third heaven* in the supernatural realms. So if there is a third heaven, then this means there is also a first and second heaven.

First Heaven

It is generally believed the first heaven refers to the earth God created and gave to man. He said: *'Be fruitful and multiply; fill the earth and subdue it. Rule over the fish of the sea and the birds of the air and over every living creature that moves on the ground'* (Genesis 1:28). The highest heavens belong to the Lord, but the earth He has given to man (Psalm 115:16).

Second Heaven

The second heaven is between the first and third heaven and this heavenly realm has become recognised as the demonic realm. This is where the spiritual forces of evil, rulers, and principalities operate, between the third heaven and earth. The demonic realm includes the atmosphere or air around us, because satan is the ruler of the kingdom of the air (Ephesians 2:2). Jesus referred to satan as the prince of this world: *'I will not speak with you much longer, for the prince of this world is coming. He has no hold on Me'* (John 14:30 & John 12:31).

The Bible speaks of there being a war in the heavens where the Archangel Michael and his angels fought against the great dragon and his fallen angels, and hurled them to earth (Revelation 12:7-9).

During Daniel's twenty-one days of prayer and fasting, there was an angel sent by God to Daniel. However, to get from the third Heaven to reach Daniel on earth, the angel had to fight a principality that was obstructing the way. This principality was known as the prince of Persia and was operating in the second heavenly realm (Daniel 10:13).

Our real battles are against the spiritual forces of evil in the heavenly realms: *'For our struggle is not against flesh and blood, but against the rulers, against the authorities, against the powers of this dark world and against the spiritual forces of evil in the **heavenly realms**'* (Ephesians 6:12). This verse reveals there are spiritual forces of evil in the *heavenly realms*, where the demonic forces in the second heaven are influencing people on earth.

Third Heaven

So what about the third heaven? Paul describes an encounter he had in the third Heaven and refers to it as Paradise: *'I know a man in Christ who fourteen years ago was* **caught up into the third Heaven.** *And I know that this man was* **caught up to Paradise**' (2 Corinthians 12:2-4). It is widely believed that the man Paul was referring to was himself, and he states that he didn't know if this experience was 'in the body' or 'outside the body'. In other words, he couldn't tell whether his whole being was in the third Heaven or if it was just his spirit that encountered Paradise.

Jesus spoke about Paradise when the thief on the cross asked Him to remember him in His Kingdom. He replied: *'Today you will be with Me in Paradise'* (Luke 23:43). We see Paradise being mentioned again when Jesus spoke to the church in Ephesus: *'To him whom overcomes I will give the right to eat from the Tree of Life, which is in the Paradise of God'* (Revelation 2:7).

Paradise is thought to be just one of the places in the third Heaven. Some prophets have testified to Paradise being the first of the realms in the third heaven and there are greater realms including the Throne Room and the Holy City (Revelation 3:21, 4:1-4, 21:10). Paul refers to us being seated with Christ in the *Heavenly realms* (Ephesians 2:6).

So the third heaven may be seen as the *highest heavens*: *'To the Lord your God belong the heavens, even the highest heavens, the earth and everything in it'* (Deuteronomy 10:14).

Some people speak about there being an *open heaven*. An open heaven is where there is little, if any, demonic activity between earth and the third Heaven. This is a connection or direct access between earth and the highest Heaven. An open heaven may occur during times of prayer and worship as people engage in God's Presence. Also, there may be some geographical places on earth that are like open heavens where the Presence of God is felt more tangibly.

Satan is a fallen guardian cherub and can only be in one place at any moment in time, for he is a created being (Ezekiel 28:16). God is omnipresent, that is He is everywhere. He created the earth and every being in it. He knows our minds and thoughts, as do His angels whom He may send to minister to us. God is omnipotent, that is all powerful, and omniscient, that is all knowing. He knows everything about us for nothing is hidden from Him (Hebrews 4:13).

Two Kingdoms

A 'king-dom' belongs to a king for it is a king's domain. Though there are many earthly kings, each having a kingdom, there is only One King of all kings and Lord of all lords, and this is Jesus. *'He is dressed in a robe dipped in blood and His name is the Word of God...On his robe and on His thigh is the name written "King of kings and Lord of lords"'*(Revelation 19:16).

There are two main kingdoms in the supernatural realm: the kingdom of darkness which belongs to satan, and the Kingdom of light which belongs to God. However, we read in the book of Revelation: *'The kingdom of the world has become the Kingdom of our Lord, and He will reign forever and ever'* (Revelation 11:15). We have a choice which kingdom we want to live in: to follow the deeds of darkness or choose the Kingdom of light. Jesus said: *'I am the Light of the world. Whoever follows Me will never walk in darkness, but will have the light of Life'* (John 8:12).

The kingdom of satan is also known as the *underworld* or *hell*. This is known as *'Sheol'* in the Old Testament Hebrew language and *'Hades'* in the New Testament Greek language. The good news is that at the name of Jesus every knee will bow, in heaven, on earth and *under* the earth (Philippians 2:10). This means *all* demonic powers and evil spirits come under the authority of the Lord God Almighty.

Some Christians don't believe there is a hell, yet Jesus refers to it a number of times in the scriptures, and there are believers who have testified to encountering hell and even written books on it. Jesus said that those who practice evil will be thrown into the fiery furnace or eternal fire, a place that was meant to be just for the devil and his angels, and there will be weeping and gnashing of teeth (Matthew 13:42, 25:41).

Spiritual Ranking

In the heavenly realms there are celestial or heavenly beings that carry various degrees of supernatural power. In the beginning God created the heavens, the earth and everything in it, therefore God has authority over everything He created (Genesis 1:1). He is the Creator.

After Jesus humbled Himself and became obedient to death on a cross, He was raised to the highest place and given the name that is above all names, that at the name of Jesus, every knee will bow in heaven, on earth and under the earth, and every tongue confess that Jesus Christ is Lord (Philippians 2:9).

Jesus said: *'I am the Living One; I was dead, and behold I am alive for ever and ever! And I hold the keys of death and Hades'* (Revelation 1:18). This means God has *all* authority and power and can choose who He gives it to. Jesus said after His resurrection from the dead: *'All authority in heaven and on earth has been given to Me. Therefore, go...'* (Matthew 28:18). If Jesus has taken back *all* authority, then satan has none!

God created a variety of angelic and supernatural heavenly beings with varying degrees of Kingdom power and authority. Those with the highest authority are thought to be the Cherubim and Seraphim who guard the throne of God (Genesis 3:24, Ezekiel 10:14, Revelation 4:8). The Seraphim are the ones who carry the fire (Isaiah 6:6) and the Cherubim carry the glory (Hebrews 9:5). Whereas the Cherubim have four wings, the Seraphim are described as having six wings. However, the Cherubim are described as the four living creatures who worship around the throne of God having the faces of a lion, ox, eagle and man. The four living creatures are described further in the books of Revelation and Ezekiel (Ezekiel 1:5-9, 10:14, Revelation 4:8).

There are the Archangels, such as Gabriel and Michael, where Michael is seen as the Chief Prince (Daniel 10:13, Luke 1:19, Jude 1:9, Revelation 12:7). Gabriel is thought to be an archangel, though there is no actual reference in the Bible that he is. The Book of Enoch, that wasn't included in the original Hebrew text, refers to there being seven archangels.

Then there are the ministering angels with different levels of ranking and authority who God sends to serve alongside His people (Hebrews 1:14, Mathew 4:11, 26:53). Each servant of God who carries an anointing will have been assigned an angel or angels to minister alongside them to advance God's Kingdom.

Beneath God's heavenly host of angels is the demonic realm. Satan is a fallen cherub, created by God (Ezekiel 28:13-16) who leads the kingdom of darkness. Jesus refers to satan as the prince of this world. Under satan are the powers, principalities and rulers of this world and the spiritual forces of evil (Daniel 10:13, Ephesians 6:12, Colossians 2:15).

Father God, King Jesus & Holy Spirit
& Redeemed Man

Seraphim, Cherubim (Living Creatures)
Arch-Angels

Various Ranking of Angels & Celestial Beings

Guardian Angels

Satan - prince of air & demonic realm (Mathew 12:24)

Principalities, rulers of darkness, evil powers (Ephesians 6:12)

High-ranking demons

Low-ranking demons (1 Corinthians 10:22)

Fallen man

Principalities are high-ranking demonic powers or rulers, that rule over geographical regions, usually nations, like the Prince of Persia. A principality may be defined as this: *'The position of authority of a prince or chief ruler'*[1] and this refers to the supreme power or sovereignty that a prince or ruler has over their state or country.

It was previously believed that a principality couldn't occupy a man, but we read about the demon-possessed man of Gadarenes (or Gerasenes) who carried Legion, representing thousands of demons (Mark 5:1-10). It is believed that Legion was a principality who governed the area. Once the man was delivered from this principality, the atmosphere over the region changed.

Kris Vallotton, author of *Spirit Wars*, says this about principalities: *'Principalities that rule the air are based in people. As these people get delivered, their spheres and realms gain freedom and the "spiritual air pollution" is eradicated'*. [2]

Likewise, territorial spirits are evil powers which rule over selected areas or territories. Jesus commanded us to *disciple nations* (Mathew 28:19). The atmosphere over a region depends on what spirits are influencing the people in the area. Hence, a nation can be changed in a day when the people surrender their lives to Jesus and accept Him as their Lord and Saviour.

There are high and low ranking demonic spirits, and these may dwell in objects, buildings, animals or humans (Revelation 12:7-10). Fallen man is a man who has fallen due to sin and hasn't yet entered into a relationship with God, or may have fallen away from his faith, and is at the very bottom, below the demons.

However, redeemed man is a man who has been born-again and filled with the Holy Spirit, and is seated with Christ in the Heavenly places. *'And His incomparably great power for us who believe. That power is like the working of His mighty strength, which He exerted in Christ when He raised Him from the dead and* **seated Him at His right hand in the Heavenly realms, far above all rule and authority, power and dominion.** *And God placed all things under His feet...'* (Ephesians 1:19-22). Paul continues: **'And God raised us up with Christ and seated us with Him in the Heavenly realms in Christ Jesus'** (Ephesians 2:6).

It is generally believed there are twice as many angels as there are demons, for a third of the fallen angels were hurled with the dragon, satan, down to earth (Revelation 12:4).

Understanding the Spiritual Realms

Man can gain spiritual power either through evil spirits operating in him (known as demonic power) or the Holy Spirit dwelling in him (known as God's Kingdom power). Christ dwelling in us means we have access to be seated with Him in the heavenly realms, above all power and authority. That is why *'He who is in us is greater than the one who is in the world'* (1 John 4:4).

When the seven sons of Sceva commanded the demons to leave a man, the demons didn't budge but instead attacked the seven sons. This was because the sons of Sceva didn't have God's authority to cast out demons for they hadn't received the Holy Spirit. Hence the demon said: *'Jesus I know, and I know about Paul, but who are you?'* (Acts 19:15). Demonic spirits recognise if a person carries the Holy Spirit or not, and the level of Kingdom authority they carry.

God will send His angels to co-labour with us as we minister to His people. *'Are not all angels ministering spirits sent to serve those who will inherit salvation?'* (Hebrews 1: 14).

People who have what is known as a 'prophetic seer' gifting will be aware of the presence of angels because they can 'see' in the spirit realm more easily than others do. Those in ministry may be more aware of the angelic realm or God's celestial beings in the atmosphere around them, especially when the anointing begins to flow and signs, healings and wonders follow.

Jesus went around preaching to the unsaved: *'Repent for the Kingdom of Heaven is near'* (Matthew 4:17), but He said to the believer: *'The Kingdom of God is within you'* (Luke 17:21). Hence, God's Kingdom is near for anyone who wants to invite Jesus into their hearts, and when we do, His Kingdom is now within us.

Jesus said: *'From the days of John the Baptist until now, the Kingdom of Heaven has been forcefully advancing, and forceful men lay hold of it'* (Matthew 11:12).

I believe God is calling us to advance His Kingdom here on earth, and we can do this as we say the words He taught us to pray: *'Your Kingdom come, Your will be done, on earth as in Heaven!'* (Mathew 6:10). As we declare these words daily in our prayers, we will start to see things shifting in the heavenly realms, as we see God's Kingdom advancing, on earth as in heaven.

Lord Jesus, I ask for a fresh revelation of Your heavenly realms and the celestial beings, including the angelic realm. Help me to see that the unseen realm is more real than the visible realm. Open my eyes to see and my ears to hear all that You want to reveal to my spirit, in Your Mighty Name.

END NOTES

[1] Collins English Dictionary
[2] Vallotton, Kris. *Spirit Wars,* p 182 *(Chosen Books, 2012)*

2

Walking in Kingdom Authority

All authority in heaven and on earth has been given to me. Therefore, go and make disciples of all nations

Mathew 28:18

God gives us a measure of His divine authority the moment we step into His Kingdom as a born-again believer and follower of Jesus. However, we *grow* in our spiritual authority as we grow in our relationship with Him. A new born-again believer is like a new-born baby in the Kingdom, and acquires more Kingdom authority as they are nurtured through the various stages of sonship. Therefore, spiritual authority increases with our spiritual growth and continues to grow until we attain the fullness of sonship, carrying the heart of the mature bride of Christ.

Kingdom authority has nothing to do with going to Bible College or gaining academic qualifications, but is gained from pursuing an intimate relationship with Jesus and living a Spirit-filled and Spirit-led lifestyle.

As we discover our true spiritual identity we can step into our Kingdom authority. This is because as we grow closer to God we become more aware of our spiritual identity and the authority we carry as His children. Hence, we grow in our Kingdom authority as a result of pursuing an intimate relationship with Father God, King Jesus and Holy Spirit.

During a season in my life, the Lord stirred my spirit to take some time-out from my medical career, so I decided to take a two month sabbatical. In this season, I spent my mornings with God, listening to Him and seeking His Presence. At the end of this season of drawing closer to God, a close friend of mine observed a difference in me. She commented that she hadn't seen me pray with such authority as she did when I prayed with her that day. I smiled as I realised how God had increased my measure of authority as a result of my drawing closer to Him. I have noticed this again and again in people who pursue a lifestyle of intimacy and divine sonship with Him.

What is Authority and Power?

The Oxford English Dictionary defines 'authority' as: *'The power of right to give orders, the right to act in a specified way delegated from one person or organisation.'* Authority is a legal or rightful power given to a person by virtue of his office or ranking, granted by someone in greater office. For example, a police officer is given authority because it has been given him by someone in legal office who is of a higher rank than himself.

The Centurion who asked Jesus to heal his servant had such faith in Jesus that he believed his servant would be healed. This was because he was aware of the power and authority Jesus carried to heal the sick and set the captives free. His reply to Jesus was this: *'For I myself am a man under authority, with soldiers under me. I tell this one, 'Go' and he goes; and that one 'Come' and he comes'* (Luke 7:8). The Centurion understood authority for he was under the authority of someone in greater office, and had been delegated a level of authority from this person.

In the New Testament, the Greek word for 'authority' or 'delegated power to act' is *exousia*[1] and refers to God's Kingdom authority being released to His people.

However, power is not the same as authority. The Oxford English Dictionary defines 'power' as: *'Strength or force exerted by something or someone, the ability or capacity to do something or to direct or influence the behaviour of others'*. In other words, power is a force or strength exerted by someone who isn't necessarily in authority or under legal authority. You can have power but not necessarily have authority. For example, a muscular person may exert their physical power to subdue another person. Or power may be used to get others to do what you want them to do. A rich individual may use the power of their wealth in order to get people to do what they want.

The enemy has no Kingdom authority because he no longer belongs to the Kingdom of God, but only has power that is given to him by man.

One of the Greek words for power is *dunamis* meaning 'dynamite', and is used when referring to the power to do His mighty works, and this is used when referring to God's 'miraculous power'[2]. However, we can only walk in God's *dunamis* power if we have received His *exousia* authority.

Kingdom Authority

Kingdom authority is authority which comes from God since He is the King or ruler of His domain. 'King-dom' means the King's domain. Jesus said before Pontius Pilate that He was a King but His Kingdom was not of this world but from another place (John 18:36). Jesus is the King of all kings and Lord of all lords that at the name of Jesus every knee will bow and every tongue confess that Jesus Christ is Lord (Philippians 2:10-11).

Hence, Kingdom authority is the authority given by God to those who have a personal relationship with Him. So when does a person have spiritual authority? A person has authority the moment they accept Jesus into their lives to be their Lord and Saviour. Many new born-again believers witness healings and miracles when they start to pray for people. God loves it when He sees His little ones ministering by faith to others, and He releases His angels to assist them as they minister to others.

God so wants to share His authority with frail men, women, and children. I have seen little children who have received Jesus in their hearts, operate with His divine authority when they have prayed for the sick. They lay hands on them and say a simple prayer like 'be healed in Jesus Name' or 'sickness go, in Jesus Name' or 'Jesus heal' and the person starts to recover. God rejoices when little ones start learning how to walk in their *exousia* authority.

Kingdom authority is from the inner man or spirit, whereas worldly authority is from the soul. The purpose of Kingdom authority is to destroy the works of the enemy and to heal the sick, cleanse the lepers, set the captives free, raise the dead and release the prisoners from darkness. It is to build up the body of Christ and advance God's Kingdom here on earth (2 Corinthians 10:8).

Whilst I was doing a medical outreach in Mozambique an old lady came to see me who presented with 'fits' for the first time in her life. On a previous visit, she had received Jesus in her heart and since then, she had started to have a fit every few hours or so, every day. She wanted some medicine but I sensed the fits were due to witchcraft and encouraged her to take authority over the fits in Jesus' name. Though she had only been a born-again believer for a few weeks, she followed the advice I gave her. Before the clinic finished, she returned with a smile on her face and said when she felt a fit come upon her, she pointed her finger and told it to go in Jesus name! And the symptoms instantly left her. After recognising the authority she carried as a new born-again believer in Christ, she wanted to go around her village and pray for those who were sick. She had the revelation that God's Spirit in her was greater than the demonic spirits operating in the people in her village (1 John 4:4).

Many think only a pastor has authority to heal the sick and cast out demons when in actuality the Lord gives authority to all His Spirit-filled believers. One of the roles of a pastor is to encourage and empower the body of Christ to walk in their God-given authority as children of the King, since Jesus is head of the church, the body of Christ.

One day, whilst prayer walking around the walls of Chester, I noticed a group of little children wearing Roman costumes with plastic swords in their hands. They were being taught Roman history and pretending to be soldiers. However, I sensed in my spirit that Jesus wanted them to know for real how to overcome the enemy. We don't have to wait until we are a certain age in God's Kingdom before we receive His authority. The enemy is prowling around looking for vulnerable little ones to destroy. The sooner we become filled with God's Spirit, the quicker we can learn how to walk in His authority and use our spiritual swords for real.

I was teaching a group of children at church on healing when one little boy bravely shared that he had been having nightmares. Another child in the group had also suffered with nightmares but testified to being healed after receiving prayer. So I asked the child who was healed to pray for this little boy. She laid hands on him and said a simple prayer of faith. The next Sunday, the little boy testified to having no more nightmares after receiving prayer. *'From the lips of children and infants You have ordained praise because of your enemies, to silence the foe and avenger!'* (Psalm 8:2).

Those who are employed by a business or company will come under the authority of their manager or boss. The boss decides what level of power and authority he will delegate to each of his workers. He will give greater authority to those who please him and whom he trusts. Likewise, God releases greater Kingdom authority on those He trusts because He has seen them walk in His ways, seek His truth, be led by His Spirit, and carry His heart for His people.

God is after our hearts and sees what is in them as He allows us to undergo various tests of the heart as part of our boot-camp training. This includes facing various trials (spiritual, emotional, mental, and physical), as we learn to overcome the ways of the enemy.

As already mentioned, Kingdom authority is not gained from going to Bible school or studying theology or on a basis of who you know. It is also not based on how much knowledge we have. Rather, it comes from an intimate relationship with God. Jesus never went to Bible College and didn't have a theology degree. He learnt directly from His Father and by reading the scriptures. '*When Jesus had finished saying these things, the crowds were amazed at His teaching, because* **He taught as one who had authority [exousia],** *and not as their teachers of the law*' (Mathew 7:28-29).

The disciples were seen as unschooled, ordinary people (Acts 4:13). Yet they walked in *dunamis* power and had *exousia* authority, as a result of coming *under* the authority of Jesus. '*When the seventy-two disciples returned to Jesus they said, "Lord, even the demons submit to us in Your Name", and Jesus replied, "I saw Satan fall like lightning from Heaven. I have* **given you authority to trample on snakes and scorpions and to overcome all the power of the enemy**; *nothing will harm you*"' (Luke 10:17-19). Jesus has given us authority to overcome ALL the power of the enemy.

Satan has power but no authority for he was kicked out of God's Kingdom as a result of his rebellion, pride, and selfish-ambition. He only has the power of a fallen cherub, and that which has been given to him by man. When Adam and Eve sinned, they gave their authority to him. When satan tempted Jesus in the desert, he showed Him the kingdoms of the world and said: '*I will give you all their authority and splendour,* **for it has been given to me**, *and I can give it to anyone I want to*' (Luke 4:6).

After Jesus took all our sin on the cross, He went down to Hades and took back the keys that Satan had stolen (Revelation 1:18). Keys represent authority, and Jesus took back the stolen authority. Hence, when He appeared to His disciples after His resurrection He declared: '**All authority [exousia] in Heaven and on earth has been given to Me. Therefore, go and make disciples….**' (Mathew 28:18). Remember, if Jesus has *all* authority, this means satan now has *none!*

Growing in Spiritual Authority

We all have a measure of authority as children of God and it is good when we are aware of the measure we carry at any moment in time in our walk with Him. Each of us has a *sphere* of authority which God has given us and this may be over our families, churches, work places, communities, or nations. Our sphere of authority is recognised especially where we see the

Holy Spirit working powerfully through us or over a designated area of responsibility.

God gives His children different measures of divine authority as they grow and mature in their relationship with Him. The greater the depth of intimacy (through yielding ourselves to Him), the greater the authority we receive. Isaiah referred to a greater level of authority, known as 'governmental authority' that rested on the shoulders of the Messiah (Isaiah 9:6). This is authority which carries a responsibility and is for those who are called to govern God's people. Governmental authority rests on those called and appointed by God to be apostles, prophets, evangelists, pastors and teachers, whose purpose is to train and equip the body of Christ (Ephesians 4:11).

However, God is the one who appoints and anoints such people to positions of governmental authority, for He is the one to release His authority to do such work in His Kingdom. Such people whom God chooses have walked with Him through seasons of brokenness, dying to their flesh, and being spiritually prepared as they journey with Him through wilderness seasons. Their hearts have been tested and refined through His fire, as they have encountered valleys and climbed spiritual mountains, and overcome the world, flesh, and enemy during this process. This was seen in the lives of those like Joseph, Moses, Esther, David, Jesus, and His disciples.

Our spiritual authority increases as we choose to pursue an intimate relationship with Jesus. The disciples carried authority because they followed Jesus, obeyed Him, and hung out in His Presence. During the seasons I have taken time-out to go deeper with God, I have noticed a growth spurt in my spirit and an increase in divine authority.

Here are some of the things I've noticed that can influence our growth in spiritual authority:

Surrendered Life

Jesus walked in governmental authority because He chose to live a fully surrendered life, even to the point of death on the cross. He demonstrated a humble servant heart:

'Who being in the very nature God, didn't consider equality with God something to be grasped, but made Himself nothing (of no reputation), taking the very nature of a bond-servant, being made in human likeness. And being found in appearance as a man, He humbled Himself and became obedient to death- even death on a cross.' (Philippians 2:7-8).

God promoted Jesus to the highest place of authority in His Kingdom as a result of His humble, servant heart and sacrificial love. Therefore, satan had no hold on Him (John 14:30).

Our willingness to yield or submit to others in authority determines the level of authority we are given. Jesus demonstrated complete submission to His Father's will and authority but also submitted, where appropriate, to the governmental authorities. He said: *'Whoever humbles himself like a little child is the greatest in the Kingdom of Heaven'* (Matthew 18:4). Those who carry significant authority in His Kingdom are those who walk in great humility. Bill Johnson once said: *'We are to rule with the heart of a servant and serve with the heart of a king'*.

It was pride, control and rebellion that led satan to fall and lose his authority in the Kingdom. Likewise, unless we allow God to address these orphan areas in our hearts, our spiritual growth and authority will be stunted. Jesus taught and ministered *with* spiritual authority because He served *under* His Father's authority. He said: *'I tell you the truth, the Son can do nothing by Himself; He can do only what He sees His Father doing, because whatever the Father does, the Son also does'* (John 5:19).

The Lord took me through a season when He was asking me to simply serve others and not focus on frontline ministry. He revealed how a servant heart is of great value in His Kingdom and is required by those He calls into ministry. During this season, I discovered how God is more bothered about the attitude of our hearts than the 'ministry' we do. He wants us to focus more on Him instead of our work. When we have truly grasped what it means to be His servant, we will no longer be bothered by the work we do, because our hearts will be set on pleasing our King. Jesus said: *'Whoever serves Me must follow Me; and where I am, My servant will also be. My Father will honour the one who serves Me'* (John 12:26). Our Father honours those who humbly serve Him and want to please Him alone.

Many years ago, while spending time with the Lord, I had a vision. In this vision, I saw a white battle ship called *His Majesty's Service* (HMS) and Jesus was the captain. He appointed people of various military rankings amongst the team to operate in different functions. As I was shown around the ship, I noticed there were Generals and Commanders who carried great authority, but as I looked into their eyes, I saw profound humility within their hearts. The authority we are given is in proportion to the humility we carry in our hearts because the Lord exalts the humble (1 Peter 5:6).

Jesus demonstrated humility as He took up a towel and washed His disciple's feet. He told Peter that unless he let Him wash his feet, he would have no part in Him (John 13:7-8). He demonstrated how He came to serve and not be served, and has called us to do likewise, with a yielded servant heart.

Spiritual Identity

Our measure of spiritual authority is influenced by our divine identity. A child may be aware of their parents and the authority their parent's carry, but not necessarily aware of their own identity. However, as they begin to grow they will start to discover their true inherited identity as sons or daughters, and not only that, but the authority they carry. The more we become aware of who we really are in God's eyes and how He sees us, the greater the authority we carry.

Authority goes hand-in-hand with nurturing our spiritual identity. Our spiritual identity is more than just the knowledge of who we are, for it requires a revelation in our hearts and spirit of what it means to be His royal princes and princesses, as sons and daughters of the King. Those who walk in Kingdom authority have a deep awareness of who they are in Christ. This is the result of walking intimately with Him, and pursuing His Presence.

I was at a mission conference where the guest speaker, Philip Mantofa, came on the main stage to speak. I had never seen or heard this man before, but I will never forget what the Lord revealed to me as this man of God walked quietly along the stage and looked intently at the audience. He did this for a few minutes in silence and as he did, I sensed he was listening to God. During these few minutes of silence, I saw in the spirit that he was a man who carried great humility and authority. I discerned in the spirit that he was a General in God's army who knew exactly who he was and the measure of authority he carried. The mighty warriors of God are those who walk in great humility with an awareness of their identity and authority, as royal sons and daughters of the King.

Prayer & Fasting

Something else that may release an increase in our spiritual authority is prayer and fasting. When we fast we are submitting our flesh to come under our spirit, as we abstain from food or other things for a period of time. Our spirit grows in authority as we yield our flesh to God and let Him be Lord in our life. Fasting can be a routine part of our lifestyle. I have not yet seen a man or woman of God who carries significant Kingdom authority who doesn't fast, for fasting has become a part of their lifestyle.

The Lord prompted me to fast during specific seasons in my life and especially during certain assignments. Fasting can help sanctify the body, soul and spirit and increases our level of spiritual awareness. It releases a greater authority for the assignments that lie ahead. As people fast, their spirit becomes sharper and more sensitive to the promptings of the Holy Spirit. *(For more see 'Weapon of Fasting' Chapter 5).*

Overcoming Tests and Trials

Jesus fasted for forty days in the wilderness and during this season He overcame trials and temptations from the enemy. He went in the wilderness *filled* with the Holy Spirit but came out of the wilderness having been promoted in the *power* of the Spirit.

Once we overcome the orphan areas in our hearts and minds (such as fear, pride, lust, control, intimidation, doubt, bitterness, addictions, and so on) we are then in a position to help others overcome. This is because the ungodly spirit behind the negative influence no longer has a hold on us. It is like climbing up a mountain. Once we have mastered how to get to the next level, we are in a position to help others reach that same level. Hence, whatever we have overcome, we now have the authority to help others overcome.

I believe we all have spiritual mountains to climb that involve overcoming trials and tests at different stages in our spiritual journey with God. As we pass each test, the lighter our burden becomes and the further we progress, and greater is the authority we carry.

David, Moses, Joseph, and the Apostles, each had their mountains to climb and obstacles to overcome before entering their governmental callings and destinies. Likewise, Jesus was tested in every way during His time in the wilderness and overcame with humility, complete surrender and obedience to God's will.

'Consider it pure joy, my brothers, whenever you face trials of many kinds, because the testing of your faith produces perseverance...Blessed is the man who perseveres under trial, because when he has stood the test, he will receive the crown of life' (James 1:2-12).

Sanctified Lifestyle

Our journey along the path of Life with Jesus is one of a sanctified lifestyle. The closer we draw to God, the more our hearts become purified. The measure of Kingdom authority is related to the level of purity and holiness in our hearts.

Jesus is looking for a pure and spotless bride, a bride who has made her heart ready for Him (Revelation 19:7). *'Just as He who called you is holy, so be holy in all you do; for it is written: "Be holy, because I am holy!"'* (1 Peter 1:16).

Waiting on the Lord & Divine Appointments

Authority may be released in greater measure when we spend time waiting on the Lord and pursuing His Presence. These times of waiting may include divine appointments or encounters with God.

The Apostles waited on the Lord in the upper room for a period of days before they had a divine encounter with Him. The *dunamis* power of His Spirit came mightily on them at Pentecost in the form of tongues of fire and a violent wind. After this encounter, they stood up and spoke to the crowds with holy boldness and *exousia* authority.

'Those who wait on the Lord will renew their strength. They will soar on wings like eagles; they will run and not grow weary, they will walk and not be faint' (Isaiah 40:31).

The Lord may invite each one of us to enter seasons where we seek His face and wait on Him. And as we respond to this invitation of deep calling unto deep, He will reach deeper into the areas of our hearts and release greater authority in exchange.

What Do We Have Authority Over?

Naturally, we become aware of the authority we carry in the workplace and home, depending on our role or function. Also, we can be a godly influence in the family, workplace, or neighbourhood, as we become aware of the spiritual authority we carry.

Authority Over Demons

All who are filled with the Holy Spirit have power and authority to overcome the works of the enemy. Jesus gave us authority to heal the sick, cleanse the leper, raise the dead and cast out demons (Mathew 10:8). Demons have to surrender to the Name of Jesus, when the words are spoken by a Spirit-filled believer. At the Name of Jesus *every* knee will bow and this includes demonic spirits (Philippians 2:10).

Remember, Jesus has given us *all* authority which means satan has none (Mathew 28:18). When Jesus released His authority and power to His disciples, it was for them to minister to others to bring salvation, healing and deliverance. When they returned from healing the sick and casting out demons, Jesus said: *'I have given you authority to trample on snakes and scorpions and to* **overcome all the power of the enemy***; nothing will harm you'* (Luke 10:19).

Demons have to surrender to those who carry the Spirit of God, though not all people who profess to be Christians or are church-goers, have received the Holy Spirit as a result of the atoning work of Christ. There was a Jewish chief priest named Sceva who had seven sons. His sons assumed they could cast out demons, probably because they saw others declaring the words *'In the Name of Jesus'*, and maybe because their dad was a man of authority. They said: *'In the Name of Jesus, whom Paul preaches, I command you to come out!'* However, one day when they tried to cast out a demon, the demon replied: *'"Jesus I know, and I know about Paul, but who are you?" Then the man with the evil spirit jumped on them and beat them that they ran out bleeding and naked'* (Acts 19:13-16). The problem was these men hadn't received the Holy Spirit, so they lacked Kingdom authority. The demon wasn't fooled by them, even though they declared the words *'In the Name of Jesus'*. Instead, the demon had more power and therefore could attack these men.

Jesus said to Peter: *'I will give you the keys of the Kingdom of Heaven; whatever you bind on earth will be bound in Heaven and whatever you loosen on earth will be loosened in Heaven'* (Mathew 16:19). The keys represent spiritual authority. We can take authority over our situations or circumstances, especially when things may seem to be going wrong or coming against us.

To bind is to tie up. I believe Jesus is referring to binding the strongman or demonic spirits in each other or in our circumstances. To loosen is to release or set free. Jesus later repeats this same word to others (Mathew 18:18-20). He said: *'If I drive out demons by the Spirit of God, then the Kingdom of God has come. Or again, how can anyone enter a strongman's house and carry off his possessions unless he first ties up the strongman?* '(Mathew 12:29). First, we are to tie up or bind the demonic or evil spirit, then we can cast it out and loosen the person from being under its influence.

I believe the authority we have in Christ is to free each other from demonic spirits, as well as setting ourselves free. This includes authority over sickness and anything we find personally attacking us or coming in the midst of relationships.

Authority Over Our Bodies

Did you know you have authority over your body? There is a saying: *'You are what you eat'*. Likewise, we are what we think or speak. If we speak curses over ourselves, then we will be affected by what we say. And if we speak blessings over ourselves, then we will be blessed. It is so easy to self-curse by speaking negative words over ourselves, such as: *'I'm stupid, ugly, a failure, will never succeed, will never have friends, will always be poor, will have this sickness for life, I hate myself, I wish I was dead or not born, etc'*. We are to recognise this behaviour to prevent ourselves from saying or thinking such negative words or word-curses to our bodies. If we have spoken any word-curses then we can break them *in the name of Jesus* and instead thank God for creating us in His image! If there is anything that is malfunctioning, then we can command it to function properly in Jesus' Name and bless it, instead of cursing it.

Many times people have asked me to pray for their symptoms but if they are Spirit-filled believers, I have encouraged them to take authority over their own bodies.

There was a lady who had been struggling to eat food. Anytime she ate she experienced upper abdominal pain. The excess acid she produced caused her intense stomach pain, and so she developed a fear of eating. First, I encouraged her to repent and renounce the spirit of fear that was behind her eating. After this, I encouraged her to take authority over her acid production. So she commanded her acid levels to come down and her stomach to produce the right amount needed to digest her food. After taking authority, she then declared the peace of God over her stomach. She blessed her stomach and thanked God for creating it. I was with her when she had her next meal and she ate without experiencing any stomach pain. She couldn't believe it. I encouraged her to walk in authority instead of fear, and she was able to eat having no more symptoms of pain.

Another friend developed intolerance to cow's milk at the age of forty. Her bowels reacted each time she drank milk so she opted for a cow's milk-free diet. I encouraged her to take authority over her gut and bind any reaction to milk, then to bless her gut, commanding it to tolerate milk again. She did and by faith drank some milk. It had no effect on her bowels and she started to drink cow's milk again.

We must be careful not to come under a medical label or speak negatively about our bodies, but instead take authority over our symptoms or body parts and command them to function normal again, as God designed them to be, in the Name of Jesus. If we thank God for our bodies and speak blessings on them instead of curses, it is powerful. There have been times when I have felt pain or numbness develop in various parts of my body for no apparent reason. I have refused to accept it, instantly rejected it and commanded the pain to leave. I then blessed that part of my body and declared it to have normal function, in Jesus' Name. In the majority of cases the symptoms disappeared, as I took authority by faith and no longer focused on the symptoms.

Obviously, I am not advising people to stop taking their medication, especially if it is a life-saving drug to prevent a medical crisis. Rather, I am encouraging you to bless your bodies instead of cursing them, and to see the positive effects from doing this. If you are taking any medicines and experience the healing power of prayer, then it is best to discuss matters further with your doctor who can advise you accordingly.

When Paul was shipwrecked on the island of Malta, a snake wrapped itself around his arm but he threw it off. Everyone thought he would die of poisoning but he didn't. He had authority to overcome any harmful effects the snake had on his body (Acts 28:5).

Similarly, Jesus was never sick, for the enemy was never allowed to have a hold on Him. The cells in our bodies respond to authority in our spoken words, whether we speak blessings or curses. Hence, we can command the cells to function normally and command the sickness, pain or cancer cells to go, in Jesus' Name, and then see God work as we speak such words with faith and authority.

Authority Over Buildings, Lands & Objects

As well as residing in humans, demons may reside in buildings, land, or objects. Buildings, including homes and churches, may contain demonic spirits. Even non-Christians have commented on some buildings as being 'haunted'. There is usually an eerie feeling, or an uncomfortable presence is felt when demons reside in places. Some people may have nightmares as a result of an evil spirit lingering in their room. This may be because there was previous abuse, evil practice, or death in the room.

Sometimes, worship may be stifled in churches or buildings because there are oppressive or ungodly spirits present. Just as God has given us authority over our spiritual homes, that is, our bodies, so He has given us authority over our physical homes or places where we work and worship. The atmosphere shifts and the aroma changes when God's Presence is there.

There are different ways we may spiritually cleanse our land or buildings. However, the best way is to be led by the Holy Spirit. Sometimes, it may be right to fast and pray with others. Other times, it may be right to repent of the previous sins linked to the land or building. After the repentance and confession of the sins of the people, we may feel led to bind the demonic spirit(s) over the land or building, commanding them to leave and never return in Jesus' Name. Finally, we can pray a cleansing over the land or defiled building with the precious blood of Jesus. Some may feel led to take communion, and sprinkle the communion wine on the land. Others may be led to anoint the walls or land with oil, or put stakes in the land with words of scripture. As we listen to the Holy Spirit, He will prompt us what to do.

Once the building or land has been spiritually cleansed, we can bless the land or building with the *shalom* or peace of God. Jesus told the disciples to say 'peace' to the homes they entered (Luke 10:5). At the end, we can ask God to cover and protect the land or building, with His angels and wall of fire (Zechariah 2:5).

On one occasion, whilst in South Sudan, we felt our mission base needed a spiritual cleansing as a result of the previous sins committed on the land. So we repented for the sins and atrocities, including any murders, rivalry, and sexual acts, then we prayer walked around the land. As we did, we anointed the fences with oil and placed prophetic scriptures in the four corners of the land. We finished by consecrating the land with Communion wine, declaring it cleansed by His blood. Finally, we asked the Lord to send His angels to guard the walls and put a wall of fire around us. There was a fresh feel on the land after doing this. However, this was something we had to repeat whenever we sensed a defiling spirit had come on the land.

God told His people that if they humbled themselves, turned from their wicked ways and sought His face, He would forgive their sins and *heal their land* (2 Chronicles 7:14).

Demons may reside in objects, such as stones, books, crystals, jewellery, fetishes, ornaments, and so on. People may have certain objects because they were given them as presents, or they believe the objects have powers to heal them and keep evil spirits away. The truth is, they probably contain evil spirits and should be destroyed so no-one else can fall victim to them. I have been in people's homes and sensed something evil coming from an ornament or object. People can be under a curse or even fall sick as a result of some demonic object being in their house. Once the object is removed and destroyed, the evil lifts and people can start to recover. We can ask God if there is anything we possess that may have evil spirits residing in it. No matter how dear it may be, it is probably best to get rid of it.

There was an African teenage boy who needed to be delivered from an oppressive spirit. The Holy Spirit revealed an object, similar to a voodoo doll, to be in his possession. After he confessed to having one, he agreed to destroy it. His symptoms lifted as he was delivered from this oppressive spirit. He was a different person and his countenance changed once he was set free.

The Lord said to the Israelites not to bring any idols or carved images into their homes. *'The images of their gods you are to burn in the fire...do not bring a detestable thing into your house, or you, like it, will be set apart for destruction'* (Deuteronomy 7:25-26). Hence, we should take note of what we allow in our buildings. In the same way we can physically cleanse our homes or land, so we can spiritually cleanse them from any spiritual defilement.

Authority Over Nature

God has given man authority over animals and nature. He told Adam and Eve that they had rulership over the fish of the sea, the birds of the air and *over every living creature* (Genesis 1:28). This is confirmed in Psalms: *'What is man that You are mindful of him? You made him ruler over the works of Your hand; You put everything under his feet; all flocks and herds and the beasts of the field, the birds of the air and fish of the sea, all that swim the paths of the sea'* (Psalm 8:5-8).

We have been given authority over every moving creature whether in the sea, air, or on the land. Jesus said we have authority to trample on the snakes and scorpions (Luke 10:18).

I was taking a walk along a beach in Mozambique when a strange dog started to run in my direction. It was barking and didn't look happy as it charged straight towards me. So I raised my hand and said in a firm voice, 'Stop, in Jesus' Name!' Then it suddenly skidded to a stop, looking straight at me. In a firm voice, I pointed my finger and said, 'Go back, in Jesus' Name!' and it turned around and went back. It simply submitted to my authority.

A missionary neighbour used to have a guard dog. One day it was fine and the next day it was acting confused, as if it was crazy. The night before it had escaped and ended up at a place nearby where there had been a gathering of witchdoctors. They were probably scared of the dog and cast curses or evil spirits on it. After my neighbour prayed and cast out these spirits, the dog started to behave normally again.

I taught a small group of Sudanese people on spiritual authority and one of the ladies gave a testimony the following week. She was walking barefoot through tall grass when a snake appeared right in front of her with its head about a meter from the ground. She pointed her finger and took authority over the snake in Jesus' Name. It simply left and slithered away.

On another occasion we were getting ready to teach and minister to children at a mission base. The only problem was that we were meeting in a room that had a tin roof and when it rains, you can't hear anything but the loud pelting noise of rain. Just before we were to start, thick dark clouds overshadowed us and released a torrential downpour along with thunder and lightning. We could have cancelled our meeting, but instead we took authority over the weather and commanded the clouds to disperse and the moon to shine forth. Within twenty minutes, not only had the rain ceased, but we could see the starry sky and moon.

In Africa, I had creatures appear in my room like frogs and centipedes, or birds would hover outside my window and appear to be looking in. On such occasions, I sensed there was an evil spirit in these creatures for they didn't behave like they normally would. The moment I took authority and commanded them to go in Jesus' Name, they either disappeared or tried to escape in the opposite direction.

James said the prayer of a righteous man is powerful and effective. Just like Elijah prayed and called down rain, so can a righteous Spirit-filled believer. *'The prayer of a righteous man is powerful and effective.* **Elijah was a man just like us.** *He prayed earnestly that it would not rain, and it did not rain on the land for three and a half years. Again he prayed and the heavens gave rain and the earth produced its crops'* (James 5:17-18). Elijah prayed as the Lord directed. Hence, the prayers of the righteous have power and authority, even over nature.

Jesus demonstrated authority over nature. He cursed the fig tree for not producing fruit, and it died. Then He rebuked the storm at sea. He said to the waves, *'Quiet! Be still!'* and they calmed down. And after He rebuked the wind, it ceased (Mark 4:39). Jesus told His disciples *if they have faith,* they could tell a mountain to be thrown into the sea and it will happen (Mathew 21:21). We simply need faith the size of a mustard seed to exercise the authority we have been given over nature.

Authority Over Regions & Principalities

As already mentioned a principality is a ruler or ruling prince over a nation or region. There are different principalities ruling over different geographical regions. For example, some regions may be strong in witchcraft, death, poverty, sex-trade industry, and so on. These are high-ranking demonic strongholds. We are not to fear them but equally I believe we should not directly take them on by ourselves because there is nothing I'm aware of in scripture which says we have authority over them.

Paul speaks about *resisting* the evil powers, rulers, and principalities by coming in the opposite spirit, and standing firm with the fruit of the Spirit (Ephesians 6:10-16). Instead of praying directly against the spirits, as some may be in the habit of doing, we may intercede for our town or nation by directly approaching God with repentant prayers. He is the one who deals with the principalities by sending His army of angels to do battle in the Heavenly realms (see Daniel 10:12).

A principality or stronghold over a nation may be the result of the governmental power or rulership in that area, and this will affect the people. Our prayers for a nation can include praying for those in governmental authority. When the Holy Spirit comes upon a group of people, the enemy has to flee or be displaced. The same applies to discipling a nation. As we minister to the people in an area, a principality can be displaced.

When Joshua the high priest stood before the Angel of the Lord and satan, the Angel of the Lord said: *'The Lord rebuke you satan!'* (Zechariah 3:2). He didn't rebuke or speak any slanderous words using his own authority. Rather, he said: *'The Lord rebuke you.'* Hence, we may pray words like, 'The Lord rebuke you!' when coming against a high-ranking demonic authority. However, I would only do this if it came across my path. I wouldn't go chasing after it.

Jesus passed by the villages that rejected Him but He didn't curse them. When the Samaritans didn't allow them to enter into their village, the disciples wanted to call down fire to destroy the village, but Jesus rebuked His disciples for thinking that way. Instead, He simply ignored the Samaritans response and continued walking to the next village (Luke 9:54).

Unless we have heard clearly from God and He has commissioned us with a divine plan of action, then it's wise not to pray directly against a principality over a region. Just because we sense an evil presence or know there is witchcraft practiced in an area, doesn't mean we should automatically start taking authority against it. However, we may do this if it has been assigned to us from God. When it comes to dealing with principalities we are entering a completely different area of spiritual warfare. I want to emphasize that this is not to stop us from praying for a region or people group or nation, for we can pray directly to God for a people group or nation, as did Daniel and Nehemiah. They prayed a repentance prayer for the sins of their people and asked God to forgive their sins and cleanse their land. We can pray likewise, and ask God to release His blessings on a nation or people group. These are safe prayers directed to God that are not coming directly against the enemy.

I have been very wary of tackling principalities and never become involved unless God has specifically assigned me to do so. There have been many people who have become casualties as a result of taking on a principality that God hadn't assigned them to in the first place. They wrongly assumed they had the authority and entered into a spiritual battle that wasn't theirs to fight.

If we take on something that God hasn't called us to, then we are not under His protective covering and may be vulnerable to enemy attack. This may result in serious issues as a result of the spiritual opposition, such as, sickness, accidents and even death.

We all make mistakes and hopefully learn from them but if we have stepped outside our sphere of God-given authority and taken on battles we were not assigned to, we can simply repent and ask God to reverse the effects that have taken place. If there have been any casualties (like sickness in the family or other forms of spiritual attack), we can ask God for His forgiveness and to bring healing and restoration where needed.

Those who are in the army of the Lord take orders from King Jesus, their Commander in Chief. He gives a strategy for each battle we are called to fight. As we obey Him, God will release His warring angels to do battle against the evil powers and principalities of darkness.

Jesus didn't say we are to pray to the angels and release them to do battle. Rather, He said we are to pray: *'Your Kingdom come, Your will be done, on earth as in Heaven'*. As we pray directly to Jesus, our Heavenly Father, and the Holy Spirit, God dispatches His army of angels according to His plans and will. Even Jesus Himself said that if He wanted an army of angels to fight for Him, He would first call on His Father. *'Do you think I can't* **call on My Father,** *and He will at once put at My dispersal more than twelve legions of angels?* '(Mathew 26:53).

Let us not confuse this with God's messenger angels who are sent to give us a specific message. We read how Mary and Daniel conversed with the angel Gabriel, and John with an angel on the island of Patmos (book of Revelation). It is scriptural to talk to angels when the angels first appear to us with a message sent by God. However, when dealing in spiritual warfare, we can ask God to release His warring angels. This may automatically happen when we pray in tongues or do warfare in our God given spiritual language. He will dispatch His angels to do warfare on our behalf, as He assigns different angels for the different missions and tasks He has called us to do here on earth.

When Daniel prayed and fasted for twenty-one days, he prayed directly to God. He didn't do warfare against the enemy but repented before God for the sins of his people. '**While I was speaking and praying, confessing my sin and the sin of my people Israel and making my request to the Lord my God for His holy hill**, *Gabriel, the man I had seen in the earlier vision, came to me in swift flight...*' (Daniel 9:20). This was a safe and powerful prayer. As a result, God sent a messenger who said: '*The prince of the Persian kingdom resisted me twenty-one days. Then Michael, one of the chief princes, came to help me, because I was detained there with the prince of Persia*' (Daniel 10:13). Here the prince of Persia was the principality over the region. As Daniel prayed a repentance prayer for the sins of his people, God sent an angel to battle with this principality. However, the angel got detained so the archangel (chief prince) Michael, was required to come to the rescue. Daniel didn't pray directly against the principality; his prayers were focused on repentance and seeking God's forgiveness for the sins of his people. As a result, God released His warring angels to do battle in the Heavenly realms. Daniel recognised the sins over his nation, and prevented the ruling spirit or principality having effect on him by coming in the opposite spirit with repentance prayer.

On one occasion, God called me to enter into such a battle. I have to admit, I didn't want to get involved but rather wanted to flee from it. I reluctantly obeyed then found out He had also called other missionaries to stay and intercede for the area and base. God doesn't usually ask us to do things alone but will connect us with others with whom He has called to pray. I heard there were many witchdoctors, sorcerers and shamanists attending a New Year celebration on the beach, just across the road from us. This was a time when they would engage with water spirits and demonic powers so they could receive greater measures of evil power. God called us to stand against these evil forces so we responded to what the Holy Spirit directed us to do.

As we began praying, some of us felt led to fast for the whole week. We consecrated ourselves before God, repented of all known sin (so we had no open door to sin by which the enemy could attack us), and prayer walked around our land. As we met to pray on New Year's Eve, I felt led by the Spirit to ask God to release thunder and lightning from Heaven, as He did for Elijah. After Elijah had contended with the false prophets on Mount Carmel, he was led by God to call down the rain. It was God's plan to release the rains on the land after a three year drought. He humbly obeyed God's strategy and saw victory (1 Kings 18:41-44).

I had never prayed this before but felt led by the Spirit to do so. At that moment in time there was clear blue sky above us and not a cloud in sight. Within a few hours or so a storm started to brew. This was no ordinary storm. There were strong winds with terrifying thunder and lightning. It was one of the most powerful, terrifying storms I have ever witnessed. The next day we heard reports that the satanists and witchdoctors were furious for their plans had been thwarted. One of them even commented that they saw power coming from our base which had stopped them being able to use their powers. It was amazing to see what God did, though scary at the same time. (I have to say it was not an assignment I enjoyed doing or would like to do again.) As a result of this, the following year the witchdoctors and satanists decided not to return to the same place but sought somewhere else to go. The next New Year was peaceful and there was no oppression felt in the atmosphere.

We all have authority to cast out demons in people and homes. We also have authority over animals, nature and the land we live on. However, when dealing with principalities or evil powers of darkness ruling over people groups or nations, it is safer not to directly pray against them in warfare prayer, but pray directly to God and be led by His Spirit. It is safe when we repent and ask God for His forgiveness, and to release salvation, healing and deliverance on the land, for this is an intercessory prayer for the people, and is not coming directly against the enemy.

A fellow believer was going to pray against the witches in his area. When I heard what he was planning to do, alarm bells began to go off in my spirit. I first asked if God had given him a strategy. He answered, no. I then asked if God had called him to do this. His reply was that he hadn't even thought to ask but just presumed it was right to come against any evil in their area. I asked if he had let his pastor know and received his approval and blessing. He hadn't. So I asked him why he was doing it. He responded that it was because he wanted to get rid of the witches in the area. I knew he was clearly stepping outside of his spiritual boundary and could get hit by the enemy if he went ahead. I advised him not to go ahead until he knew that God had assigned him to do such a thing, and to seek God's Wisdom and Council, instead of his own 'wise' thoughts, because there are right and wrong ways of doing things.

In a similar way, we can seek strategy from the Lord when ministering to someone who practices witchcraft. If the person wants to know Jesus, then we can lovingly pray for them and bring them into His Kingdom, as they repent and renounce their evil practices. However, if they don't want to know Jesus, then we can privately pray for their salvation. We can pray they will encounter God's love and receive healing in their hearts.

We are commanded to heal the sick and cast out demons, but few are called and designated to deal with principalities or ruling spirits over regions. Battles over regions are won when we humbly align our hearts with the will of God and obey His instructions. It may be we are to disciple a nation by reaching out to the people one by one before the battle is won over a region.

God has given His sons and daughters spheres of divine authority to advance His Kingdom, and more is released the deeper we grow in our relationship of sonship with Him.

Heavenly Father, thank You for the divine authority You give us as children in Your Kingdom. Give me a fresh revelation of the sphere of authority You have given me and how to use it in everyday life. I repent for the times I have stepped outside my boundaries of spiritual authority. Please forgive me for doing this (name such occasions). I am sorry for not seeking Your will on the matter and ask You to restore the lives of those affected by this. Lord, show me how to pray in the power of Your Spirit and discern what is on Your heart for Your people. May Your Kingdom come and will be done on earth as in heaven, in Your mighty Name.

END NOTES

[1] Exousia (Greek 1849): *Strong's Exhaustive Concordance; Red Letter Edition*
[2] Dunamis (Greek 1411); *Strong's Exhaustive Concordance; Red Letter Edition*

HE WHO OVERCOMES

3

Operating With the Sword of the Spirit

For the weapons we fight with are not the weapons of the world. On the contrary, they have divine power to demolish strongholds.

2 Corinthians 10:4

Jesus is our Lord of Hosts, *Jehovah Sabaoth,* or Captain of the army of the Lord. Battles are taking place right now between the angelic hosts and evil forces in the Heavenly realms. *'For our struggle is not against flesh and blood, but against the rulers, against the authorities, against the powers of darkness and against the spiritual forces of evil in the Heavenly realms'* (Ephesians 6:12).

We only have one enemy, satan. Therefore, our battles are not against flesh and blood, as we tend to think, but are in the spiritual realm. Hence, we overcome by seeking the Lord's perspective and will on a matter, and responding in the Spirit. This means we need to be aware of the enemy's schemes in order to respond in the opposite spirit.

One morning, as I was waking up in South Sudan, I saw in the Spirit three words, 'SPIRITUAL MEDICAL OPERATION'. The words were in capital letters and looked white and fluffy in texture, like cotton wool. Next, I saw the word 'MEDICAL' had a line drawn through it and above it was written the word 'MILITARY'. I was puzzled at this very clear word from God.

The term *Spiritual Military Operation* had a specific meaning and I discovered it related to the military assignments that were discussed in the 'strategy room' with the Generals. The Lord was training me as a warrior in His army during my service on the mission field in this war-torn nation.

Military Intelligence is a term used in the armed forces where information of strategic military value is analyzed concerning an enemy or area, and with regards to performing military tasks and operations. In God's Kingdom, there is *Divine Intelligence* where the Lord reveals His strategy and plans to those He has anointed and appointed for specific divine assignments. This is received through revelatory-knowledge along with His wisdom, counsel, and discernment.

Prophetic prayer warriors are like the spiritual military air force for they shift the spiritual atmospheres and advance God's Kingdom through warfare prayer, and declaring His Kingdom come and will be done. As we pray in the Spirit, God responds by releasing His warring angels to do battle in the heavenly realms against the evil forces. Prayers are powerful and can bring enemy strongholds down and quench demonic activity, especially when we pray together in the unity of the Spirit.

During a prayer meeting, the Lord gave me a picture. In this picture I saw each prophetic intercessor was like a fighter pilot in a military jet. As we gathered together to pray in the Spirit, our fighter jets formed the shape of one huge military jet. This was the power of prayer, as we prayed together in the unity of the Spirit.

Jesus disarmed the powers and authorities and made a public spectacle of them having triumphed over them by the cross (Colossians 2:15). The battles in the Heavenly realms are far from over. *'From the days of John the Baptist until now, the Kingdom of Heaven has been forcefully advancing, and forceful men lay hold of it'* (Mathew 11:12).

Though we have victory through the cross, the battle isn't over yet, for we still have ongoing battles to fight. However, He has provided us with various spiritual weapons to discern and oppose the attacks of the enemy.

Jesus said: *'In the world you will have trouble. But take heart! I have overcome the world'* (John 16:33). He warned that many would be persecuted for their faith, and even families and friends may betray them, but to stand firm and they would receive eternal life (Luke 21:12-19). We stand firm by knowing who we are in God's Kingdom and by holding on to His Word and promises. Never forget, He who is in us is greater than he who is in the world (1 John 4:4).

Let us look at the divine weapons God has given us. This involves the various ways we may operate with the Sword of the Spirit through prayer and worship.

Power of Prayer & Worship

Our prayer language is developed from an intimate relationship with God. It is not a one-way conversation but a two-way conversation that flows from a place of intimacy with Him. I used to think prayer was simply my words or thoughts spoken to God, until I realised He also wanted to speak to me. Hence, prayer is a divine connection where our spirit connects to God's Spirit, and this includes discovering how to *listen to Him, engage in His Presence,* and *pray in the Spirit*.

Likewise, worship is a form of prayer as we come into God's Presence and surrender our hearts and minds to Him. It is not about singing religious songs. The first mention of worship in the Bible is the Hebrew word *'Shachah'* and this is when Abraham *bowed down* to worship God, as he was getting ready to sacrifice his son Isaac to Him (Genesis 22:5). Hence, one of the meanings of worship is to bow down or prostrate oneself as an act of homage and reverence before God.

Engaging in His Presence

True worship brings us into the Presence of the Lord. This is because we encounter His Presence when we worship Him in Spirit and in truth. As we carry His Presence in our hearts, we are in a place of continual fellowship with Him. Engaging in His Presence is actually a spiritual weapon because the enemy flees from the Presence of the Lord. *'If you make the Most High your dwelling- even the Lord who is my refuge- then no harm will befall you, no disaster will come near your tent. For he will command His angels concerning you, to guard you in all your ways'* (Psalm 91:9-11). The safest place to be is in His Presence. This is the result of a surrendered lifestyle, as we yield ourselves to Him.

Moses asked God who He would send to be with them, to guard and protect them whilst crossing the desert. And God replied: **'My Presence will go with you and I will give you rest'** (Exodus 33:14). His Presence manifested as a cloud by day and fire by night, and this is how He led the Israelites through the desert. Whenever we engage in His Presence we enter a place of divine rest. It was the angel of His Presence that saved the Israelites from destruction: *'In all their distress He too was distressed, and* **the Angel of His Presence saved them**' (Isaiah 63:9).

Each time we engage in God's Presence, we are preparing our hearts to operate under the power and anointing of His Spirit, instead of through our flesh.

Sword of the Spirit

What is the sword of the Spirit? It is the very word of God that comes out of our mouths. *'Take the mighty razor-sharp Spirit-sword of the spoken word of God'* (TPT Ephesians 6:17). The words we speak carry power, like that of a sharp two-edged sword. Hence, we operate with the sword of the Spirit when we speak *words* from the heart of God.

Jesus is the Word of God, for in the beginning was the Word and the Word was with God and the Word was God (John 1:1). Here, the Greek for 'Word' is *Logos* - Jesus is the Logos. However, the Greek for 'word' when referring to the sword of the Spirit as the *word* of God in Ephesians 6:17, is *Rhema*. Paul was referring to the sword of the Spirit as the *Rhema* word or Spirit-breathed word, and this has cutting power.

The Book of Revelation describes Jesus as the Word of God with a sharp sword coming from His mouth: *'He is dressed in a robe dipped in blood,* **and His Name is the Word of God.** *The armies of Heaven were following Him, riding on white horses and dressed in fine* *linen, white and clean.* ***Out of His mouth comes a sharp sword with which to strike down the nations'*** (Revelation 19:13-15).

There are two Greek words that describe the swords mentioned in the scriptures. *Rhomphaia* is the Greek word used when referring to a short sword and *Machaira* is the Greek word used when referring to a long sword. The sword that comes from the mouth of Jesus is described as a *Machaira,* or a long powerful sword (Rev 1:16, 2:12, 19:25). This type of sword is as long as the body and is used in long-distance fighting. The sword referred to in Ephesians 6:17 and Hebrews 4:12 is described as a *Rhomphaia* or short sword. The short sword is the length of the fore-arm and more like a dagger or long knife that is used in hand-to-hand combat.

The Word of God is alive and powerful. It pierces and circumcises our hearts like a two-edged sword. It judges the thoughts and attitudes of the heart (Hebrews 4:12). It brings conviction of sin as well as revelation to our hearts and minds, for it is not dead or passive, but alive and active. As we speak God's Word in the Spirit, it is like a sword coming out of our mouths. It can pierce the hearts of His people with truth and revelation, as well as quench the fiery darts of the enemy, for it has a cutting edge.

His word is truth and quenches the lies, fears, false accusations, and deceptions that come from the enemy. Jesus prayed for His disciples: *'Sanctify them by the truth; Your Word is truth'* (John 17:17). When Jesus was tested and tempted by satan in the wilderness, He responded each time with the word of God, declaring: *'It is written..!'* (Luke 4:8). The sword of the Spirit came out of His mouth as He spoke with the Word of truth. And it is His Word of truth that exposes the lies, deceptive thoughts, and false beliefs from the enemy.

When God speaks His Word, it will not return to Him empty but will accomplish and achieve the purpose for which it was sent (Isaiah 55:10). He compares it to being like fire and a hammer: *"Is not My Word like fire",* declares the Lord, *"and like a hammer that breaks a rock in pieces?"'* (Jeremiah 23:29).

The Holy Spirit may breathe His *Rhema* Word into our spirit through a word of scripture or a word directly from the mouth of the Lord, and our spirit comes alive as we hear and receive it.

The words we speak from our mouth are like a two-edged sword, and that's why the words we say over others or ourselves can be powerful, especially when we speak or pray from the heart of God. However, when we speak with anger, hatred, judgement or bitterness in our hearts, then the words we speak are more likely to carry evil power and become word-curses. *'With the tongue we praise our Lord and Father, and with it we curse men...my brothers this should not be'* (James 3:9-10).

When the angel Gabriel appeared before the priest Zechariah and told him that his wife Elizabeth would bear a son named John, Zechariah expressed doubt since his wife was old and well past her child-bearing years (Luke 1:18-20). As a result of these negative words of doubt and unbelief, the angel silenced Zechariah. I believe this was not some kind of punishment, but rather a divine protection on the baby, so Elizabeth would give birth to John. These negative words could have prematurely aborted the birth because they may have been spoken as 'word-curses', hence Zechariah's mouth was sealed so this wouldn't happen. This was demonstrating the power of the words we speak and how they release blessings or curses.

Many years ago, a senior pastor revealed to me that the words I spoke carried power, and I was to be aware of this and careful of what I said. So often we are unaware of the power of the tongue and may casually say a negative word that acts like a curse. There is life or death in the power of the tongue (Proverbs 18:21). As we become more self-aware of the words we speak and what we say, we will learn how to use our swords more effectively in God's Kingdom.

God's Word is not only a sword, but it nurtures our spirit and builds up our spiritual muscles. Jesus opposed the enemy in the desert by declaring the Word of God: *'It is written, man does not live on bread alone but on every word that comes from the mouth of God'* (Mathew 4:4). As we feed on the Word of God, we protect our minds from the lies and fears of the enemy. We overcome as we declare His Word - the source of all truth.

'All scripture is God breathed and useful **for teaching, rebuking, correcting and training in righteousness***, so that the man of God may be thoroughly equipped for every good work'* (2 Timothy 3:16). His living word not only teaches, but rebukes us and trains us for battle, and to walk in righteousness.

God's Word speaks life and releases hope and faith, for it quenches the words of the enemy that bring hopelessness and death. He is calling us to be His vessels who deliver His living word to His people, releasing life instead of death, and His truth spoken in love, and to quench the fiery darts of lies and fears from the enemy.

The sword of the Spirit is a powerful weapon, so let us see the various ways we may warfare with the sword of the Spirit through our prayer language and worship.

Thanksgiving & Praise

David knew the power behind thanks and praise: *'We enter His gates with thanksgiving and His courts with praise. Give thanks to Him and praise His name'* (Psalm 100:4). Giving thanks and praise brings us into His Presence. We 'thank' Him for all He has done in our lives and the lives of others and for what is yet to come, and for His unconditional love. On the other hand, 'praise' causes us to lift our voices to Him, as we shout praises to His name. We praise Him for who He is and tell Him He is worthy of all honour, praise and glory. Hence, we lift up our hands and voices and shout aloud when we praise Him.

There is always something to thank and praise God for. The best place to operate in warfare prayer and worship is by engaging in His Presence. We engage in His Presence by humbly posturing ourselves before Him, and focusing our mind, heart and spirit on Him. Thanks and praise is a key to turn our hearts towards Him and engage in His Presence. If we give God thanks for at least five things, this will enable our hearts to engage with His Spirit. He enters our hearts by *faith* (Ephesians 3:17).

Did you know that whenever we give God thanks and praise, it releases a stirring in the Heavenly realms? This is because He responds each time we lift up our weapons of thanks and praise to Him. Whenever the living creatures give thanks and praise to Him who sits on the throne, the twenty-four elders fall down, take off their crowns and worship Him saying: *'You are worthy, our Lord and God, to receive glory and honour and power, for You created all things, and by Your will they were created and have their being'*. Day and night the living creatures never stop saying, *'Holy, holy, holy, is the Lord God Almighty, who was and is and is to come'* (Revelation 4:8-11). The angels, living creatures and elders worship God around His throne saying: *'Worthy is the Lamb, who was slain...'* (Revelation 5:12).

As we regularly engage in thanks and praise, God releases His warring angels to do battle for us. Paul and Silas could have moaned and groaned after they were beaten and arrested and put in prison, but instead they chose to give thanks and praise to the Lord. They thanked and praised Him, even in pain and with bruised bodies, and this caused a stirring in the Heavenly realms, such that the chains of all the prisoners fell off, and they walked out free. *'About midnight, Paul and Silas were praying and singing hymns to God and the other prisoners were listening to them. Suddenly, there was such a violent earthquake that the foundations of the prison were shaken. At once, all the prison doors flew open and everybody's chains came loose'* (Acts 16:25-26).

King Jehoshaphat saw a huge army coming against him and knew that without God's help he would be defeated. So he turned to God and bowed down in worship. The Lord gave him a strategy and he obeyed. King Jehoshaphat's weapons were worship, thanksgiving and praise. He appointed men to praise the Lord for the splendour of His holiness. The worshippers went out at the head of the army saying: *'Give thanks to the Lord, for His love endures forever'*. And as they began to give thanks and shout praises to God, the Lord set up ambushes against their enemies (2 Chronicles 20: 18-22).

We are to give thanks and praise in *all* things and not just for the good things we experience in life. This includes the most difficult and uncertain times we face (Philippians 4:6, 1 Thessalonians

5:18). God is greater than any crisis or difficulty and He can turn anything around for the good, because God works in all things for the good to those who love Him and have been called according to His purpose (Romans 8:28).

As we daily practice thanking and praising Him from the moment we awake to before going to bed, we will see His hand move in our lives and help us overcome our circumstances. Even if something bad has happened, we can thank Him, knowing He is greater, and trust Him to act. *'A righteous man will have no fear of bad news; his heart is steadfast, trusting in the Lord'* (Psalm 112:7).

Thanksgiving and praise are mighty weapons that bring down enemy strongholds. God acts quickly in our times of difficulty when we choose to thank and praise Him instead of complaining, moaning, or becoming angry with Him.

The little children were shouting: *'Hosanna to the Son of David'*, as Jesus entered the temple. He said: *'From the lips of children and infants, You have ordained praise'* (Mathew 21:16). We, as children of God, should never stop thanking and praising Him.

There was a pastor from another country who was imprisoned for his faith. He had been in prison for eight years as a result of being seen with a Bible. I was at a conference where we were asked to pray for his nation to receive the gospel, and for him to be set free. We gave God thanks and praise for this man. During the evening we had word that he had just been released from prison. Thanksgiving and praise sets the prisoners free (Psalm 102:20-22).

Warfare Praise & War Cry

There have been times when I have worshipped alongside fellow believers and we have suddenly entered into a marching rhythm during the praise and worship. It is as if we are marching on a battle ground and overcoming the enemy through the words we are proclaiming and declaring in the Spirit. This is *'warfare praise'*.

Once when I was reaching out to some street children in Africa, we had a time of praise and worship. I had prayed that God would release a spirit of praise in their hearts. These little children, between five and twelve years of age, were shouting aloud to God, praising Him with songs in their tribal language. They had spontaneously started to sing praises before the group leader arrived and they didn't just sing, they shouted at the top of their voices. I smiled as this scripture immediately came to mind: *'From the lips of children and infants You have ordained praise because of your enemies, to silence the foe and the avenger'* (Psalm 8:2). The praise that was being shouted from the mouths of these little ones was causing havoc in the spiritual realm and bringing silence to the enemy! Without even knowing it, they were doing warfare praise.

Joshua brought down the walls of Jericho with the shouts from the people and the blowing of trumpets but he first had to follow God's strategy in order for this to happen. On the seventh day of marching around the city, the people were to give a 'war cry'. This is a shout when battle is being declared or when victory is being taken.

Joshua told them, *'"Do not give a war cry, do not raise your voices, do not say a word, until the day I tell you to shout. Then shout!"...On the seventh day they marched around the city seven times in the same manner. On the seventh time around, when the priests sounded the trumpet blast, Joshua commanded the people, "Shout! For the Lord has given you the city!"...When the trumpet sounded, the people shouted and the wall collapsed'* (Joshua 6:10-21).

Here we see warfare praise through the sounding of trumpets and also a war cry shout from the people. The result was that the walls fell down. I believe the six days they silently marched around the city, the wall of Jericho was being weakened in the spiritual realm. Walls represent spiritual strongholds. The wall or stronghold was then of sufficient weakness to be torn down through a warfare cry. It wasn't the physical aspect of the shout that brought the walls down, but rather what had been taking place in the spiritual realms. The stronghold had been weakened through prayer and sounding the trumpets for six days. Therefore, it was ready to fall on the seventh day when the war cry was made and God released His army of angels.

When trumpets or shofars are blown by a prompting of the Holy Spirit, there is a significant change in the spiritual atmosphere over a meeting or area. I have been in worship meetings when someone has blown a shofar and I have witnessed an immediate change in the spiritual atmosphere as the peace of God fell like a blanket. It's as if any demonic spirits have to depart as the peace and Presence of God fills the whole place. I believe something like this was happening when the priests blew the trumpets each day in Jericho. They were shifting the spiritual atmosphere.

Whilst in Mozambique with Iris Global, I took a group of mission students on a two-week outreach in another war-torn nation. One day during the outreach, we gathered together for a time of prayer and worship before we were due to minister in a village. I had sensed in my spirit there would be opposition in the village so we spent some time engaging in God's Presence before we went. The team were feeling tired and not wanting to do anything, especially pray (a tactic of the enemy when a battle is around the corner). So we spent a few minutes praying for one another, and as we did this, the spirit of tiredness and apathy quickly lifted. The team suddenly broke out into spontaneous praise and holy laughter. What followed next as we were praying in the Spirit was amazing and something I had never experienced before. We all stood up simultaneously, under the prompting of the Holy Spirit, and lifted our arms high in the air as if we were holding spiritual swords in our hands. Then all together, unrehearsed and at exactly the same moment, we all gave out a loud war cry. It lasted for a few minutes as we shouted at the top of our voices the words the Holy Spirit put in our mouths. It was powerful and I sensed the walls falling down in the spiritual realm. Something had broken and I could see we were ready to march forward in battle to help deliver the people of this village from the hands of the enemy into the hands of Jesus. It was an awesome experience where the Holy Spirit led us in a simultaneous battle cry. We were now ready to advance, for the victory had been won in the Heavenly realms.

Worship in Spirit & Truth

There may be times when we worship God with our lips, but our hearts and minds are distant, and as a result, we don't enter His Presence. Jesus pointed this out: *'These people honour Me with their lips, but their hearts are far from Me. They worship Me in vain; their teachings [on worship] are but rules taught by men'* (Matthew 15:8, Isaiah 29:13). He said: *'A time is coming when true worshippers will worship the Father in Spirit and truth, for they are the kind of worshippers the Father seeks.* **God is Spirit and His worshippers must worship in Spirit and in truth'** (John 4:23-24).

I was at a conference in London where the professional worship band was playing loud music. Though everyone was clapping and singing the words on the screen, I somehow didn't sense the Presence of God - just what sounded like a lot of banging and noise. Then the guest speaker, Heidi Baker, came on stage to speak, but instead she started to worship all over again, along with an African guitarist. As Heidi bowed down on her knees and worshipped before God, the Presence of God fell in such a tangible way that everyone broke out singing in different spiritual languages. There was such a tangible Presence in the midst that the audience took over the worship. They were now worshipping in the Spirit as they sang in different spiritual languages.

It felt so powerful and sounded heavenly, as if there were angels worshipping in our midst. This opened my eyes to true worship in the Spirit. I realised it was not about being performance based or producing 'loud' or 'good' music. Rather, true worship is simply bowing down before God as we usher in His Presence. Our audience consists of just One Person – King Jesus.

True worship is where our hearts are engaged with God and we want to bow down, kneel, or prostrate ourselves before Him. Healing and miracles break out as we worship God in His majestic Presence. There is no sickness when in His glory realm. He is looking for true worshippers who want to seek His face and hunger for His Presence. These are powerful moments where we witness signs and wonders, as well as the inner beauty of being in His Presence.

When David played his harp before Saul, the tormenting spirits departed. This was because David knew how to access the Presence of the Lord through worship (1 Samuel 16:23). Many have been healed and delivered of demons when entering corporate worship. Demons cannot stand to hear true worship; they shriek and have to leave whenever the Presence of God comes. When we bow down to worship Him, no longer bothered about ourselves, then He will come and the enemy will flee.

Praying in the Spirit

Praying in the Spirit is something to do on *all* occasions and not just when we feel like it (Ephesians 6:18), and is opposite to praying in the flesh. When we pray in the flesh, probably nothing will happen, simply because we haven't learnt to pray from our heart and spirit. When we pray in the flesh we babble saying what we want and hope God is listening. It is our carnal nature that is operating.

However, when we discover how to pray in the Spirit, our spirit comes alive as we speak to our Heavenly Father, knowing He hears us. Then we will see God's power at work and His Kingdom come as we pray in accordance with His will. Jesus taught us to pray: '*Your Kingdom come, Your will be done, on earth as in Heaven*' because it is powerful when we declare His Kingdom come and will be done, instead of our own.

When we are struggling to pray in our natural language, we can always pray with our spiritual language. '*We do not know what we ought to pray for, but the Spirit Himself intercedes for us with groans that words can't express*' (Romans 8:26).

If we ask God, He will give all Spirit-filled believers a spiritual language, the gift of praying in tongues (1 Corinthians 12:10). This is a supernatural prayer language to help us pray in the Spirit, especially when we don't know what to pray. I don't understand it, but He does. It is a gift of the Holy Spirit that connects with my spirit as I pray in this language, and then returns back to Him. The enemy is barred from knowing what conversation I am having with God for it is Spirit to spirit, hence it is powerful.

Sometimes the tongue language may be in another known language (like when the disciples spoke in different tongues on the day of Pentecost), or it may be in a supernatural language which only God and His angels understand. '*For anyone who speaks in a tongue doesn't speak to men but to God. Indeed no-one understands him; he utters mysteries with his spirit'* (1 Corinthians 14:2-3).

Many times I find myself praying first in my spiritual language and then in my natural English. The two go hand-in-hand, especially when interceding or praying for someone. Paul encourages us to pray with our spirit and then with our mind (1 Corinthians 14:15). Praying in tongues is edifying for ourselves and also when praying for others. It is a powerful tool to connect us to the Spirit of God. *'Dear friends,* **build yourselves up** *in your most holy faith and* **pray in the Holy Spirit***'* (Jude 1:20).

Whenever people ask me to pray for them, I usually begin by praying in my spiritual language. This enables me to be led by the Spirit how to pray for them. Sometimes, God may want to do something different from an individual's request, or perhaps address the root issue instead of the symptoms.

At various times when I have walked down streets, I have started to pray in tongues. My spirit has been activated by God's Spirit to intercede though I don't know what I am praying. My spirit stays focused on God as I am walking down that street.

Also, I believe God can give us a *warfare language*. At times when I have been praying in the Spirit, I have broken into a warfare tongue, where my spirit rises within and it feels like I am engaging in a spiritual battle. There is a holy boldness and authority that rises up within my spirit and the words sound different to my other spiritual language.

I was ministering to a group of pastors in South Sudan when I felt the Lord wanted to release a warfare prayer language for some of them. So I laid my hands on them, and prayed for the Lord to release a warfare tongue, and they suddenly prayed with such boldness and authority that some started to sweat droplets as they prayed in various languages

Likewise, I have seen counterfeit tongues. This happens with people who are not Spirit-filled that are praying with a counterfeit or demonic tongue. The language sounds more like a monotonic chant and has an uncomfortable edge when heard.

When we may spiritually discern this, we can bind the spirit and if the person is willing to renounce it, they can receive God's Spirit instead. Once I saw an African man stand up and pray with a warring spirit, but something didn't feel right. My colleagues sensed it was a demonic warring spirit, so they took authority over it and cast it out. The man's appearance completely changed after he was set free and received the Lord in his heart.

The gift of tongues is powerful when used for personal prayer and worship, as well as for corporate prayer and ministry. It is a powerful weapon in warfare prayer. Praying in tongues can build up our spirit, especially during dry seasons. It can help us pray in the Spirit when ministering to others and is a powerful intercessory tool for breaking down enemy strongholds.

Prophetic Acts, Declaration & Proclamation

God may speak to His body through prophetic words, visions, scriptures or even through a spiritual language. Usually, if a person prophecies with a spiritual tongue, then God brings understanding of His word with the gift of interpretation. Also, the Holy Spirit may lead us to do 'prophetic acts' or speak words of 'prophetic declaration' or 'prophetic proclamation'.

A prophetic act is when someone responds to what the Spirit may be revealing or saying to them, and as they do, there is a spiritual release or breakthrough in the Heavenly realms. They are usually simple acts that release Kingdom power. The Lord has prompted me to cleanse rivers or consecrate lands using either anointing oil or consecrated wine, followed by declaring them cleansed in the name of Jesus. This is a simple prophetic act and is profound when in obedience to God's Spirit.

On one occasion when I was with a Sudanese bishop and group of pastors, we felt led to consecrate an African river known for its witchcraft. We poured some consecrated wine into it and declared it cleansed with the blood of Jesus. Later, we heard a neighbour (who did not know what had taken place) testify to seeing a water spirit (python or something snake like) coming out of the river.

When Joshua followed the orders from the Lord to march around Jericho seven times and then shout the war cry, he was performing a prophetic act. Elisha did the same when he poured salt onto the defiled river and it became cleansed and once more safe to drink (2 Kings 2:21). Prophetic acts are simple to do but they carry great authority and breakthrough power in the spiritual realm. The Lord gives a simple word or picture to act out and, as we do, He releases spiritual breakthrough.

A prophetic proclamation or declaration is when we proclaim or declare a word from God over a situation, event, place, person or even a nation, and as we speak it forth, so it will come to pass. It is very powerful. In the Old Testament, it was the prophets who proclaimed or declared such words as they prophesied over people and nations. However, God can use any Spirit-filled believer, like you or me, to do the same.

One prayer which God put on my heart to pray and declare over the lives of the African children was that each child would not die but live and accomplish all that the Lord had planned and purposed in their lives. I would declare life and health over them, speaking it into being and coming against any sickness and death. So when the Lord gives us words to declare or proclaim, or simple acts to do, we will see Him move mightily in return.

Power in the Name of Jesus

The first time I witnessed a healing using the powerful Name of Jesus I happened to be working as a children's doctor on a ward in Uganda. There was a lovely little girl who had miliary TB (tuberculosis finely scattered throughout both her lungs). She was on the maximum treatment we could offer but was deteriorating on both the oxygen and anti-TB therapy. The last thing I could think of doing was to pray for her. Suddenly, as I was praying, a spirit of boldness came upon me and I heard myself commanding the disease to leave her body in the *Name of Jesus!* I couldn't remember praying with such boldness like this before. Nothing profound appeared to happen at that moment but the following week when I was on the critical ward I noticed she wasn't there. I looked in the death book but her name wasn't there either. I finally went to the recovery ward and there she was, sitting up with her mum. Both of them were looking at me and smiling. Their beaming faces said it all! She was now off the oxygen and making a great recovery. Something had shifted when praying *in the Name of Jesus* that led to her breakthrough for healing. Jesus said: *'**In My Name** they will drive out demons; they will place their hands on sick people and they will get healed'* (Mark 16:17). Demons and sickness have to submit to the powerful Name of Jesus.

Peter said it was faith in the name of Jesus that healed the crippled beggar: *'By faith in the **name of Jesus** this man you see and know was made strong. It is **Jesus' name** and the faith that comes through Him that has given this complete healing to him'* (Acts 3:16).

There have been testimonies where people in desperate situations have shouted out the name 'Jesus' and, as they did, there was a supernatural response where they were suddenly rescued from their disaster. One lady, a missionary in Uganda, saw some gunmen coming up to her and about to kill her. As they pointed their rifles at her she cried out 'Jesus!' and their rifles pointed upwards. They couldn't kill her and she is alive to tell the testimony. Another friend was about to be pulled under the waters when white water rafting along the river Nile, so he shouted 'Jesus!' Suddenly, he felt a hand lift him out of the river and put him on the bank. There is power in the name of Jesus to rescue and protect us.

When David fought Goliath, he didn't use a sword but a small pebble and said: *'I come against you in **the Name of the Lord Almighty**, the God of the armies of Israel'* (1 Samuel 17:45-47).

Jesus prayed His Father would *protect* His disciples by the *power in His Name* (John 17:11). The disciples were commanded by the priests and Sadducees never again to speak or teach in the Name of Jesus for they feared its power since people were being miraculously healed (Acts 4:18). This led the disciples to rejoice even more and ask God for even greater boldness to proclaim His Name.

There is power in the Name of Jesus. We can break a curse in the powerful Name of Jesus. Jesus said we can ask Him for anything in His Name and He will do it, if it is in accordance with His will (1 John 5:14). God said: *'He will call upon Me and I will answer him; I will be with him in trouble, I will deliver him and honour him'* (Psalm 91:15). Jesus prayed that His Father would protect us by the power of His name: *'Protect them by the power of Your name, the name You gave Me'* (John 17:11).

Power in the Blood of Jesus

During an outreach in Mozambique, it was interesting to see the reaction of a woman, who happened to be a witchdoctor, when she noticed a red cross on our medical tent. Her response was one of fear as she looked at it and ran away shrieking, *'The blood of Jesus!!'* It made me realise how satan and his evil hordes fear the blood of Jesus for they know its power to overcome and conquer any demonic power.

There is divine power in the blood of Jesus because it is so pure and holy that nothing unclean can touch it or penetrate through it. Demons shriek at it and flee. His blood cleanses us from all filth, sickness and sin and enables us to become pure and holy. It is like 100% supernatural bleach that gets rid of all demons and spiritual germs and purifies us from all sin (1 John 1:7).

The saints overcame the enemy by the *blood of the Lamb* (Revelation 12:11). There is life in the blood. It supernaturally cleanses from all our sins (Leviticus 17:11). For by His wounds we have been healed (1 Peter 2:24). This healing is for our bodies, souls and spirits.

Christ's forgiveness and healing is received when we partake in the Communion. As we receive His body and blood by faith, we receive both cleansing and healing. There is power in the blood of Jesus. Hence, it heals, cleanses, and protects us from the enemy.

His blood can cover and protect us from demonic spirits, especially as we minister to others. Some may choose to put the cross between themselves and the participant, whilst others may cover themselves with His blood.

I think it is wise to cover ourselves with His blood before we go out to minister or battle in the Spirit. Likewise, after taking part in spiritual warfare or ministry, we can cleanse ourselves from any demonic slime we may have come into contact with. They overcame by the blood of the Lamb.

Prayer & Fasting

Fasting is when we abstain from the things which please or feed our flesh, that is, our body and soul. Instead, we choose to hunger in our spirit for more of God's Presence, through prayer and worship.

Fasting can be a powerful weapon when receiving an assignment from God or engaging in a spiritual battle, where we see God's power work through us in greater measure. It is powerful and can bring breakthrough in our life and the lives of others.

Fasting releases miracles. The demon behind the epilepsy would only come out with prayer and *fasting* (Mathew 17:14-21). When Daniel received a vision of a great war, he prayed and fasted for twenty-one days. During this time, there was a battle going on in the Heavenly realms between an angel and a principality- the prince of Persia. Note that Daniel didn't war against the principality. He simply focused on God and prayed to Him concerning the situation. God sent His angels to do the battle. It took the length of the fast, twenty-one days of warfare prayer, until the archangel Michael defeated the prince. The angel was then able to explain everything to Daniel (Daniel 10:2-14).

It was while the church at Antioch was praying and fasting, the Lord spoke to them and said: *'Set apart for me Saul and Barnabas for the work which I have called them'* (Acts 13:2). Here prayer with fasting released a calling and commissioning.

In the natural when we fast, our bodies undergo a detoxification process which is actually beneficial to our bodies and health. If our bodies are undergoing a detoxification and clean up, our spirits are also undergoing a similar process of sanctification. Fasting enables us to become holy vessels where God can release greater power and anointing for the work He has commissioned us to do. Hence, prayer after fasting can have significant outcomes.

Satanists fast to gain more demonic power for spiritual breakthrough. However, they pray and fast to gain demonic power to see families break up, divorces take place and to bring destruction, even death, on people, churches or ministries. If they fast to gain demonic power, think how more powerful it is when Christians fast to bring Kingdom breakthrough in people's lives. (For more on fasting read Chapter 5).

Word of Testimony

The saints overcame satan by the blood of the Lamb and by the *word of their testimony*. Some translations read the *word of His testimony* (Revelation 12:11). I think both are correct since a testimony bears witness to the power, authority and character of God. It testifies to His truth. Testimonies are powerful tools to use in God's Kingdom, especially when reaching out to non-believers or others in their faith. Many have acted upon a testimony, thinking 'if God can do it for them, He can do it for me', and then witnessed God do it.

The testimony of Jesus is the spirit of prophecy (Revelation 19:10). When we prophesy in the Spirit, we are speaking from the heart of God to the spirit of man. Prophecy testifies to the nature and character of God and is the witness of Jesus.

John said he was on the island of Patmos because of the word of God and the testimony of Jesus (Revelation 1:9). The testimony of Jesus is declaring what the Holy Spirit puts in our spirit to say. We are testifying to the truth and word of God. It is the *rhema* word of God in us. The word of testimony releases faith and this in turn can bring salvation, deliverance and healing in the lives of those who hear. No-one can argue against a word of testimony from God. It carries weight and substance, and signs and wonders will accompany it.

Binding & Loosening

Jesus said to Peter: *'I will give you the keys of the Kingdom of Heaven; whatever you* **bind on earth will be bound in Heaven, and whatever you loose on earth will be loosed in Heaven***'* (Mathew 16:19). Some translations include the words 'will have been bound' and 'will have been loosened'. This means what we bind and loosen has already taken place in the Heavenly realm. Since there is no sickness, disease or demons in the third Heaven (God's Heavenly realm), then we can bind all sickness, disease and demonic spirits on earth. As we cast it out, we are loosening the person from the bondage they are in. Or we can pray to loosen them from their sickness or demonic spirits in the Name of Jesus.

I heard a preacher once say binding and loosening was only for Peter and it didn't apply to us. How far from the truth! Jesus spoke these words first to Peter but then He went on to speak these exact same words to other followers (Mathew 18:18).

Jesus says we are to drive out demons by the Spirit of God but bind up the strongman first (Mathew 12:28-29). When we bind up a demonic spirit, we are essentially telling it to be quiet and not allowing it to manifest in any way. Then we can cast it out, that is, if the person wants to be set free.

However, if the person doesn't want to acknowledge or renounce the demonic spirit, then we can still bind it. This is a good thing to do before we are due to meet up with someone who may be struggling with certain strongholds (like lust, pride, fear, jealousy, gossip, control, deception, intimidation, or any negative spirit, etc.). We can take authority and bind each spirit from rearing its ugly head before we meet them. This allows the other person to be open to hear God and we may find the conversation becomes more fruitful.

I met up with an old friend who wasn't a Spirit-filled believer and the conversation contained things I didn't want to hear. I felt defiled after I left. The next time we met, I prepared myself and took authority over the spirit of lust and perversion. This time we had a lovely conversation and my friend was more open to hear things about God. These demonic spirits were not allowed to show their ugly head for I had bound them or zipped their mouths from speaking and influencing my friend's mind.

However, I found that binding a spirit doesn't last forever; it is only for a period of time, usually a day. We have to keep on binding an evil spirit each time we meet up with someone, until they are willing to be delivered from it. Many times I will be in a room with others and sense an evil spirit manifesting like pride, control, performance or jealousy. I will silently bind this spirit and command it to stop affecting the person's thoughts, in Jesus' Name. Then minutes later, the person may forget what they were saying or the conversation changes and the ungodly spirit is no longer having an influence. It is easy to do as we pray with authority.

Breakthrough Prayer

There are situations in life where we need a breakthrough. God may give us a strategy, as He did with Joshua and the walls of Jericho. It may require fasting and praying, or persevering in prayer until breakthrough is seen. In other cases, we may need to approach His courtroom, asking for His mercy and forgiveness or to bring justice where needed (see Chapter 10, *Accessing the Courts of Heaven*).

I also believe there is an angel of breakthrough whom the Lord assigns to be with those He has called to bring revival or spiritual breakthrough in the nations. Certain individuals with such callings may have a 'breaker anointing' if the angel of breakthrough has been assigned to them.

'One who breaks open the way will go up before them; they will break through the gate and go out. The King will pass through before them, the Lord at their head' (Micah 2:13).

Prophetic Blessings

I was attending a conference where Roy Godwin, the former executive director of Ffald-y-Brenin retreat centre in Wales, was speaking on the power of *'blessing prayers'*[1]. He shared many testimonies on releasing a prophetic blessing simply by praying as the Holy Spirit led him to bless others.

He released blessings by saying, *'I bless you, in the name of Jesus, to...'* and would pray for a person to know all truth and bear much fruit in their lives. Also, he would bless them with regards to health, finances, family relationships etc, as he felt led by the Spirit to pray. It was a simple yet profound prayer, for the testimonies that followed were outstanding. These prophetic blessings were mainly prayed for non-believers and would release breakthrough in their lives, as well as healing and God encounters.

So I decided to test it out on a fellow believer at church. The Holy Spirit led me to pray a blessing on someone I didn't know well, and I simply released a blessing as I felt led to pray. I may have prayed something like this: *'I bless you in the Name of Jesus, to encounter God's love and know Him in a deeper way. May you be the head and not the tail, and discover all truth and bear fruit in the Kingdom. May He bless your relationships and bring unity in the family....'* The person started to cry and said it was powerful as these words ministered to her spirit.

How powerful it is when we choose to say words that bless instead of words that curse. It is a choice to speak positively instead of negatively and to bless instead of curse. Negative words are harmful, especially when they condemn, judge, criticise, accuse, complain, moan, or think it's doom and gloom, and release a sense of heaviness in our spirit. However, when we choose to bless and see situations as opportunities to pray, our hearts feel lighter and are free from oppression.

The Lord instructed Aaron how to release a priestly blessing on the Israelites. He said to say this prayer, known as the Aaronic prayer: *'The Lord bless you and keep you; the Lord make His face shine upon you and be gracious to you; the Lord turn His face toward you and give you peace'*, but God finishes by saying these words: *'So they will put My name on the Israelites and I will bless them'* (Numbers 6:22-27). If we pray a blessing in the *Name of Jesus* and pray according to His will for His people, then He will bless them. The key is to bless in the Name of Jesus for it is the Lord who blesses and not us.

Prophetic blessings may be released over people, churches, shops, businesses, neighbourhoods, and territories, and carry power when they are prayed from the heart of God.

These are the various ways we may operate by using the sword of the Spirit, with the words we utter from our mouths. They are the spiritual weapons that are available for us today, as we yield our hearts to God and invite His Spirit to lead us in prayer and worship.

Lord Jesus, teach me how to pray more effectively in the power of Your Spirit. Give me a greater revelation of the power of the words I speak, especially during prayer and worship. I ask for a prayer language to enable me to pray in Your Spirit (if you don't already pray in a spiritual tongue then you can ask by faith with thanksgiving, and start babbling as the words come out of your mouth). Thank You for the power there is in Your Name, Your blood and Your Word, to release healing, breakthrough and freedom. Teach me how to become a prayer warrior in Your Kingdom and carrier of Your Presence, in Jesus' mighty name!

END NOTES

[1] Roy Godwin: *The Way of Blessing;* (CPI group UK, 2016)

4

Recognising Your Spiritual Armour

Let us put aside the deeds of darkness
and put on the armour of light

Romans 13:12

Whilst serving in the war-torn nation of South Sudan, I discovered that the way to resist the 'enemy' is by responding in the opposite spirit. This meant I was to love instead of hate, to forgive instead of judge, to be kind instead of selfish, to humble myself and not think I knew more or was greater than others, and to pray for my enemies including those who spoke against me or hurt me.

Jesus commanded us to *love* our enemies. He said: *'Love your enemies, do good to those who hate you, bless those who curse you, pray for someone who mistreats you...do to others as you would have them do to you'* (Luke 6:27-31). Jesus taught us to respond in the opposite spirit with the heart of God, instead of reacting with our flesh from an orphan heart.

Armour of Light

Paul figuratively speaks about us putting on the armour of light, but what is the armour of light? These words refer to clothing ourselves or coming under the Lord Jesus Himself, instead of putting on or coming under the deeds of sin and darkness. The armour of light can represent the glory or manifest Presence of Jesus, and this exudes from our innermost being when we choose a lifestyle of abiding in His Presence. The armour of light is so bright that it can blind the eyes of the enemy. The rays are so brilliant, that the enemy can't see you, but only Jesus and His angels. This is because it carries divine weight and authority, as well as protection.

Hence, the *armour of light* refers to daily engaging in His Presence and by doing so we overcome the deeds of darkness (Romans 13:12). The deeds of darkness may include drunkenness, sexual sin, jealousy, anger, dissension, and unforgiveness. However, we wear the *armour of light* when we choose to respond with the heart of God and display the fruit of His Spirit.

I believe our spiritual armour is not something we take off and put back on again, but rather it is something we wear constantly for it is part of our spiritual lifestyle. In doing this, we are clothing ourselves in Christ Jesus, and this provides a divine protective covering.

Resisting Principalities

'Put on the full armour of God, so that you can take your stand against the devils' schemes. For our struggle isn't against flesh and blood, but against the rulers (principalities), against the authorities, against the powers of this dark world and against the spiritual forces of evil in the heavenly realms. Therefore, put on the **full armour** *of God, so that when the day of evil comes, you may be able to stand your ground, and after you have done everything, to stand'* (Ephesians 6:11-13).

In this passage, Paul instructs us to put on our *full* armour so we may stand or resist the principalities and powers of evil that are in the world. The various parts of armour he describes are fruit of the Spirit, and each fruit is nurtured as we yield each orphan area of our hearts to Jesus. Once we learn how to operate in the fruit of the Spirit, we can resist the spiritual forces of evil, including the principalities. A principality only has a hold on us if we allow it to, and this is through opening our minds and hearts to sinful actions and negative thoughts.

One day the Lord gave me a fresh revelation concerning principalities. This came at a time I was getting ready to return to the war-torn nation of South Sudan. Principalities are essentially high-ranking demonic powers that rule over designated areas. Their aim is to gain rulership over the people within that area. They can attack or rule us if we open our hearts to them by harbouring any unresolved sin. Hence, we overcome by not allowing sin to enter our hearts. We do this by daily surrendering our minds and hearts to Jesus as we die to self and take up our cross and follow Him. If we have no open doors in our heart (such as, jealousy, judgement, resentment, fear, pride, or any door open to 'self'), then the enemy can't come in.

This means we can *resist* any demon or principality by simply choosing to come under the power and influence of God's Spirit, as we surrender ourselves to Him. As we wear our armour, the fruit of His Spirit, we will resist the enemy by choosing to love, serve, be generous, honour, obey Him, and so on.

'Bless those who persecute; bless and do not curse... Do not pay anyone evil for evil...Do not take revenge, my friends, but leave room for God's wrath, for it is written: "It is Mine to avenge; I will repay", says the Lord. On the contrary: "If your enemy is hungry, feed him; if he is thirsty, give him a drink. In doing this, you will heap burning coals on his head". **Do not be overcome by evil, but overcome evil with good'** (Romans 12:14-21).

Jesus resisted all principalities including the *prince of the air*, satan himself, because He was without sin. Hence, satan had no *hold* on Him (John 14:30).

One thing the Lord made clear to me before engaging in any spiritual battle was to deal with any unresolved sin in my heart. This is because unresolved sin creates chinks or holes in our armour. Only then could I take up my position in Him and come under His authority and protection.

The fruit of the Spirit, which is the character and nature of God, is the lifestyle we are called to live. It is our spiritual armour. We are not to take it off but live with it every day from here to eternity.

Spiritual Armour - Fruit of the Spirit

The spiritual armour described in this passage is fruit of the Spirit: *'**Stand firm** then, with the belt of **truth** buckled around your waist, with the breastplate of **righteousness** in place and with your feet fitted with the readiness that comes from the gospel of **peace**. In addition to all this, take up the shield of **faith**, with which you can extinguish all the flaming arrows of the evil one. Take the helmet of **salvation** and the **sword of the Spirit**, which is the **Word of God**. And **pray in the Spirit** on all occasions'* (Ephesians 6:14-18).

Our spiritual armour includes other fruit not mentioned in this passage, such as, love, joy, patience, kindness, goodness, faithfulness, gentleness, self-control, compassion, mercy, grace, humility, meekness, forgiveness, unity, honour, obedience, submission and a servant heart (see Exodus 34:6, Galatians 5:22-24, Colossians 3:12, 1 Peter 4:1-11).

Let us take a look at how the fruit of the Spirit can be our spiritual armour.

Clothed in His Presence

God's Presence is more than a deep sense of inner peace. It is our spiritual armour! It is when we rest in His Presence that we can overcome the storms or battles taking place around us.

I believe it is our goal to discover how to become carriers of His Presence and overcome the enemy from this place of inner peace. In this place of abiding in Him we become seated with Christ in the Heavenly places, and this means satan is put under our feet (Ephesians 2:6). God's Presence quenches all fears and demonic manifestations, because the safest place to be is in His Presence.

David knew how to come into the Presence of the Lord. He was a warrior and a man after God's own heart. He prayed this prayer: *'One thing I ask of the Lord, this is what I seek: that I may **dwell** in the house of the Lord all the days of my life; **to gaze upon the beauty of the Lord** and to seek Him in His temple'*. He then continues: *'For in the day of trouble He will keep me **safe in His dwelling**; **He will hide me in the shelter of His tabernacle**'* (Psalm 27:4-5).

David hungered to dwell in the Presence of God. He knew that living under the shelter of the Most High was a place of safety and refuge. Psalm 91 powerfully describes how to overcome the battles around us by dwelling in His Presence. '*He who **dwells in the shelter of the Most High** will **rest** in the **shadow of the Almighty**'* (Psalm 91:1). To 'dwell' means the same as to 'abide' or 'rest' in His Presence. Natural rest is when we take a break or stop what we are doing. However, spiritual rest is about coming into God's Presence as we align our hearts with His. To come under the shelter of the Most High or be in the shadow of the Almighty refers to coming under the weighty Presence of God. His Presence can be both within and upon us. When we choose to abide in His Presence we come under His divine protection. We remain hidden under His wings or the wings of His angels, as we choose to follow Him.

Many times I have had the picture of walking under a huge wave. I had always viewed it as ministering under the power of His Spirit, until one day I saw it with fresh revelation. The wave suddenly turned into a wing and I was actually walking in its shadow. The words came to me: '*Life is to be one of walking beside Me, under the shadow of My wing and not just focused on ministry. Ministry is to be an overflow from walking with Me. This creates waves where others may receive My Spirit. As you abide in Me, you are walking under the shadow of My wing*'.

Being under the shadow of His wing not only gives us comfort and protection, but there is an anointing that comes from resting in His Presence. This is like Peter's shadow, where anyone who came in contact with his shadow was healed, because they were actually coming under the anointing and Presence of God that overflowed from him.

When the Presence of God overshadows people it creates a ripple effect on those around them. It is like a wave generating more waves and ripples. When He is with us, we will carry an overflow of His Presence that others may encounter. The most important thing is that we don't focus on the waves or the effect they have on those around us, but we keep our eyes focused on Him. As we remain hidden under His wings we become overshadowed by His Presence.

Love

Love is a weapon for there is power in love. It is a manifestation of His Presence. It sets us free from fear for perfect love *casts out fear* (1 John 4:18). God is love. Hence, whoever lives in love, lives in God and God in Him (1 John 4:16). We are to do everything in love (1 Corinthians 16:14). Jesus said the first and greatest commandment is this: *'Love the Lord your God with all your heart, all your soul and with all your mind'* (Mathew 22:37-39). And the second is to *love* your neighbour as yourself. Hence, we are *commanded* to love, and this is the greatest of all the commandments!

Jesus commands us to fight our enemies *with love* and be perfect as our Heavenly Father is perfect. This means to love others as God loves us (Mathew 5:44). It is love that delivers us from fear: *'For God didn't give us a spirit of fear but of power, love and of self-discipline'* (2 Timothy 1:7).

It doesn't stop there for we are to bless our enemies and not curse them. If our enemy is hungry, feed him; if he is thirsty, give him a drink. In doing this we are heaping burning coals on his head. We are not to be overcome by evil but overcome evil with good (Romans 12:9-21).

If we speak in tongues or prophecy or intercede, but lack love, then it is powerless and like a clanging gong. This is because love is more than a feeling. Love is patient, love is kind. It does not envy, it doesn't boast, it is not proud. It is not rude or self-seeking. It is slow to anger and keeps no record of wrongs. Love doesn't delight in evil but delights in the truth. It always protects, always trusts, always hopes and perseveres. Love never fails (1 Corinthians 13:1-13).

The love of God in us is so powerful that it can melt away any fear from the enemy. In a powerful vision I saw a witchdoctor coming to attack me with a sword and spear in his hand. He was full of anger and hatred and was going to kill me. Then I saw a massive outpouring of white light coming down from the throne of God. It fell on me and covered me like a downpour, and as I reached out to my enemy with the power of God's love, he started to cry and fell to his knees. He let go of his weapons as he fell to the ground and received the love of Jesus. He then joined sides with me and was no longer my enemy, but my friend.

There is power in love. It melts away the fear and hatred from our enemies. It is God's love that enables us to turn from our sinful ways and become adopted as His spiritual sons and daughters in His family. It is love that changes the hearts of His people. The main thing the enemy lacks and doesn't want us to have is God's love.

Before Jesus died, He told His disciples the greatest love anyone could have was to lay down his life for his friend (John 15:13). And then He demonstrated such sacrificial love for you and me. Our spiritual foundation is to be built on love for love conquers all (Ephesians 3:17).

Peace

Whereas natural peace is the absence of noise, supernatural peace is the Presence of God Himself. Jesus is the Prince of Peace therefore peace is a Person (Isaiah 9:6). When Gideon encountered the Angel of the Lord face-to-face, he thought his life was finished for no-one survived seeing the face of God. But the Angel of the Lord said: *'Peace! Do not be afraid. You are not going to die'*. After this Gideon built an altar and called it *'The Lord is Peace'*, which in Hebrew is *Jehovah Shalom* (Judges 6:23-24).

It is the peace of God in us that enables us to walk through the storms in life. Jesus overcame the storms because He was at total peace. When we carry His peace, we can take authority over the waves and storms around us.

Paul says: *'The God of peace will soon crush Satan under your feet'* (Romans 16:20). Our feet have been fitted with the Gospel of peace (Ephesians 6:15). Wherever we place our feet, we can speak His 'shalom' over any house, town or area. Jesus said: *'When you enter a house, first say, "Peace to this house". If a man of peace is there, your peace will rest on him; if not, it will return to you'* (Luke 10:5).

When we allow fear to enter our hearts, we are not operating from the Spirit of God and that is why we may see nothing happen or struggle to hear Him. Peace overcomes fear and with His peace we can take authority over demonic spirits.

Jesus didn't shout at demons when commanding them to leave, but He spoke with authority. Demons are not deaf! They do not respond to noise but authority. Some Christians shout at demons from a place of fear. The demons don't need to know who we are by our shouting because they can see God's Spirit in us, and it is His Spirit they submit to (Acts 19:13-19).

I was called to see someone in church who seemed to be 'fitting'. She was lying on the floor and her body was shaking. Others gathered around and shouted at the demon telling it to come out. Nothing happened. I was asked to come and help but I felt uncomfortable at the way those around her were shouting. I didn't feel the peace of God but instead stress and fear in the atmosphere. So I knelt down beside her and gently whispered in her ear, *'In the Name of Jesus, I command you to stop and leave her'*. Within ten seconds, she stopped shaking, opened her eyes and regained consciousness. We are to overcome demonic spirits with God's authority expressed with His love and peace, instead of shouting with fear.

Paul prayed a powerful prayer to quench fears and anxieties: *'The Lord is near. Do not be anxious about anything, but in everything, by prayer and petition, with thanksgiving, present your requests to God. And the* **peace of God** *that transcends all understanding, will* **guard your hearts and minds** *in Christ Jesus'* (Philippians 4:7). Here the Greek word used for 'guard' is a military word. Hence, peace is a warfare weapon that protects and guards the battles that go on in our hearts and minds. It is His peace that directs our paths and helps us overcome the circumstances around us.

Joy

Paul suffered much persecution for his faith, yet commanded us to be joyful always (1 Thessalonians 5:16). And he prayed that the God of hope would fill us with all *joy* and *peace* as we trust in Him, so we may overflow with the *power* of His Spirit (Romans 15:13).

Before His death, Jesus prayed for His disciples to be filled with the *full measure of joy* (John 17:13). I believe joy is a weapon that strengthens our inner being, and His joy would enable His disciples to overcome the persecution that was coming. It was for the joy set before Him that Jesus endured the cross (Hebrews 12:2). We can ask God for His joy in our times of difficulty so it can give us inner strength to persevere until the end.

Nehemiah told God's people: *'Do not grieve. For the* **joy of the Lord is your strength**' (Nehemiah 8:10). When we are filled with the joy of the Lord, it energizes us and gives us an inner strength. Joy comes from a deep sense of God's Spirit within us.

After the Ark of the Covenant had been returned, David rejoiced with thanksgiving and praise to God. He declared: *'Splendour and majesty are before Him;* **strength and joy in His dwelling place**' (1 Chronicles 16:27). David knew the joy of the Lord was his strength, but it came from seeking His Presence: *'You fill me with joy in Your Presence'* (Psalm 16:11).

A few years after being on the mission field, God showed me how to advance in enemy territory with His joy. I had never thought you could have joy when in battle. I had always thought it was a time to be serious when contending with the enemy. However, God taught me something different. I was about to go to South Sudan, when Heidi Baker prayed for me. She prayed that God would release His Spirit of joy in me as I stepped into this dark nation. Then I started to laugh; and I laughed from deep within, such that it gave me abdominal cramps. It was spiritual laughter that my mind couldn't comprehend.

Next, with my eyes still shut, I saw a huge transparent angel standing in front of me. The angel had blond curly hair and looked young and handsome, and was about seven foot tall. Each time the angel touched me, I burst into holy laughter. I asked the Lord, who was this angel? The Lord replied it was His angel of Joy. I had no idea there was an angel of joy! I then asked the Lord if this angel would be accompanying me to South Sudan and He said yes! Angels are warriors. This angel was His warrior of joy! What a revelation.

Wherever we go or whatever our battle, we can fight with His joy, for His joy is our strength. I believe if there is an angel of joy, there must be warrior angels for each fruit of the Spirit. How amazing is that!

Faith

Faith is a choice in our spirit. It is being sure of what we hope for and certain of what we do not see (Hebrews 11:1). When we hope for something, it is like shooting an arrow in the air, not knowing where it is going or the outcome. Faith, on the other hand, is when we have a certainty in our spirit, for we can see or sense in the Spirit the outcome. God gives us this assurance that He is going to act in accordance to what He has revealed to our spirit.

Faith believes in the unseen realm and in the impossible. If God says it will happen, then it will happen, no matter how impossible it may seem! If the thought comes from Him, then we are to stand with faith that it will come to pass on earth as it is in Heaven.

Faith is both a defensive and an offensive weapon. It defends as a shield by extinguishing the flaming arrows of the enemy (Ephesians 6:16). However, faith is like a sword for we advance by faith in His Word. We can both defend ourselves and attack the enemy, with faith. We stand in faith. Wobbly knees and eyes that look back at the enemy with fear or anxiety quench our faith. However, if we stand upright, looking forward with our eyes on the Lord, we will resist the devil as we stand firm in our faith (1 Peter 5:9).

Faith quenches the flaming arrows of the enemy. The arrows may be *fear, doubt, anxiety, lies, accusations, temptations, false guilt,* etc. We daily walk by faith by choosing to stand on the Word of God and what He reveals to us by His Spirit, because faith comes through hearing and hearing through the Word of God (Romans 10:17). Here, the Word is the *rhema* word or Spirit-breathed word.

Hearing through the Spirit-breathed word of God enables us to see through our spiritual eyes instead of through our natural ones. Just as Elisha opened the eyes of his servant to see what was taking part in the spiritual realm around him, so we can ask God to open our eyes to see with our spirit and respond by faith accordingly.

We are to live by faith and not by our natural sight (2 Corinthians 5:7) and then we will see God do amazing things in our lives and in the lives of those around us. It is the righteous who live by faith (Romans 1:17). We just have to look at how Jesus lived and we will see that He demonstrated a life of complete faith in His Father. He kept telling His disciples not to fear or doubt, but to have faith.

Faith increases as we choose to live a Spirit-led life. This means we choose to see and hear things in the Spirit and respond by faith. Faith has nothing to do with reason, logic or commonsense. It is of the Spirit and not our flesh. It is risk taking, and believes in the outrageous and impossible. It moves in the opposite direction to man's ways of thinking. It has complete trust in God and steps out in total obedience to His word and Spirit. Without faith, we can't advance God's Kingdom. When Jesus returns, He will be looking for those who live, not by reasoning or common sense, but by faith (Luke 18:8).

Truth

Jesus said: *'I am the way, **the truth** and the life'* (John 14:6). *'If you **hold to My teaching**, you are really My disciples. Then you **will know the truth, and the truth will set you free'*** (John 8:32). Jesus is the source of all truth. And He sent us the Holy Spirit who is the Spirit of truth: *'When the Counsellor comes, whom I will send to you from the Father, the **Spirit of truth who goes out from the Father**, He will testify about Me'* (John 15:26).

He later says: *'But when He, **the Spirit of truth, comes, He will guide you into all truth.** He will not speak on His own; He will speak only what He hears, and He will tell you what is yet to come'* (John 16:13). It is the Spirit of truth that guides us through life and sets us free from the lies, deceptions, and false beliefs of the enemy.

One of the names Jesus was given in Revelation was *Faithful and True* (Revelation 19:11). It is interesting how these two words are used in different translations. In Psalm 91:4, the New International Version (NIV) reads: *'faithfulness will be your shield'*, whereas, in the New King James Version (NKJV), it reads: *'truth will be your shield'*. Truth is like a shield for it quenches the fiery darts or lies from the enemy. It not only sets us free, but keeps us free as we declare it. Hence, walking in the truth releases greater faith and freedom.

Truth is like a belt firmly fastened around our waists, holding everything together (Ephesians 6:14). The truth of God quenches all lies, fears and false beliefs, and frees us from satan's clutches. When we feed on the Word it helps us live by the truth and walk in the Spirit. However, though the truth is powerful, it is not always spoken in the right way. Sometimes, we may speak the truth with a spirit of judgement, condemnation or anger, and this can cause more harm than good. The truth is well received when it is spoken in love and with God's conviction (Ephesians 4:15).

Before His death, Jesus prayed for His disciples to be *sanctified* by the truth: *'Sanctify them by the truth; Your Word is truth'* (John 17:17). The truth helps to keep our hearts and minds pure and free from ungodly thoughts, lies, or deception.

Nowadays we are seeing more people who are being persecuted for speaking out the truth, especially in Western countries. Many are losing their jobs or being suspended from work, simply because they spoke out the truth or bore witness to the truth. Many fear speaking the truth because of the persecution that may follow if they do. Jesus spoke the truth, even in His last hour before facing the cross. However, great is the reward in heaven for those who stand firm to the very end on the truth.

Wisdom & Discernment

There is worldly wisdom and discernment, and God's wisdom and discernment. The wisdom of the world is based on man's opinion and thoughts and worldly culture, and this is contrary to God's. God's ways and thoughts are different to man's (Isaiah 55:8). God's wisdom and discernment can only be revealed to our hearts through His Spirit, and this helps us to resist the temptations, fears and deception in the world.

Wisdom is found on the lips of the discerning (Proverbs 10:13). *'My Son, **preserve sound judgment and discernment**, do not let them out of your sight; they will be life for you, an ornament to grace your neck. **Then you will go on your way in safety, and your foot will not stumble'*** (Proverbs 3:21). We can ask God for His gifts of wisdom and discernment and He will freely give them to us, if we ask with faith (James 1:5, 1 Corinthians 12:8-10).

His wisdom and discernment have helped me through times of trials and testing, and also when making strategic decisions or ministering to others.

'The fear of the Lord is the beginning of wisdom' (Proverbs 9:10). *'Do not be wise in your own eyes; fear the Lord and shun evil'* (Proverbs 3:7). Wisdom comes when we choose to fear the Lord and rely on Him instead of our own understanding.

For every thought that crosses our mind, spiritual discernment enables us discern if the thought is from the flesh, satan, or God. Discerning in the Spirit helps us to walk in safety, make the right decisions, avoid fears, lies and deception, and follow along the path God has called us to walk with Him. (See *'Growing in Wisdom & Discernment'* Chapter 8).

Repentance & Forgiveness

Many times during ministry, I have witnessed the power of repentance and forgiveness in freeing someone from bondage. When we experience hurt, pain, or commit sin, it is like a rope or chain being tied around us, but the keys of repentance and forgiveness can free us from these chains of bondage. Any sin leads to bondage or imprisonment, including mocking: *'Now stop your mocking or your chains will become heavier'* (Isaiah 28:22). However, repentance and forgiveness (to others or ourselves) can release chains and free us from physical, emotional and spiritual bondage.

Healing and freedom are released when we confess our sins and pray for each other (James 5:16). Negative thoughts are like toxins that attack our bodies and cause stress, sickness, and disease. However, we walk in freedom through repentance and forgiveness. If we confess our sins, God will forgive us and purify us from all unrighteousness (1 John 1:9).

Nehemiah and Daniel came before God as they identified with the sins of their people and chose to stand in the gap by repenting for their sins. This is known as *Identification Repentance Prayer.* Breakthrough was seen as God released His mercy instead of judgement. As a result, Nehemiah was given favour and authority to rebuild the walls of Jerusalem, and Daniel was given a message and a vision by the angel Gabriel concerning the future of God's people (Daniel 9:1-23).

After Solomon dedicated the temple and prayed, God replied: *'If My people, who are called by My Name, will humble themselves and pray and seek My face and turn from their wicked ways, then I will hear from Heaven and will forgive their sin and heal their land'* (2 Chronicles 7:14). Repentance from sins can bring healing not only to our bodies but also to our land. Healing the land affects the crops, and this will affect our finances and health. A nation can be changed in a day through Identification Repentance Prayer.

Likewise, generational sins and curses are passed down the blood-line until they are broken through repentance and forgiveness. Generational sins may affect an individual, a family, a church, or even a nation.

There was famine for three successive years during King David's reign, so he sought the Lord to find out why. The Lord said it was due to the sin of his predecessor King Saul and his 'blood-stained house'. Saul's sin had been passed down to David through the royal line and affected his nation, until the sin was dealt with through David's prayers of repentance (2 Samuel 21:1).

While I was in a war-torn nation, I was aware of the people suffering through famine, displacement and deaths as a result of their corrupt dictator leadership. Tribes were fighting each other over cattle and there was ongoing tension. Then one man, who was a pastor from a tribe in the north, felt led by God to stand in the gap for his people. He arranged a big gathering for the local churches and government officials to attend and spoke bravely to his people by addressing their issues and the need to repent before God. The people identified with their sin and wholeheartedly repented before God. There was a shift in the spiritual atmosphere as they did and great rejoicing followed. Two weeks later, a political war broke out where the opposing party was fighting for government leadership. Many lives were lost as a result of this political battle. Militia groups broke out and all the states of this nation ended up coming under the attack of these militia groups, except the state whose people had got on their knees in prayers of repentance. God saved their land from being attacked by the enemy.

When we confess our sins and seek God's forgiveness, He will heal and restore our land. He is looking for those who will stand in the gap and repent for the sins of their people. Then He will cleanse our land and deliver us from the hands of the enemy.

Servant Heart & Humility

A servant heart is of great value to God, especially when it comes with humility. I believe all God's children, especially those called to leadership, require the fruit of humility. If I am not willing to serve, then I am not fit to lead. When we discover our true identity in Christ we discover what it means to serve. The Lord gives us His grace as we surrender all pride, striving, achievement, and the need to be in control.

When Jesus taught His disciples on humility He said: *'The **greatest among you will be your servant**. For whoever exalts himself will be humbled, and **whoever humbles himself will be exalted**'* (Mathew 23:8-12). Jesus came not to be served but to serve and He demonstrated this as He washed His disciples' feet (John 13:1-12).

Our true identity is not in what we do but how God sees us. Our work is our assignment and not our identity. We are to see each other as brothers and sisters in Christ and relate to one another this way. One of satan's weapons is pride and we oppose this with God's grace and humility. Pride will pull us down, but humility will lift us up. We *clothe* ourselves with humility (1 Peter 5:5-6).

One of the areas we struggle with is that of offense. We have probably been offended by someone or something at some point in our lives. Offense is a form of pride and will trip us up and make us fall. When we allow ourselves to become offended we are shifting the blame to someone else by pointing the finger at them. The truth is that an area of pride in our orphan heart has been triggered and this is to be addressed.

To overcome any offense we simply yield this area of hurt or pain in our heart to Jesus and allow Him to heal us. As we let it go and give it to Him, He transforms our hearts. The outcome is we are no longer affected by the words that were said or the actions that were done. Jesus never allowed Himself to be offended by man, for He could discern the orphan and ungodly areas in their hearts. He either ignored their comments or actions, or challenged them with a righteous response.

Some may pray with a sense of pride or superiority in their hearts, instead of a heart of humility. True humility is when we know God's greatness and are willing to yield to Him. Warriors for God do battle on their knees. Humility is not a sign of weakness, but of power. Those in God's Kingdom who walk in great humility are those who carry the greatest authority. The meek are those who do not rely on their own strength, but yield themselves to God and lean on Him.

Jesus could have fought the enemy with thousands of angels but He didn't. Instead He humbled Himself to death on a cross and, in doing so God exalted Him to the highest place (Philippians 2:8). When we fight the enemy in our own strength, we will be defeated. However, if we choose to surrender our will and flesh to God, we will overcome. *'Submit yourselves to God. Resist the devil and he will flee'* (James 4:7). The enemy can no longer attack what we have crucified in our flesh, but he can attack the things we haven't surrendered to God.

Grace

God invites us to live by His grace instead of our own power and strength. Grace is God's power at work in us to do what we can't do in the natural. It is an inner strength and ability to do what we are unable to do in our natural strength. Grace is given to us by God but He only gives it to the humble in heart. Living by grace enables us to rely on the power of His Spirit instead of our own strength and abilities.

The apostles moved in the power of the Spirit for great grace was upon them (Acts 4:33). Grace carries power. Jesus said: '*My grace is sufficient for you, for **My power** is made perfect in weakness*' (2 Corinthians 12:9). John knew Jesus as one who was full of grace and truth (John 1:14-17).

Instead of relying on our own strengths and abilities to do God's work on earth, we are called to live not by might nor by power but by His Spirit (Zechariah 4:6). This is the power of His grace at work in us.

Self-Control

Self-control is a fruit of the spirit and is different to the need to always be in control which is of the flesh. Self-control is when we control our thoughts, words and actions. It is the ability to hold back from saying or doing anything we would regret or that may hurt others. However, a person who operates with a controlling spirit is someone who always needs to be in control and control others. This may be seen as a form of witchcraft.

Wherever we lack self-control, it opens the door in our hearts to temptation and sin. Hence, self-control prevents us from falling into sin or temptation. Peter taught us to be self-controlled, clear minded and alert, in order to pray (1 Peter 4:7, 5:8). Our minds can be influenced by alcohol, sex, pornography, violence, drugs, anger or negative thoughts, but self-control helps us to stay alert and not fall into the enemy's den (1 Thessalonians 5:8).

Many times, when we lose self-control due to an outburst of anger, it may be there is a root to this ungodly fruit. The Holy Spirit can reveal the root and heal our hearts, as we choose to forgive others where needed.

It takes the fruit of self-control to be able to act in God's Spirit instead of react in the flesh. Simon Peter reacted to Jesus' arrest by cutting off the ear of the high priest's servant (John 18:8).

Instead of impulsively reacting to the people around us we can take a deep breath and respond with the fruit of self-control.

Patience & Perseverance

It is so easy to want to rush into things and run ahead of God but God wants us to wait for His timing because it is always perfect. He is outside of time for He knows the past and the present, as well as the future. If we try and jump into things too soon, we can cause a premature delivery or spiritual abortion to God's plans. However, perseverance enables us to become mature and complete, and not lacking anything (James 1:4). *'Blessed is the man who perseveres when under trial, because when he has stood the test, he will receive the crown of life'* (James 1:12).

Jesus always waited for His Father's timing. He was never in a rush. Even after Lazarus had died, He waited a few days before telling His disciples to get up and go with Him to the tomb. God has a strategy and purpose that requires us to wait on Him and step out when He gives us the green light and says, 'Go!'

'Those who wait on the Lord will renew their strength; they will soar on wings like eagles, they will run and not grow weary. They will walk and not be faint' (Isaiah 40:31). As we wait on the Lord, He does deeper work in our hearts and this strengthens our innermost being.

Patience means giving our reins of control to God instead of trying to take charge ourselves. Sometimes, when we get frustrated and impatient about something, it may be because we don't feel in control. There was a time when I felt frustrated in life during a season of transition for I didn't know what was happening in my life and felt out of control. I feared the unknown future because I had no idea what was going to happen in my life. However, during this season the Lord kept asking me to give the control reins to Him. Did I trust Him with my future? It was another area of dying to my flesh, a part that wanted to be in control.

'Wait for the Lord, be strong and take heart and wait for the Lord' (Psalm 27:13).

Renewing Our Minds

Helmets protect the heads from injury or attack. The helmet of salvation may be seen as protecting our thoughts as we journey along the path of salvation. Our minds are being renewed as we become hearers of His word and Spirit and discerners of His truth. This protects our minds from coming under any lies, gossip, deception, criticism, fears, or other negative things we may see or hear. Instead, we can take captive these thoughts by cleansing our minds and imaginations with the power of His blood, and choosing to focus our thoughts on His Word and Spirit instead. Negativity can enslave us or even destroy us, for it can be like a self-destructive weapon. Whereas, when we choose to speak words that release life instead of death, this can help us and others walk in freedom. We can repent of the repeated negative words we constantly say and ask the Lord to cleanse our minds and hearts with the power of His blood.

Honour One Another

Honour is one of the Ten Commandments. We are to honour our parents so we may live long and receive His blessings (Exodus 20:12). In the natural, we honour those who have status or rank, such as the royal family, famous people, leaders or our boss. However, as children of God, we are called to honour God's people. That means we choose to show respect to the downcast, the poor and the rejects of society.

God is willing to raise the poor from the dust and lift the needy from the ash heap and seat them with princes (Psalm 113:7-8). We honour one another when we choose to see everyone through God's eyes, and love through the eyes of His heart. As God's royal children we can learn to honour others, and this includes honouring those who have made mistakes or fallen because of sin. We are to see them as God sees them, not judge them for their sins, but honour them, simply because they are a child of God (Romans 12:9).

Obedience & Righteousness

Obedience is part of our artillery. One of the enemy's strongholds is rebellion. Hence, obedience to God's will protects us from falling due to the sin of rebellion. When we choose to disobey God then we are stepping out of His divine covering and are at risk of coming under a curse, but when we choose to obey Him, then we stay under His covering and receive blessings (Deuteronomy 28). Does this mean that if we are hit by the enemy then we have disobeyed God or sinned? Not necessarily. We can still get hit by the enemy even when we are doing His will for we are in a spiritual battle.

'When you pass through the waters, I will be with you, and when you pass through the rivers they will not sweep over you. When you walk through the fire, you will not be burned; the flames will not set you ablaze. For I am the Lord, your God' (Isaiah 43:2).

Sometimes, we may need to ask others to cover us in prayer. Joshua only overcame the Amalekite army when Moses was praying for him on the hill top (Exodus 17:11).

Obedience is better than sacrifice! *'Does the Lord delight in burnt offerings and sacrifices as much as in obeying the voice of the Lord?* **To obey is better than sacrifice,** *and to heed is better than the fat of rams.* **For rebellion is like the sin of divination** *and arrogance like the evil of idolatry'* (1 Samuel 15:22-23).

David knew well that obedience to the will of God mattered more than sacrifice (Psalm 40:6-8). The truth is, we can make offerings to God but still be disobedient to His will. To live in obedience to the will of God will include personal sacrifices along the way. Hence obedience matters more than offerings.

Being obedient is a key attribute to being a warrior for the Lord. To be in the army of the Lord means our hearts are fully surrendered to His will and willing to take orders from Him. All soldiers are trained to follow orders and stay in alignment with what they are commanded to do. If they step out of line, their life can be in danger. We are called to be obedient even unto death, as we willingly lay down our lives for God. When we say yes to being in His army, in effect we are declaring our life is no longer our own but His. We belong to Him.

Jesus' biggest battle was in the garden of Gethsemane. When He asked His Father to take the cup of suffering away from Him, He said: *'Not My will but Yours be done!'* God is looking for His faithful and obedient servants who will stand with Him until the end, not looking back or choosing to go their own way.

Sadly, there are many Christians today who opt out of the will of God as it is too much for them. There is a cost to obeying His will but a far greater reward that awaits us in Heaven. Instead of focusing on the cost we simply have to be willing to pay the price. Life on earth is temporary like a drop in the ocean compared to life in Heaven which is eternal.

Jesus told His followers that unless they ate the flesh of the Son of Man and drank His blood then they had no life in them. Many couldn't accept this, and no longer followed Him (John 6:53-66).

God may ask us to lay down things for Him we don't want to. This may be relationships, work, homes, possessions, roles or anything we idolize, that is things we put before God and can't live without. Jesus always obeyed His Father and did His will even when it cost Him His life. God will ask different things from each one of us. We have a choice. We can surrender and obey, or not. He rewards those who are righteous and obey Him. Never forget, He always has our best interests at heart and knows what is best.

One of God's names is the Lord our Righteousness or *Jehovah Tsidek* (Jeremiah 23:6). Living a righteous life is not about going to church or doing good things. Rather, it is choosing to do what is right in God's eyes. As we cast our eyes on Jesus He will guide us along the right path, the path of righteousness (Psalm 23:3).

Self-righteousness is based on what we think to be right but from a self-centred opinion or the flesh. Whereas the fruit of righteousness is simply doing what is right in the eyes of God. The breastplate of righteousness is worn when we hold onto what is right in His eyes and this will protect our hearts (Ephesians 6:14). This same verse in The Passion Translation reads: *'Put on holiness as the protective armour that covers your heart'*. James said the prayer of a righteous man is powerful and effective (James 5:16).

Jesus said: *'Blessed are those who hunger and thirst for righteousness, for they will be filled'* (Mathew 5:6). When we seek first the

Kingdom of God *and* His righteousness, then all the other things will be given to us (Mathew 6:33).

We read in the Old Testament how God brought victory in every battle when the kings did what was right in His eyes. To do what is right means not only to seek Him but to obey His will.

Boldness

After the apostles had been threatened to never speak or teach the Name of Jesus, they asked God to increase their boldness to proclaim His Word: *'Now Lord, consider their threats and enable Your servants to **speak Your Word with great boldness**... After they prayed, the place where they were meeting was shaken. And they were all **filled with the Holy Spirit and spoke the Word of God boldly'*** (Acts 4:29). God didn't give us a spirit of timidity, but of power, love and a sound mind (2 Timothy 1:7). The Spirit of God will release boldness in our spirit to stand against the enemy and speak His Word without fear or shame.

There was a little old lady who came for ministry who had been abused as a girl and this had caused her to live in shame, fear, and timidity all her life. As a result, she had a stutter and was very withdrawn. I witnessed God do some outstanding divine heart surgery in this lady's heart. He healed her emotionally, mentally and spiritually and, when she stood up to testify to what God had done, she spoke with a spirit of boldness like never before. Everyone was stunned at the work of God as they witnessed a divine boldness in her heart.

Unity in the Spirit

Jesus said whenever two or more gather together to pray in His Name, He is with us (Mathew 18:19-20). There is a greater Presence of God when passionate lovers of Jesus gather together to pray and worship in the Spirit. He loves it when we are united by His Spirit. Whenever we are joined together in the Spirit it causes the intensity of His fire to increase. And when many flames come together it becomes like one huge burning fire. God does mighty things when we pray together in the unity of the Spirit.

Recognising Your Spiritual Armour

Jesus sent out His disciples in pairs when they went to heal the sick and bring the lost into the Kingdom (Luke 10:1). There is wisdom here for one can be interceding while the other is ministering. Also two minds are better than one when listening to God and discerning His Spirit.

When I was preparing the medical team for the different outreaches in Africa, one of the things God showed me was that the team was to operate in the unity of the Spirit in order for His power to flow through us and for His protection to be over us. A friend had a prophetic picture of the team holding hands but being attacked by a swarm of mosquitoes carrying malaria. Holding hands represented a superficial joining of the flesh. However, when the team became joined at the elbows there was a spirit of unity that the swarm of mosquitoes couldn't penetrate.

Just before Jesus died, He prayed a powerful prayer for all believers, that we may be one with Him as He is with the Father. If we are united to Jesus and the Father, then are spirits can be united through the Holy Spirit to one another. He continued to pray that we may be brought to complete unity so the world would know that the Father sent Him (John 17:21-23).

Superficial unity is of the flesh, but true spiritual unity comes through prayer and worship. Washing each other's feet, praying for one another and taking Communion together, are ways to be united in His Spirit. When we are in unity with one another and God, there is divine protection and the enemy cannot attack us. But where there is division, disunity, disloyalty, gossip, or sin, then the enemy can get through that crack or chink in our armour and attack. We can be united in the Spirit and still agree to disagree on things. God has made us to be different but when we come together in His Name and pray for one another, then we become united in the power of His Spirit.

It is powerful when we contend for unity in the Spirit with those whom we are working with or ministering alongside. Unity releases protection and anointing: *'How good it is when brothers live together in unity! It is like precious oil poured on the head'* (Psalm 133:1-2). One man can put a thousand to flight but two men can put ten thousand to flight (Deuteronomy 32:30).

David Overcoming Goliath

David enquired about Goliath and fearlessly said to Saul that the Lord who delivered him from the paw of the lion and bear would deliver him also from the hand of Goliath (1 Samuel 17:37). David was seeing Goliath not through his natural but through his spiritual eyes. David was just a teenager, but spiritually he was a giant. He was well equipped for warfare as a result of his ongoing lifestyle of prayer and worship.

David knew in his spirit that God was far greater than Goliath, so instead of retreating in fear he advanced with holy boldness and the fear of the Lord. He carried spiritual authority as a result of his intimate relationship with God. He proclaimed the battle was not by sword or spear (flesh), but the battle was the Lord's (1 Samuel 17:47). Here he was uttering the word of God with the sword of the Spirit as he declared God's truth. He ran forward with the stones knowing that the Lord was with him and God's warring angels knocked out Goliath.

David couldn't fight with Saul's armour because it was different to his own. David's armour was the fruit of the Spirit which had increased as a result of his time spent in the secret place with God. He had developed the spiritual muscles of faith along with the fear of the Lord, and fired God's word with a spirit of boldness. He was fully armed as he walked in spiritual authority and declared the truth in the powerful Name of Jesus.

Like David, God has called us to be giant slayers. This is from a lifestyle of being in the secret place with Him and abiding in His Presence. Our spiritual armour is developed as we hang out with God and allow Him to address the orphan areas in our heart. In effect we are clothing ourselves in Him, the armour of light, as we pursue His Spirit and rest in His Presence.

Lord Jesus, help me to recognise the orphan areas of my heart as I yield my heart to You. Reveal the chinks in my armour and how to overcome through Your Spirit. May Your Spirit transform my heart and mind as I daily seek Your Wisdom and Revelatory-Truth. Teach me how to walk in Your ways and hear Your Spirit, and nurture my heart with the fruit of Your Spirit. Give me a heart that passionately seeks Your Presence, and obeys Your will whatever the cost, to the very end.

5

Weapon of Fasting

This kind of demon is only cast out through prayer and fasting

Matthew 17:21

When God called me to serve Him on the mission field I somehow knew that fasting was to become a part of my lifestyle. Since I could no longer avoid it I decided to look at the reasons why I should fast. There are many reasons why we should fast and the enemy tries to discourage us from doing so because he doesn't want us to know the truth or power behind fasting. Where food may dull the spirit, fasting will sharpen it.

Fasting is one of the most powerful weapons for spiritual breakthrough. Not only that, but it draws us closer and deeper in our relationship with God. Jesus didn't say *'if'* but *'when'* you fast because fasting was something the disciples were to adopt as part of their lifestyle (Matthew 6:16).

What is Fasting?

Fasting is abstaining from the things that please or feed the desires of our flesh (body and soul) for a period of time *and* instead hungering for more of God's Presence. In effect, we are feeding or feasting on His Spirit as we submit the flesh (body and soul) to our spirit, and surrender our spirit to the Holy Spirit. When we fast we are focusing on the spirit instead of the flesh and this helps to fine tune our spirit to hear Him more clearly.

Fasting increases our spiritual appetite as we hunger for more of His Presence. It is an important tool when seeking spiritual breakthrough, healing, direction, divine strategy, and for sharpening our spiritual senses. God can work through our hearts in greater measures as a result of fasting. The Lord showed me that fasting is like a power-drill that breaks through our spiritually dry grounds to access the deep rivers of His Life-giving water.

Fasting was something I avoided until I realized it was a spiritual weapon. It is recognized as one of the spiritual disciplines that draws us closer to God. The more we fast the easier it becomes, as our flesh learns to yield to our spirit.

However, I would like to point out that fasting is *not* a way to lose weight or to draw attention to ourselves. It is *not* a hunger strike or a way to manipulate God to get what we want. God sees our hearts and responds accordingly. If we struggle with any kind of fasting or think fasting is not for me, then we are probably living a flesh-led life instead of a Spirit-led life.

Reasons to Fast

It is a Command

When Jesus spoke to His disciples about fasting He didn't say *'if'* but *'when'* you fast: '**When you fast** *put oil on your head and wash your face, so that it will not be obvious to men that you are fasting, but only to your Father who is unseen; and your Father,* **who sees what is done in secret, will reward you**,' (Matthew 6:17). Father God rewards all who fast in secret with the right attitude of heart. When Jesus was questioned why the disciples didn't fast He replied: '*How can the guests of the Bridegroom mourn while He is with them? The time will come when the Bridegroom will be taken from them;* **then they will fast**' (Matthew 9:15).

When the Lord calls us to follow Him fasting becomes part of our lifestyle. This may be on a regular basis as well as for specific times and seasons. For some, this may be a day every week and for others, it may be three to five days a month or a whole month each year. It is between you and God how often you fast and how you fast. When we fast on a regular basis, for example for a day a week, it helps our flesh to come under the influence of our spirit and this keeps us more Spirit-focused instead of flesh-focused. It is a bit like going to a spiritual gym to keep our spirits 'healthy' and fully yielded to God. In effect, we are showing the enemy we are not under the rulership of our flesh or the world but God.

Changes are coming in the world and some have already started. The spiritual discipline of fasting will help prepare our hearts and spirits to be ready for such times as these.

Turn our Hearts Back to God

The Lord said: *'Return to Me with all your heart, with fasting and weeping and mourning'* and Joel replied to the people: *'Blow the trumpet in Zion, declare a holy fast, call a sacred assembly. Gather the people, consecrate the assembly; bring together the elders, gather the children, those nursing at the breast'* (Joel 2:12-17). The Lord called His people to turn their hearts back to Him and to cry out to Him with prayer and fasting. When they did He forgave their sins and blessed their land once again.

The Lord sees our hearts when we turn to Him in prayer and fasting. He responds by turning things around for good as we choose to follow Him. The first command is to love the Lord our God with ALL our heart, mind, soul and strength. Fasting helps to turn our hearts back to Him.

Spiritual Breakthrough

After Jesus reached thirty years of age He started His full-time ministry with a forty-day fast. This fast was God ordained. Straight after He was baptized with the Spirit in the river Jordan, He was then led by the Spirit into the wilderness. During this fast Jesus faced many tests and trials, along with temptations, but He constantly kept His mind and Spirit focused on the Word of God.

Jesus underwent the same tests, trials, and temptations that the Israelites did when they were in the desert but He overcame each one. After achieving this spiritual breakthrough He was ready to enter His ministry, but now in the *power and anointing* of the Spirit (Luke 4:1-14).

This was a significant season of spiritual breakthrough where Jesus overcame the tests and trials of the enemy. Fasting is an excellent tool or spiritual weapon to see breakthrough in our lives or the lives of others, as we overcome such tests and trials.

Fasting is like a power drill to break through the dry and hard ground until fresh water or oil comes gushing forth. Hence, we are not to give up but persevere until breakthrough occurs.

Daniel was a man of prayer and fasting. When he saw God was grieved by the sins of the people, his response was to stand in the gap and intercede, through prayer and fasting (Daniel 9:3-16). Next, Daniel had a vision concerning a great war and this led him to pray and fast for three weeks. During this fast, he ate no choice food or meat or wine, but just vegetables (Daniel 10:2-3). From day one of his fast, warring angels were dispatched to battle in the Heavenly realms. The Archangel Michael was warring against the principality over the Persian region (or the prince of Persia). Finally, on day twenty-one, an angel arrived and said to him: *'The prince of the Persian kingdom resisted me twenty-one days. Then Michael, one of the chief princes, came to help me, because I was detained there with the prince of Persia'* (Daniel 10:13). It took twenty-one days of spiritual warfare, through prayer and fasting, before breakthrough occurred over the demonic strongholds operating over this nation.

There was a time when I felt immense spiritual opposition to my calling and ministry and this was confirmed by a word given to me by a credible prophet, Isabel Allum. Isabel prophesied, *'Just like Daniel fasted for twenty-one days and the arch-angel Michael came to intercept against the prince of Persia, the Lord will wage war on your behalf and end the tug of war in the spirit realm.'*

After hearing this word I felt prompted to go on a Daniel fast. Two days after the fast finished, I was invited to a prophetic conference with fellow prophetic warriors. It was a divine appointment where I received both prophetic words and ministry, and at the end of this special gathering, I knew in my spirit that this battle was finally over and the enemy was defeated.

Fasting is a way to see breakthrough in our ministry, health, families, finances, churches, or even nations. When people ask me to pray for them to see a breakthrough in their health or life, I usually invite them to fast, because I believe fasting helps to release breakthrough.

People may feel led to fast when seeking a financial breakthrough. There was a Christian Healing Retreat centre that was struggling to pay their staff's wages, so the leadership team sought God in prayer and fasting. The day the wages were due to be paid, the exact amount of money appeared in their account, and all the workers received their wages. They had no idea where the money had come from, but prayer and fasting released the necessary finances.

As well as doing individual fasts, we can partake in *corporate fasts*. Corporate fasts are when groups of believers come together in prayer and fasting to see breakthrough in a specific area or for a certain person. Esther arranged a corporate fast where her people fasted for three days to deliver the Jews from the clutches of death (Esther 4:12-16). This was known as a 'complete' fast because they fasted from water as well as food.

I signed up to take part in a fifty-day church fast where people took it in turns to pray and fast each day. The results were amazing. There was a shift in the prayer and worship, as the believers had caught something during this season of pressing deeper through prayer and fasting.

A lady with a prophetic ministry was on a flight when she noticed the person sitting next to her wasn't eating their food. So she asked the person why they weren't eating and the person replied that they were fasting. As she enquired further, it turned out that this person was a satanist. Satanists fast in order to gain greater demonic power for spiritual breakthrough. However, their breakthrough is in the demonic realm. They pray and fast to see families break up, divorces take place, and to bring sickness and destruction on people, churches, and ministries. If they fast to gain demonic power, think how powerful it is when Christians fast to bring Kingdom breakthrough in people's lives, churches and nations! Knowing this truth opened my eyes to how fasting is a powerful weapon we are no longer to ignore.

Spiritual Direction

Another reason to fast is when we are seeking spiritual direction, for fasting helps to tune our spiritual senses to hear, see, sense, and discern more clearly. I have benefitted from fasting when seeking God's will or direction in my life. He has replied to my hunger and desire to do His will by revealing the next steps.

While the church at Antioch were praying and fasting, the Lord spoke to them and said: *'Set apart for me Saul and Barnabas for the work to which I have called them'* (Acts 13:2). Here prayer and fasting released a commissioning. People can hear God more clearly when praying in the unity of the Spirit. Jesus said when two or more come together in His Name, He is with them (Matthew 18:20).

During the time of lockdown from the Corona Virus pandemic in 2020, my spirit felt led to do a three week Daniel fast on the lead up to Pentecost. When Pentecost came, nothing dramatic happened and I wasn't sure the reason behind the fast. Then a few days later, I sensed I was to be in a certain place at a certain time, at a natural beauty spot that I frequently visited to spend time with the Lord. So I tested it out and went to the location at the specified time. It seemed like a normal day and nothing extraordinary happened, until I decided to walk back via the river route. I made my way back across a footbridge overlooking the shallow depths of the river and saw hundreds of tiny silver fish on both sides of the bridge. I assumed it must be breeding season. Then as I continued to walk alongside the river edge, I suddenly noticed a twelve foot dark shadow following me upstream. It was moving at my pace and no more than a few feet from the river's edge.

I started to laugh as I saw hundreds of hand size silver fish jumping out of the water swimming alongside me. So I said, *'OK God, You have got my attention!'* Next, I sensed Him ask me this question: *'What do you call a group of fish?'* I replied: *'A school'*. Immediately, I sensed Him say: *'I want you to start a new online school for beginners and intermediate learners on healing'*. The tiny fish I saw across the footbridge represented the beginners and the hand sized fish represented the intermediates. This tied in well with two books I had just published in the Kingdom Medicine series (*Foundation For Healing*[1] for beginners and *Kingdom Tools*[2] for intermediates).

I laughed for I knew these were not my own thoughts and something that I certainly wouldn't think of doing. The Lord had directed me to start a new ministry involving online teaching and training. This was the result of the three week fast followed by the prompting of the Spirit, to be in a certain location at a certain time. I loved the way God communicated this to me through nature, knowing my love for the outdoors and prayer walking with Him. I immediately responded to this assignment.

Whenever I feel I have reached a plateau in my walk with God, or I'm not sure where I am going, then I usually fast. Fasting is a way of humbling ourselves before God, knowing our need for His counsel and direction, as well as revealing how desperate we are for Him.

One time, during a season of transition, I felt desperate to know where God was in my life. So I fasted as my spirit cried out to Him, and I continued until He answered me. Suddenly, on the third day, I was overwhelmed by His loving Presence. It was as if His Presence crashed into my room like a mighty wave and overshadowed me. Suddenly, the 'power drill' effect of fasting had struck the oil of His Presence. He revealed to my spirit that I was in His will and right where He wanted me to be. This was going to be a season of just me and Him walking together through the wilderness.

After this, my relationship with God went to a much deeper level. God was delighted in my hunger for more of Him and seeking His face. Fasting draws our heart and spirit closer to Him.

Healing & Deliverance

I believe fasting is a weapon for healing and deliverance. Fasting is like moving up in gears when contending for breakthrough. Fasting releases miracles. The demon behind the fitting boy would only come out with prayer and *fasting* (Mathew 17:14-21).

The famous healing evangelist Smith Wigglesworth was asked to pray for a Welsh man who was dying of Tuberculosis (TB). He did, but the man wasn't healed. As Wigglesworth was walking up the Welsh mountains the Lord told him to go back and pray for this man. However, this time he fasted and asked a group of fellow elders to join him in fasting. As he fasted, he came up against the demon that was behind the disease. The symptoms of TB came upon Smith Wigglesworth himself and he spent the night battling in the spirit until it finally left him. He overcame the spirit behind the man's TB through fasting and prayer. When he went back to the man who was dying, he and the fellow believers followed the Lord's strategy. They simply joined hands around the man and said one word, 'Jesus'. They quietly repeated the name Jesus until the man had an encounter with the Lord Himself, repented of his sin and jumped off the bed, healed and set free.[3]

In some cases, it may be wise to fast before ministering to an individual. Fasting prepares our hearts and fine tunes our spirit to hear God and minister under His anointing. People may fast before ministering at conferences. Some fast for weeks beforehand since battles are going on and the enemy is trying to stop the move of God's Spirit or block people coming.

Prayer and fasting release supernatural power and may create an open heaven for God's angels and Spirit to come in power. I have noticed the difference when attending conferences where there has been prayer and fasting beforehand compared to conferences where there has been little or none. Miracles, healings and heavenly encounters are the norm where prayer and fasting has prepared the way for the Lord.

I would like to point out that sometimes we may fast and pray for healing and nothing happens or the person dies. David prayed and fasted before God for Bathsheba's child to live, but the child died (2 Samuel 12:16). Fasting doesn't guarantee healing or breakthrough and there may be reasons for this that we may not understand, but I believe no fasting is wasted.

Freedom from Idol Worship

Another reason we may fast is to break free from idol worship. Without realizing, we may have allowed things to influence our lives or take over our time and therefore restrict or stifle our relationship with God. God may lovingly ask us to fast from such things for a period of time. This may be from musical instruments, electronic games, social media, TV, or whatever we seem to spend a lot of our time doing.

When I worked as a Doctor in the National Health Service I would turn on my TV every evening after I came back from work as a form of relaxation. This seemed a normal part of life until I took a sabbatical. The first thing the Lord asked was for me to fast from watching TV for six weeks. At the end of the six weeks I turned on the TV and realized how much rubbish was on it and how it polluted my mind and dulled my spirit. I saw how my spiritual senses had become sharper and clearer during this six week fast. So from then on I decided to watch very little TV and to use my evenings to draw closer to Him.

Sanctify Ourselves for Engaging in Battles

God may ask us to fast before entering or engaging in a spiritual battle. Through fasting we sanctify our body, soul and spirit as we yield every part of our self to the Lord.

Jehoshaphat, King of Judah, was alarmed when he saw a huge army coming against him. So he enquired of the Lord and immediately proclaimed a fast for the people of Judah. During the corporate fast Jehoshaphat humbled himself before God and waited for His response. God replied and gave Jehoshaphat a strategy to overcome the enemy. The Lord told Jehoshaphat that the battle belonged to Him. However, he still had to take his place in God's army and follow His orders. As he humbly obeyed the Lord, the battle was won (2 Chronicles 20).

Holy Communion is another way to sanctify ourselves as we partake in the body and blood of Jesus. Many take Communion on a daily basis when fasting, as they feed on the body and blood of Jesus. There is power in the Communion and it can prepare our spirits for the battles ahead.

Battles are to be fought in the Spirit-realm and not in the flesh (Ephesians 6:12). Hence, we prepare by humbling ourselves, knowing the battle is the Lord's and we are under His authority and guidance (2 Chronicles 20:15). Pride has no place in spiritual warfare. We will fall if we fight with pride or in our own strength. Since the battle is spiritual, it means we rely on God's army of angels and Heavenly beings to fight for us as we pray in the Spirit.

On one occasion God called me to engage in a battle I didn't want to get involved in but rather flee. I had just finished a season of medical outreaches in Mozambique and was ready for a well earned break when the Lord asked me to fast and engage in a spiritual battle. I was very tired and it was during the last two weeks of the year in the run up to New Year. I started to sense an evil presence in the atmosphere outside our base. It was getting thicker and more intense each day and I just wanted to get on a plane and flee to England for a break. God had other plans and encouraged me to stay and pray around the base during this time, for I was here for such a time as this. I reluctantly obeyed, then found out He had also called other missionaries who were prophetic warriors to stay and intercede for the area and base.

I heard there were many witchdoctors, sorcerers and shamanists attending a New Year celebration just across the road from us (this I have referred to in Chapter 2). This was a time when they would engage with water spirits and demonic forces so they could receive greater measures of evil power. God called us to stand against these evil forces, so we responded as the Holy Spirit directed us to do. The Lord gave us a strategy to prayer walk around both missionary bases and lay hands on the fenced walls.

God gave me divine grace to fast during this time for He removed my desire to eat. I was somehow not hungry during the fast and my appetite returned when it was all over. So we consecrated ourselves before God, repented of all known sin (so we had no open door to sin by which the enemy could attack us), and worshipped and prayed around our bases.

Finally, as we met to pray and worship on New Year's Eve, I felt prompted to ask God to release thunder and lightning from Heaven. I had never prayed like this before but felt led by the Spirit to do so. At that moment in time there was clear blue sky and not a cloud in sight. Within a few hours a storm started to brew. This was no ordinary storm for suddenly there were strong winds with terrifying thunder and lightning. It was one of the most powerful and terrifying storms I have witnessed.

The next day we heard reports, that the satanists and witchdoctors were furious for their plans had been thwarted. One of them even commented that they saw power coming from our base which had stopped them using their powers. It was amazing to see what God did. The following year the witchdoctors and shamanists decided not to return to the same place but went somewhere else instead. The next New Year was peaceful and there was no oppression or heaviness felt in the atmosphere.

Fasting was an opportunity to purify ourselves, close any open doors in our heart to the enemy, and to humbly posture ourselves under the leadership and authority of the Lord, as we followed His strategy and commands. The battle was won!

Types of Fasting

There are different types of fasting and these can be divided into *food-fasts* or *non-food fasts*. However, the common ones mentioned in the scriptures refer to the food fasts. We can ask the Holy Spirit *what type* of fast, *when* to fast and *how long* to fast.

Normally the hardest days to fast are the first few days when our body is craving the desires of the flesh. Once we have broken through the first few days then it usually becomes easier. It is a bit like the initial muscle pain we feel after a work-out in the gym. The pain eases as our muscles become stronger.

Types of Food Fasts

There are three types of food-fast mentioned in the scriptures.

Total or Esther Fast

A complete or total fast refers to no food *and* no drink. This is known as an Esther fast and is usually no more than three days long. This is because there can be major health risks after taking no fluids for more than seventy two hours. It is well known that the kidneys may malfunction and go into failure if no fluids have been taken for more than 3 days.

The best example is when Esther did a three day complete fast, abstaining from food and drink, and invited the Israelites to do likewise (Esther 4:16). The result was spiritual breakthrough where Esther had favour with the king to fulfill her God given assignment, to free the Israelites from captivity and death.

Food Fast

Another type of fast is a *food fast*, where food is abstained but drinks are allowed. Some may drink water or juices, or gradually wean from taking juices and hot drinks to water alone. This fast may be from a day up to forty days, though some may choose to fast for longer. It is wise to start gradually with a food fast especially if you haven't fasted before, and to be Spirit-led if you are thinking of doing a long fast. It is advisable to have a medical check-up beforehand if there are any health issues. However, a food fast is not advisable for anyone who has an eating disorder such as anorexia.

During a food fast a person may feel dizzy if their sugar levels become low. In such cases, a person may eat a piece of bread or fruit or something else, until they feel fine again. It is good to drink less caffeine before a food fast to prevent getting headaches as a result of caffeine withdrawal.

It is my understanding that Jesus fasted from food but not water during His forty day fast in the desert. Some may disagree, but Scripture only mentions Him not eating food, being tempted with food and feeling extremely hungry at the end. It does not mention that He fasted from water, was thirsty or tempted with water. Strictly speaking He would be dead if He fasted from water for more than four days unless He was supernaturally sustained. Since He came to show us the way to follow Him, it makes more sense that He fasted from food but not water during that length of time.

Partial Fast or Daniel Fast

The term 'Daniel fast' has been used when referring to a partial fast, such as a single meal a day, or just eating fruit, bread, soup or vegetables. It includes no choice food such as meat, wine, desserts, or other enjoyable foods. (Vegetarians may argue that vegetables are enjoyable food).

A Daniel fast is the best example of a partial fast where Daniel ate vegetables and abstained from meat, rich foods, and alcohol. Some people may prefer a partial fast for various health reasons and others may choose a partial fast because of their daily physical demands. Partial fasts, generally speaking, are more tolerable because the body is less likely to experience any dizzy episodes or caffeine withdrawal headaches.

Non-Food Fasts

For those who struggle or are unable to fast from food there are non-food fasts. The non-food fasts include abstaining from TV, sports or games, personal interests, social media, and so on. Essentially, we are giving God our time and attention instead of focusing on the things we would usually do. Therefore, a non-food fast can be a fast from anything.

One year, the Lord prompted me to give my evenings in the month of January to Him. Nothing happened during the first week as I worshipped and focused on Him, but I chose to continue out of obedience to Him. However, during the second week, I sensed His Presence begin to enter the room as if He was sitting beside me on the settee. From then on He would be there with me each evening and I looked forward to engaging in His Presence. After the ten day waiting period it became easy to access His Presence for He would turn up and be there for me. The Lord was testing my heart to wait on Him and desire His Presence more than anything else. As I did, He drew closer to me and my heart drew closer to Him.

A non-food fast that is beneficial to everyone is a fast from *'negative speech'*. I encourage you to do this if you haven't already done one. This means resisting critical speech, judgmental words, gossip, moaning, disapproval, and complaining. We may see things shift and change if we choose to give thanks and praise, and to bless or pray for our enemies, instead of cursing them. This is a great spiritual exercise to help a person break free from negative thinking. It is best done if there is someone to whom we may be accountable, such as a spouse, friend or family member, and this person can point out every time we say a negative word. This enables us to become more self-aware of what we say and to change our way of thinking and speaking.

Benefits of Fasting

Here are some of the benefits to our body, soul and spirit when we fast.

Healthier Bodies

There are physical as well as spiritual benefits to fasting. In the natural when we fast from food, our bodies undergo a process of detoxification and start utilizing energy from our fat reserves. It has been scientifically proven that a day of fasting from food every week is beneficial to our health. If our bodies undergo a process of detoxification and clean up, then our spirits are probably undergoing a similar process of sanctification.

Fasting enables us to become holy vessels where God can release greater power and anointing for the work He has commissioned us to do. Daniel and his men were healthy and strong when they fasted from meat and wine during their partial fast. *'At the end of the ten days they looked healthier and better nourished than any of the young men who ate the royal food'* (Daniel 1:15).

Pre-operation Preparation

I usually advise people to fast before they come for ministry for inner healing. This is because I don't want them to be dependent upon me, but to take responsibility for themselves by showing God how seriously they want to be healed and set free. It is a bit like the preparation before a surgical operation where patients are told to fast (not to eat or drink for a certain period of time before an operation). Those who are unable to fast from food can do a partial fast or fast from other things such as TV, alcohol, social media or whatever takes up a chunk of their time. The time of fasting is an opportunity for us to prepare our heart, mind and spirit to be more receptive to the Lord.

One lady decided to fast before we met for prayer. She had an amazing download from the Lord concerning the spiritual and emotional roots behind her symptoms. As a result she came spiritually prepared for the ministry.

Increase in Spiritual Authority & Anointing

During a fast, God not only does a deeper, sanctifying work in our hearts, but releases more of His authority to overcome the enemy. Fasting releases spiritual authority. Our spirit grows in authority when we yield our flesh to God and let Him be Lord in our life. As we fast from our flesh, our spirit becomes sharper and more sensitive to the promptings of His Spirit. Whereas food and the desires of the flesh may dull the spirit, fasting can sharpen the spirit. Many may feel called to fast before taking on a spiritual assignment especially where spiritual breakthrough may be required to advance God's Kingdom. I believe fasting increases our divine authority to accomplish the assignment. After Jesus' forty day fast He left the desert in the *power* of the Spirit to begin His ministry.

Overcome Temptation

Fasting helps us to resist or overcome temptations. Jesus fasted forty days in the desert and resisted all temptations from satan. Temptation speaks to our flesh and that is why when we fast and surrender our flesh to our spirit, we are saying 'no' to temptation!

Life Transformation

Fasting can transform our hearts and lives as we contend for things in the kingdom. It is a way to be Spirit-led instead of led by the desires of our flesh. God not only draws us closer to Him, but releases Kingdom mysteries and greater revelations as we turn our hearts to Him in prayer and fasting.

Fasting sharpens our spirit and increases our ability to discern. When we contend for things through prayer and fasting God can bring deliverance and transformation. Also, prayer and fasting can release divine protection when we are interceding for a person or situation.

A person felt a sudden urge to pray and fast for a friend who was on the mission field. She sensed in her spirit something wasn't right and her friend might have been in danger. It turned out that her friend was at risk of being attacked by men. During the same time this person prayed and fasted, God had protected her friend.

Supernatural Food

Jesus said to His disciples: *'I have food to eat that you know nothing about'* (John 4:32). *'Man doesn't live on bread alone but on every word which comes from the mouth of God'* (Matthew 4:4). Jesus has supernatural food, manna from Heaven, which will sustain us and supply the power and energy our body needs. He said this to those who overcame the ungodly teachings of Balaam and the Nicolaitans: *'I will give you some of the hidden manna'* (Revelation 2:17).

There are testimonies of people who have stayed alive by simply taking Communion and eating nothing else. There is a mystery behind fasting and taking Communion that we are not to ignore but instead should explore.

Sometimes, the benefits of fasting may be seen during the fast or at the end of the fast. At other times, we may not see the benefits until much later. Fasting is beneficial to our body, soul and spirit. It can release healing as well as spiritual breakthrough and direction for it is like a spiritual power drill. It is a mighty weapon for spiritual battles and draws our hearts into a deeper place of communion with God.

END NOTES
[1] Angela Walker: *Foundation For Healing; Kingdom Medicine Vol 1*, (2020)
[2] Angela Walker: *Kingdom Tools; Kingdom Medicine Vol 2*, (2020)
[3] Robert Liardon: *Smith Wigglesworth Prayer, Power and Miracles;* p204-7 *(Destiny Image Pubisher 2005)*

6

Power In the Blood

They overcame him by the blood of the Lamb and by the word of their testimony

Revelation 12:11

The cross and blood of Jesus are to be central in our lives if we want to serve God and overcome the ways of the enemy. The life we are called to follow is the way of the cross. Many are called but few are chosen. The chosen ones are those who obey God's will and follow Him, and this includes the willingness to lay down our lives for Him.

The Cross

There may be seasons in our life where we encounter the cross in a real and tangible way. This is usually a God ordained time in our spiritual walk and journey with Him, and may occur as we go through what appears to be valleys or wilderness seasons.

Some Christians believe the cross is just about what Jesus did for us. However, I believe it is not just what He has done for us but includes what we are willing to do for Him. He is inviting each one of us to lay down our lives for Him, just as He did for us.

Many times I had read in the scriptures about daily taking up the cross to follow Jesus yet my heart hadn't encountered such a lifestyle. Then one day, Jesus made this scripture very real to me and put the question to me Himself.

It happened one Sunday morning at church. I met as usual with others to pray before the service, but this time my eyes were drawn to a white box. On the small white box was a red cross with the words 'First Aid'. I was intrigued about why the Lord had drawn my attention to this. Then the following words came to me: *'It is all about My cross. You will reach out to My people and give them 'first aid' by choosing a life laid down for Me. And through My cross you will bring them into My Kingdom and I will heal them.'*

Jesus was calling me to lay down my life for Him, including my medical career, and serve Him by doing basic or 'first aid' medicine in Africa. Later I realised His cross was to be the centre of my life, for at the centre of the cross is His love, forgiveness, and healing power. He invites us to lay down our lives for Him if we truly want to follow Him.

Shortly after this we entered into worship and I became overwhelmed by His Presence. Tears streamed down my face and it was as if it was just Him and me in the room as everything faded in the distance. The worship song being sung was all about the cross and His dying love for us.

Suddenly, I had a vision where I saw Jesus on the cross. He seemed three times the size of a normal man and was looking down to me. His eyes were full of sacrificial love as He spoke these words to me: *'Ange, I have sacrificed My life for you. Will you sacrifice your life for Me?'*

Everything in my life flashed before my mind: my medical career, possessions, home, relationships and finances. Was I willing to lay all of this down for Him and truly let it go? There was no going back or holding on to anything anymore. It was as if I had nothing but Him.

I realised the cost to follow Jesus involved laying down my life for Him. It was HUGE. It was everything I had, everything that I was and everything that mattered to me. This was the real price I had to pay to follow Jesus. This is what it means to follow Him to the cross and completely surrender ourselves, even the right to our own lives. It costs us everything just as it cost Jesus Himself *everything*!

Just before Jesus took up His cross, He said to His disciples: *'Greater love has no-one than this, that he lays down his life for his friends'* (John 15:13). This is true love for it is sacrificial. God is love and He demonstrated His sacrificial love for us by asking His one and only Son to lay down His life for us, so that we may be redeemed from our sins and come back into a loving relationship with Him. We minimise or forget the pain and suffering that our Father God went through to see His one and only Son suffer on the cross. Not only that, but Jesus was willing to obey His Father's will and endure the cross, for the joy set before Him (Hebrews 12:2).

When we say 'yes' to taking up our cross, we are saying 'yes' to abandoning ourselves to the things of this world, including our flesh and selfish desires. It will cost us, just like it cost Jesus, *everything*. Jesus had only been in fulltime ministry for three years when He knew it was His time to leave earth. There was only one right way that He was to die and that was the way of the cross.

Willing to be His Witnesses

The Greek word for 'witness' in Acts 1:8 is *martus* or martyr. Jesus told His disciples that they would be His witnesses to the ends of the earth. He was meaning that they would not only be testifying to who He was, but be willing to die for their faith if required.

Jesus said this to His disciples: *'If anyone wants to follow Me, he must deny himself, pick up his cross and follow me'* (Matthew 16:34). And, *'Whoever finds his life will lose it, but whoever loses his life for My sake, will find it'* (Matthew 10:39). He said: *'I tell you the truth, unless a kernel of wheat falls to the ground and dies, it remains only a single seed. But if it dies, it produces many seeds. The man who loves his life will lose it. While the man who hates his life in this world, will keep it for eternal life. Whoever serves Me must follow Me, and where I am, My servant will also be. My Father will honour the one who serves Me'* (John 12:24-26).

HE WHO OVERCOMES

The greatest love a man has is to lay down his life for his friends (John 15:13). Jesus demonstrated this to us on the cross and invites us to choose to live a sacrificial life as a demonstration of our love for Him.

This is a powerful way to overcome the attacks of the enemy, because when we lay down our lives for Jesus, then the enemy has nothing to attack, for our lives are no longer our own. We overcome by choosing to yield our lives to Him: *'They **overcame** by the blood of the Lamb and the word of His testimony; they did not love their lives so much as to shrink from death'* (Revelation 12:11).

Many are called but few are chosen. Those who are chosen are the ones who say 'Yes' to the cross and a crucified life. Paul had discovered this truth: *'I consider everything a loss compared to the surpassing greatness of knowing Christ Jesus, My Lord, for whose sake I have lost all things'* (Philippians 3:8).

There may be things that the Lord asks us to lay down for Him and seasons where we encounter deeper measures of the cross, until our lives have become a fragrant love offering for Him. How many of us have sung the well known hymn 'When I Survey the Wondrous Cross' and obeyed the words in the final verse? *'Were the whole realm of nature mine, that was an offering far too small, Love so amazing, so Divine, demands my life, my soul, MY ALL'*.

One of the powerful ways to overcome the enemy is to no longer focus on self, or the things of the world, but Jesus. Hence, we overcome by the blood of the Lamb, the word of His testimony, and by willingly laying down our lives, even unto death (Revelation 12:11). Jesus overcame all the works of the enemy because He always did the Father's will and spent time alone with the Father. He overcame the power of death by humbling Himself before the Father and being obedient, even unto death on a cross (Philippians 2:8).

I have met mighty men and women of God who carry such Kingdom authority yet walk in great humility, because they have encountered the cross. Hence, their lives are no longer their own but have been totally yielded as a love offering to Him.

It doesn't really matter when we die, as long as we have completed God's will for us. Jesus, at thirty-three years of age, had almost completed His Father's will and was about to enter the last chapter, 'The Cross'.

Vision of the Crucifixion

During a time of private prayer one morning, I entered into a vision of the events leading up to Jesus' crucifixion. It came unexpectedly and was like watching a film. At first I saw the legs of Roman soldiers marching by. They were wearing their full Roman outfit and each had a sword or spear in one hand and a shield in the other. I could hear the sound of their marching. Crowds were gathered around making much noise and trying to press in closer to see Jesus. There was a stirring in the atmosphere. The soldiers tried to control the crowds and create a path for Jesus to walk down. He then fell with the cross on His back. He looked bruised, severely beaten and had gashes on His back. You could see the red swollen marks where He had been beaten, with blood oozing from His broken skin. One of His eyes was swollen and bruised and His face looked disfigured. All He was wearing was a piece of cloth wrapped around His waist. As He fell, He looked utterly exhausted and in so much pain. Every muscle seemed to be in spasm from the excruciating pain He was experiencing. Then I saw a man come to His aid. He took the cross from Jesus and Jesus stared deeply into his eyes. As He did, His Spirit spoke to this man's spirit, for He uttered no word. As Jesus continued, He was mocked, spat upon, laughed at and humiliated as things were thrown at Him. He was insulted and ridiculed by the voices around Him. He seemed powerless with nothing to defend Himself. He kept quiet and said nothing but continued His walk to the cross. Insult and abuse kept being hurled His way. His own men even betrayed Him, but He still chose to say nothing.

As Jesus reached Golgotha, He was thrown to the ground. His feet were grabbed and held tightly as a huge rusty nail was hammered through them. The pain was like an electric shock as it spread throughout the rest of His body. As the nails pierced His hands, shock waves of pain were felt throughout. The intensity was almost too much to bear. As the cross was lifted up, the intensity of the pain increased. His hands and feet had nothing to hold onto except the nails.

Darkness covered everywhere and the winds and rains increased. Most of the crowds had now left but there were some who stood by the cross, weeping, unable to leave Him. Jesus, now feeling very much abandoned, cried out, *'My God, My God, why have You forsaken Me?'* He could no longer feel His Father's Presence and felt such abandonment and rejection. At the same time, as His weary body hung on the cross, there was something else taking place that was unknown to those around. Jesus was in the midst of an intense, almighty battle in the Heavenly realms with satan and all his hordes of demons. It took a sacrificial Lamb without mark or blemish to overcome all the powers and forces of darkness. Jesus saw that the people who had beaten and crucified Him didn't know what they had done, for the true battle was taking place in the Heavenly realms. He prayed: *'Father, forgive them, for they know not what they do'* (Luke 23:34).

During His last three hours, Jesus willingly took all sin, all guilt, all shame, all curses, all sickness, all hurt, abuse, rejection and pain upon Himself. It was immense and indescribable. Only He and His Father knew what He was experiencing and the overwhelming burden He had to carry. His Father grieved to see His Son in such pain, but knew this was the only way that He could draw mankind back to Himself.

Then it was over. The enemy had finally been defeated. Jesus said, *'It is finished!'* and as He did, He breathed a huge sigh of relief saying: *'Father, into Your hands I commit My Spirit!'* As He breathed His last breath, the ground started to tremble and the rocks split apart. There was thunder and lightning as the temple curtain was torn in two from top to bottom. Now He had to take back the keys of death and hell which had been stolen by satan, before He could return to His Father. He was to take back all authority that had been His from the very beginning. The enemy now realised that he had been defeated. Jesus had won the battle through the power of His unconditional love and perfect sacrifice as He lay down His life in obedience to His Father's will. The vision ended.

The Greek word for 'it is finished' in John 19:30 is *tetelestai* which translated means *'I end, I fulfil, I accomplish, I pay'*. The word was apparently used in business when settling accounts or paying off debts in full. In doing so, papers would be stamped with *tetelestai* meaning 'paid in full'. Jesus cancelled the written code that was against us, the debt we had to pay for our sins, by nailing it to the cross. *'He forgave us all our sins, having cancelled the written code, with its regulations, that was against us and stood opposed to us; He took it away, nailing it to the cross. And having disarmed the powers and authorities, He made a public spectacle of them, triumphing over them by the cross'* (Colossians 2:13-15).

When Jesus said 'it is finished', He had paid in full the debt we owed for our sin. The battle was over. Satan had now been defeated. Victory was won.

Rejection & Betrayal

Most of us will probably experience rejection and betrayal at some point in our lives. Some may be in denial of it, since it is buried deep within. Others may be very conscious of it for it is like a sore wound.

There was a time when I experienced rejection and betrayal which came unexpectedly and like a shock. I couldn't understand why such a thing could happen, but it did. Through it I came to understand more of Jesus' suffering heart and what He went through on the cross. I could sense how He may have felt when He was mocked, scorned, beaten, spat upon, humiliated and yes, even betrayed by His own men. Also the abandonment He may have experienced by His own Father when He cried out: *'My God, My God, why have You forsaken Me?'* (Mathew 27:46). I could start to feel in my heart some of the pain and suffering that Jesus must have felt, but more so, I knew He understood my pain because of what He underwent. It was a time to walk in brokenness before God and to understand more of His suffering heart. *'The sacrifices of God are a broken spirit; a broken and contrite heart, O God, You will not despise'* (Psalm 51:17).

With love and intimacy comes suffering. It is not uncommon for obedient men and women of God to experience persecution for their faith or even betrayal by close friends. What is most important is not what has happened but how we deal with it and overcome with the grace of God to enable us. We have a choice. We can moan and complain and grow bitter and resentful in our hearts and remain in the pit of self-pity and rejection; or we can reach out to Jesus and take hold of His hand, letting Him pull us out. Since He was once there Himself and has now overcome, with love and forgiveness, we too can overcome.

Surrendering Our Life

Jesus said to His disciples: *'If anyone would come after Me, he must deny himself and take up his cross and follow Me. For whoever wants to save his life will lose it, but whoever loses his life for Me, will find it. What good will it be if a man gains the whole world yet forfeits his soul? Or what can a man give in exchange for his soul? For the Son of Man is going to come in His Father's glory with His angels and then **He will reward each person according to what he has done**'* (Mathew 16:24-27).

The things that matter most to us are likely to be the things God will ask us to lay down for Him. This may be our reputation, respect, pride, control, ownership of possessions, our identity in what we do, our work or ministry, or our relationships. This is because they are blockages to our relationship with Him from going deeper and preventing us from fulfilling what God has in store for us.

For some this may mean living by faith or travelling to the nations, or it may mean bringing His Kingdom into the workplace to change the spiritual atmosphere. For others, it may be a calling to pioneer and develop new things, or perhaps to raise up God's children. As we lay down our lives for Him and hold onto nothing of this world, He will do amazing things in each of our lives and take us on adventures we never thought we would experience. As we let God be in control of our lives and look to Him for our security, we will definitely not go unrewarded both in our time on earth and in the eternal life to come.

Before Jesus took up His cross He prayed for His Father to take the cup of suffering away from Him, and then said: *'Not My will but Yours be done'*. Our cross is about surrendering our lives to God and doing His will. Jesus is our rock, our hope, our salvation, our security, our healer and deliverer, our defender and protector, our Lord, our husband and our resurrection life. In order for our lives to be in alignment with His will, we are required to surrender everything to Him. And in exchange for our completely surrendered life, we will enter into His resurrection-glory.

Power in His Blood

There is 'life in the blood' (Leviticus 17:11,14) and where there is life there is power. This means there is power in the blood of Jesus. The saints overcame *by the blood of the Lamb*. We are not to underestimate the power in His blood.

Passover & the Last Supper

The Lord's last supper with the disciples was on the night of the celebration of the Feast of Unleavened Bread. '*Then came the day of Unleavened Bread on which the Passover lamb had to be sacrificed. Jesus sent Peter and John saying, "Go and make preparations for us to eat the Passover... I have eagerly desired to eat this Passover with you before I suffer. For I tell you, I will not eat it again until it finds fulfilment in the Kingdom of God"'* (Luke 22:7-23).

Jesus had *eagerly* waited for this moment. He was going to take the place of the lamb that was to be sacrificed at the Passover meal. He changed history when He became the One and only sacrificial Lamb for all mankind (Hebrews 9:26). He was pure and without blemish for He had committed no sin. He had only done what His Father had asked because He loved Him and obeyed His commands. Since He was without sin, the prince of this world had no hold of Him (John 14:30-31).

Jews celebrate the Feast of Unleavened Bread in remembrance of the Passover. This took place the night that Moses took God's people out of Egypt and freed them from Pharaoh's control. The Lord told Moses to tell His people to take an animal, preferably a lamb that was without defect and a year old. Then they were to slaughter the lamb and take some of the blood and put it around the doorframes of the homes where they were eating. They were to eat the animal roasted with bitter herbs and bread made without yeast in haste and get ready to leave, because it was the night that the Lord was going to *pass over* Egypt. On this night, the Lord was going to pass through Egypt and strike down every firstborn and bring judgement on all the gods of Egypt. The blood was to be a sign so He would *pass over* their homes and not bring destruction to them. This was to be the same night that Pharaoh finally instructed Moses to get up and leave Egypt with God's people. It was the Exodus (Exodus 12).

Since Jesus was holy and pure without spot or blemish, He could become the sacrificial Lamb to take away the sin of the world. God was willing to offer His One and only Son who was without sin as a perfect sacrifice, so that we may receive the forgiveness of our sins and be able to come into a relationship with our Heavenly Father (John 3:16-17). This act of Jesus shedding His blood once and for all would provide freedom for us from the hands of the enemy.

The Holy Communion or Eucharist

In the Gospel of Luke we read: '*On the night of the last supper He took bread, gave thanks and broke it and gave it to them saying, "This is My Body given for you; do this in remembrance of Me". In the same way after the supper He took the cup saying, "This cup is* **the new covenant in My blood**, *which is poured out for you"*'(Luke 22:14-20). The Gospel of Mathew adds that the blood is poured out for many for *the forgiveness of sins* (Mathew 26:28).

During Communion it is good to ask God to examine our hearts so we may repent and forgive where needed. As a result of our forgiveness to others, then we may receive forgiveness through the power of His blood (1 Corinthians 11:28, Matthew 5:23).

Jesus told the Jews and His followers that whoever eats His flesh and drinks His blood abides in Him and He in them. Many of His followers left Him when hearing this. He said: '*I tell you the truth, unless you eat the flesh of the Son of Man and drink His blood, you have no life in you. Whoever eats My flesh and drinks My blood has eternal life and I will raise him up at the last day. For* **My flesh is real food and My blood is real drink. Whoever eats My flesh and drinks My blood remains in Me and I in him. This is the bread that came down from heaven**' (John 6:53-59).

In the Old Testament, the consecrated bread which the priests ate each Sabbath in the Holy place was also known as the bread of the Presence. The Lord told Moses: '*Put this bread of the Presence on this table to be with Me at all times*' (Exodus 25:30, 2 Chronicles 4:19).

Jesus said that He is the bread of life and that His body and blood are both *real*. There is life in the blood of Jesus. *'Whoever eats My flesh and drinks My blood **abides** in Me and I in him'* (John 6:56, NKJV). It was only when Jesus broke bread with the two disciples whom He had conversed with on the road to Emmaus, that their eyes were opened and they saw it was the risen Lord (Luke 24:30).

Many people today take *Communion* in remembrance of what Jesus did but don't believe it is the body and blood of Jesus. Instead they see it as being symbolic. However, there are other Christians who believe they are receiving the body and blood of Jesus. They believe something happens to it in the supernatural realm, whether before or after taking it. I believe that the Communion is a mystery and that something supernatural does take place after taking it, otherwise Jesus would have said this is 'symbolic' or 'representative of My body and blood'. But He didn't. He said, *'This **is** My body'* and *'This **is** My blood'*. He also said this cup is *the new covenant in My blood*. Here He is declaring a new covenant replacing the old one or the law given by Moses. As we take Communion we are saying 'Yes' to our commitment to Jesus. It is as if we are setting ourselves apart for Him until He returns for His bride.

A baby is yoked to its mother via the umbilical cord. This is so the toxic waste products produced by the baby's body can be exchanged for the good healthy nutritional substances delivered through the mother's blood. In the same way that a baby is yoked via the umbilical cord to its mother, so we are to be yoked to Jesus through His blood. His blood removes our toxic waste or sin in exchange for His healthy nutritional substances we receive from His Spirit. As we remain yoked to Him, we can receive cleansing by His blood and abide in His Presence.

I believe the bread and wine become His body and blood for many have testified that they have received healing when they have taken part in the Eucharist (or Communion). This wouldn't happen if it was just symbolic. I have taken communion many times when led by the Holy Spirit to do so and received cleansing and healing both physically and spiritually. There is power in the blood of Jesus for it is real and there is a mystery behind it that we can't ignore.

What Can the Blood of Jesus Do for Us?

There is power in the blood of Jesus. Here are some of the things that are freely available for us through the power of His blood.

His Blood Cleanses and Sanctifies Us from All Sin

The blood of Jesus purifies us from *all* sin (1 John 1:7). How much then will it cleanse our consciences from acts that lead to death so that we may serve the living God! (Hebrews 9:14). We have been made holy through the sacrifice of the body of Jesus, that is, we have been made holy through His blood (Hebrews 13:12). Without the shedding of blood there is no forgiveness (Hebrews 9:23). In the Old Testament it was the blood of animals that made atonement for man's sins (Leviticus 17:11). How much more does the blood of Jesus make atonement for our lives? John said: '*He is the* **atoning sacrifice for our sins,** *and not only for ours but also for the sins of the world*' (1 John 2:2).

One day whilst I was out walking with God, I was meditating on the power of His blood. It came to mind to ask Him what it would feel like to have a drop of His blood fall on me. I asked in faith completely believing He would reveal it to me and the next minute I experienced something quite extraordinary. My body felt a purity and cleanliness throughout, like it had never felt before. It was like some powerful supernatural bleach had just washed over and through me. I felt whiter than the whitest of colours. It felt amazing. I actually felt like a spotless bride.

His blood is like supernatural bleach that kills all known germs (or delivers from sickness and demons) and removes all stains (or sin) leaving a radiant, translucent white, bright colour without any spot or blemish. His blood sanctifies us from all that is not of Him.

Purchased by God & Redeemed

'*Do you not know that your body is a temple of the Holy Spirit, who is in you, whom you have received from God? You are not your own; you were bought at a price. Therefore, honour God with your body*' (1 Corinthians 6:19-20). Jesus has redeemed us from sin by being a sacrifice of atonement for us through the shedding of His blood (Romans 3:23-25). It is through His sacrificial blood that we can be brought back into relationship with God and be made one again with Him. John testifies to the love of God being shown to us when He sent His one and only Son into the world as an atoning sacrifice for our sins (1 John 4:9-10).

It was the twenty-four elders standing before the Lamb at the throne of God who sang: *'You were slain, and with Your blood You purchased men for God from every tribe and language and people and nation'* (Revelation 5:9). If we were purchased with the blood of Jesus, then our lives belong to God, they are no longer our own. God keeps reminding me that I belong to Him and my life is now in His hands. That is His desire for all of us. We are to belong to Him and not the world, for man didn't purchase us but God did.

Our Royal Inheritance

Through His blood we have been adopted into His royal family. If we are led by the Spirit of God then we have been adopted as children of God which means we are His heirs (Romans 8:14-17). *'You have made them to be a kingdom and priests to serve our God, and they will reign on the earth' (Revelation 5:9-10).* We have been called to be His kings and priests, as we choose to set ourselves apart for Him and lay down our lives for Him. The more we come to know the ways of God, the more we will understand our royal identity in Him.

Access into the Presence of God (into the Holy of Holies)

'Therefore, brothers, since we have confidence to enter the Most Holy Place by the blood of Jesus, by a new and living way opened for us through the curtain, that is His body...' (Hebrews 9:1-28).

As Jesus gave His last breath on the cross the curtain of the temple was torn in two (Luke 23:45). This was representative of the curtain that separated the Holy place from the Most Holy place (or Holy of Holies) in the temple or tabernacle. It was now no more. Jesus had made it possible for us to have direct access to the Father by His death on the cross. Therefore, we do not need to wait for the Day of Atonement for the high priest to enter the Holy of Holies or to see a priest. Instead, we can have direct access to

God through Jesus our High Priest. The veil has become His torn flesh and we now have access to the Father through Him.

Heals our Sicknesses and Infirmities

Isaiah 53 prophesies He took up our *infirmities* and carried our *sorrows*. Our infirmities refer to our sicknesses, and our sorrows refer to our emotional pain. He was pierced for our *transgressions* and crushed for our *iniquities*. Here, transgression refers to our own sin, and iniquities are the sins passed down our bloodline or generational sin. *'And by **His wounds we are healed**'* (Isaiah 53:4-5). Our body, soul and spirit can receive healing through the power of His blood.

In the Old Testament, Isaiah prophesied that by His wounds *we are healed.* This was in the present tense but became the past tense in the New Testament. After Jesus' death Peter said: *'He Himself bore our sins in His body on the tree so that we might die to sins and live for righteousness; by **His wounds you have been healed**'* (1 Peter 2:24). By faith we can claim this truth as we step into our healing through the power of His blood. There is atonement in the blood of Jesus.

Protection by the Blood

As previously mentioned, the Israelites were protected from death and destruction by marking their doorposts with the blood of a lamb. The enemy cannot penetrate the blood of Jesus, so we can receive divine protection as we place the blood between ourselves and any demonic power or sickness.

On one occasion I asked a friend to join me in praying for a woman who I felt needed to be delivered from a spirit of infirmity that was behind her sickness. I quickly, but silently, put the blood of Jesus between me and the sick person, but my friend did not. The woman got set free and healed. I was fine but my friend felt an oppressive spirit come on her because she hadn't covered herself with the blood of Jesus. She was fine after prayer, but this showed the importance of protecting ourselves with His blood when we are ministering to people or entering enemy territory.

Break all Curses

Jesus took all curses on the cross by becoming a curse for us. *'Christ redeemed us from the curse of the law by becoming a curse for us, for it is written: "Cursed is everyone who is hung on a tree!"'* (Galatians 3:13). Hence we can break the power of a curse spoken over us or someone else through declaring the blood of Jesus: *'I break this curse by the blood of Jesus!'* Also, a curse can be broken when we pray in the Name of Jesus: *'I break this curse in the Name of Jesus!* It is as simple and as powerful as that.

Redeems Us from the Sins of Our Forefathers

We are redeemed from the sins of our forefathers with the precious blood of Christ. *'For you know that it was not with perishable things like silver or gold that **you were redeemed from the empty ways of life handed down to you by your forefathers, but with the precious blood of Christ, a lamb without blemish or defect**'* (1 Peter 1:18-19). The blood of Jesus can break off any generational curse and cleanse us from all generational sin. We do not have to live under the sins and curses of our forefathers but can be set free through His blood. We have redemption and the forgiveness of sins through His blood (Ephesians 1:7). We have been set free from our sins by His blood (Revelation 1:5). However, it is not automatic, but can be done as we repent for the sins and ask for His forgiveness, through the power of His blood.

Unity in the Spirit through the Blood

Jesus told His disciples to take Communion not once but on a regular basis until He returns. As we come together as a group of believers and participate in His Communion, I believe there is a unity in the Spirit. When people gather together to take Communion and are willing to repent of their sin as well as forgive one another, then unity is restored amongst the group of believers. Communion can be a powerful way to restore unity where there has been division in the body and family.

Victory in the Blood

We overcome by the blood of the lamb (Revelation 12:11). There is victory in the blood. Jesus defeated Satan at the cross: *'And having disarmed the powers and authorities, He made a public spectacle of them, triumphing over them by the cross'* (Colossians 2:15). We have authority from God to overcome all power of the enemy, even death itself, through the power of Jesus' blood! Death has lost its sting for it has been swallowed up in the victory. Jesus overcame all death through His blood which was shed on the cross for us.

During an outreach in Mozambique, it was interesting to see the reaction of a woman of another faith when she noted a red cross on our medical tent. Her comment was one of fear as she looked at it and shrieked 'The blood of Jesus!' and then ran away. It made me realise how satan and his evil hordes fear the blood of Jesus for they know that it will overcome and conquer any demonic power or evil spirit. They cannot penetrate the blood of Jesus because it is pure and holy. Instead, they shriek back in fear and dread and run from it.

Satanists, witchdoctors and sorcerers obtain their evil power through blood, but the blood comes from 'sacrifices' of animals or even humans, especially child sacrifices. Animal or human blood is used to gain more demonic power. Jesus, who was without sin, sacrificed His own blood, which was pure and spotless, so we could be redeemed from the clutches of satan and be brought back into a love relationship with God.

There is victory over satan with the blood of Jesus. The blood of Jesus not only cleanses us from sin, and heals us of all sickness and infirmities, but it unites, protects and overcomes the works of satan. Let us never underestimate the power in the blood.

Lord Jesus, Thank You for the power there is in Your blood. Help me not to underestimate or forget the power in Your blood to cleanse, redeem, heal, protect, unite, and overcome the works of the enemy. Lord, I ask for a greater revelation of Your blood and the cross, and what it means to daily take up my cross for You. Show me the things to lay down for You so my life may become a love offering for You. In Your Name I pray.

7

Overcoming the Battle of the Mind

We take captive every thought to make it obedient to Christ

2 Corinthians 10:5

The biggest battle we have to face is what goes on between our two ears: the battle of the mind. In fact enemy strongholds are built on the way we think be it fear, pride, rebellion, control, unbelief, criticism, insignificance, rejection, and so on. Satan is constantly trying to feed our minds with temptations, distractions, lies, fears, guilt, or negative thoughts about ourselves, others, or God. His mission is to draw us away from intimacy with God and into bondage, because he is out to steal, kill and destroy God's people (John 10:10).

*'The weapons we fight with are not the weapons of the world. On the contrary, they have **divine power to demolish strongholds**. We **demolish arguments** and **every pretension** that sets itself up **against the knowledge of God** and we take captive every thought to make it obedient to Christ'* (2 Corinthians 10:4-5).

The enemy strongholds are seen as 'arguments' and 'pretensions'. Arguments may be seen as being arrogant, boastful, or persuasive thoughts. Pretensions may be seen as false beliefs, lies, or deceptions. Both arrogant and deceptive thoughts oppose the knowledge of God. Hence, we take captive such thoughts that wage war in our minds between the flesh and spirit, and instead we yield our thoughts to God to acquire the mind of Christ.

The things we fall victim to are usually the things we believe to be true when they are lies, misperceptions, or pretensions from the enemy. All enemy strongholds are based on a lie, false belief, or negative thought. Hence, they distort the way we think and behave. This is known as deception. Satan is the father of lies and deceiver of all things (John 8:44). Negative thoughts may attack our minds like fiery arrows, especially during vulnerable or tough times, but even during good times.

Spiritual Strongholds

There are natural and spiritual strongholds. A natural stronghold is a fortified place where one seeks protection from the enemy. Hence, a natural stronghold is seen as a place of refuge. In the Old Testament, there were strongholds on both sides of the battlefield on both the attacker's and defender's ground. David referred to his strongholds as places where he took refuge (1 Chronicles 12:8). However, he also referred to God as his stronghold: *'The Lord is the stronghold of my life- of whom shall I be afraid?'* (Psalm 27:1).

A spiritual stronghold may be Godly or demonic. God's strongholds are our weapons, for they are the nature and character of God, the fruit of the Spirit. However, the enemy's strongholds are the weapons the enemy uses to attack our minds based on lies, fears, prideful thoughts, and negative emotions. These negative thoughts may torment our minds and hold us in emotional, physical, mental, and spiritual bondage.

Interestingly, the word for stronghold is mentioned around fifty times in the Old Testament, but only once in the New Testament. In the Old Testament it refers to both the physical and spiritual strongholds, whereas in the New Testament, it is referred to as an enemy stronghold. However, when we usually speak of a stronghold, we are referring to a demonic stronghold. Paul said: *'The weapons we fight with are not the weapons of the world. On the contrary, they have divine power to demolish strongholds'* (2 Corinthians 10:4).

Trees & Branches

Trees don't just appear in our gardens but like all plants they start from a seed. A seed has to be watered and nurtured until it becomes a plant and eventually grows over the years and becomes a tree that produces fruit. This is the same with regard to strongholds developing in us. A person first receives a seed in their hearts and allows it to grow or be nurtured each time they rehearse or declare the words and beliefs, until it eventually grows into a tree. Our hearts and minds can nurture seeds that produce Godly fruit and seeds that produce ungodly fruit.

Just because we respond now and again with a negative word or thought doesn't mean we have a stronghold in this area. A spiritual stronghold is like developing a tree in our spiritual gardens, where the trunk represents the main spiritual issue. The fruit it produces are seen as the 'symptoms' or negative attitudes of our heart. The roots include the hidden or deep seated wounds and hurt emotions.

Each of us may struggle with certain strongholds and this is especially seen when a stronghold has come down the bloodline and been a part of a person's belief system from early on. Other strongholds may be rooted in deep painful memories or traumatic events.

For example, those who have developed a stronghold of unforgiveness may produce the symptoms or fruit of anger, resentment, bitterness, judgement, jealousy, hate, and so on. The fruit is more visible to others and seen in a person's attitude of heart. Toxic fruit is produced by toxic roots. The roots are usually hidden, but the Holy Spirit who searches our innermost being, can shine His light on the roots. Unforgiveness may have roots of rejection, self-hate, or a victim mindset. If we want to stop producing the bad fruit, then we have to address the toxic roots.

The Lord knows why we produce such fruit for He knows our past and sees the roots. With the help of the Holy Spirit, we can recognise and deal with the roots, and for everything we uproot, we can replace with a seed from the Holy Spirit to produce Kingdom fruit in our heart. The Holy Spirit may bring to our attention the orphan areas in our heart as we address a particular stronghold.

We may have deep wounds which develop over a short period of time that are not necessarily strongholds but more like wounds from an acute injury.

There was a time when a person deeply wounded my heart that caused both emotional pain and grief. I found myself forgiving them for many things that had contributed to the pain, including the various things they had said or done. When the last issue was dealt with, it was as if there were no more toxic feelings and the wound was healed. As a result, I no longer felt any negative feelings or pain in my heart towards this person. Instead, I felt a peace and God's love for them again.

However, a person may have developed a stronghold of unforgiveness if they have harboured resentment, bitterness, anger, or hatred towards an individual or people for most of their life. This can be dealt with through choosing to forgive each person as needed, including forgiving self. Then the negative or toxic fruit can be given to Jesus (such as anger, hatred, bitterness, resentment, jealousy, etc) and the person can receive cleansing and forgiveness through the blood of Jesus. In exchange, they can receive His peace and love towards others and also themselves. These seeds of peace and love may be nurtured as the person develops a forgiving heart towards others.

Another stronghold for some may be pornography. The fruit produced includes lust, masturbation, false comfort, false power and perverted thoughts. However, there may be a root of rejection, abuse, lack of love, or perhaps someone to forgive who introduced the person to pornography.

I met a person who struggled with the stronghold of fear. She would over-react with anxiety and fear in any given situation. It turned out that she had suffered traumatic events in her childhood and her mother was a very anxious and fearful person. Hence, there was a generational root as well as roots from trauma in childhood. The healing was a process as each issue was addressed and her heart and mind were gradually being renewed with God's healing love and revelatory truth.

Each stronghold is based on negative thought patterns, wounded emotions, and ungodly attitudes. We replace each negative thought by giving it to God and asking Him for His truth. By doing this, we are gradually renewing our minds with the mind of Christ. Our wounded emotions are healed as we forgive those who hurt us and then release our pain and hurt to Jesus. As we do this we can receive cleansing and healing through the power of His blood, and He will restore our hearts to become one with Him.

Spiritual Blind Spots

In the natural, we all have what is known as a 'blind spot'. This is the area (or spot) in our right and left visual fields where there is no visual input. This is where the optic nerve has to pass through the optic disc. We are usually unaware of having this defect since the visual input from the rest of our optic field compensates. Just as we have natural blind spots we also have *spiritual blind spots*.

Being born-again and filled with the Holy Spirit doesn't make us exempt from having demonic strongholds. Usually the things that are holding us captive are the things we cannot see but others can see in us. These are our spiritual blind spots. It is much easier to see faults in someone else than it is in ourselves. This is why Jesus tells us to remove the plank from our own eyes before we move the speck from our brother's (Matthew 7:3-5).

I think for every critical or 'fault finding' thought we have against someone we probably have the same, if not more, faults ourselves. This is because we usually see in others the same issues we are struggling with, and that is why Jesus said to first remove the planks from our own eyes.

Why do some people irritate us? It is probably because something in us has been triggered that *we* are to deal with. One challenging thing to do is to ask those who are close to us or know us well, about our strong and weak points? Get ready to be surprised. When I dared to ask the question myself, I couldn't believe some of the remarks I received from those whom I love and had given permission to speak into my life. It is good to pay attention, especially when more than one person is saying the same thing!

On one occasion, I was feeling irritated by a fellow missionary, so I brought the issue to God. To my surprise, the Lord revealed that the reason I was feeling irritated was because I had the same plank in my own eye. The irritant I saw in this person, I had myself!

The Lord convicted my heart to deal with my own issues first, then I would not react so much when I saw the same issue in others. This was a huge lesson. So, when I get frustrated or worked up about anything, I simply ask God to shine His light on my own heart and deal with the area in my heart first.

It is important to bring our spiritual blind spots into visibility so we can do something about them with the grace and help of the Holy Spirit. Most of the time we operate from our conscious level, but there is so much activity going on continually in our subconscious level. This is why we are usually unaware of the ways we behave to others unless it is drawn to our attention.

Familial Strongholds

It is true to say that we are usually not aware of the ungodly strongholds we carry, especially when they are so familiar to us. This may be because we have grown up with them or inherited them from our parents or the generations before them. We have become so familiar with them that we are unaware they are ungodly. For example, it may be thoughts of self-pity, criticism, judgment, emotional manipulation, control, fear, pride, rejection, inadequacy, jealousy, lust, and so on.

Being able to recognise them enables us to deal with them. Don't forget we have the Holy Spirit, as well as our brothers and sisters in Christ, to reveal any strongholds and how they may manifest in our lives.

We can always ask God what our ungodly strongholds are. If we think we have none, then the first two that may require addressing are pride and deception. Most of us will have been offended by someone or something at some point. We react to an offense with pride in our heart; *'How dare you say that about me,'* *'Did you hear what they said? They said I was ...'* , *'Look what they have done...'* Our reaction is clearly one of pride. If we think we have no pride, then we will not get offended by what others say or do. Only Jesus was without sin, hence He had no demonic strongholds! The prince of this world had no *hold* on Him (John 14:30).

Overcoming Strongholds

A plant or young shoot with shallow roots is much easier to uproot than a tree with deep roots. The same applies to the various strongholds we have allowed to grow in our 'spiritual garden'.

Recognising a stronghold is the start but then choosing to live in the opposite spirit is the daily challenge. One person may struggle with unforgiveness or fear, whereas another may struggle with pride or intimidation. We all have issues, whether major or minor, and each of these can be addressed and uprooted from our spiritual gardens. One way of overcoming strongholds is to apply something known as the five R's:

> **R**ecognise
> **R**epent
> **R**eceive forgiveness
> **R**enounce
> **R**eplace.

The first thing is to *recognise* we have an issue, as the Holy Spirit reveals the unclean or ungodly areas in our heart. Next, we *repent* as we choose to turn away from this pattern of behaviour and no longer come under it. Then we ask God to forgive us, as we forgive those who have passed the sin to us or in some way contributed to the sin. We may have to forgive ourselves for coming under it. Once we have forgiven from our hearts, then we can *receive God's forgiveness*, through the powerful blood of Jesus. This is not to be rushed but received in our hearts. Sometimes, it may help to imagine ourselves (with our sanctified imaginations) standing under a heavenly waterfall. As we picture this image, we can imagine the sanctified water cleansing and washing off all defilement from our body, soul and spirit. This is what the cleansing power of the blood of Jesus does, as we receive it by faith. We are now in a position to rebuke and *renounce* any spirit(s) behind the stronghold, commanding them to leave in Jesus' Name, e.g the spirit of fear, spirit of bitterness etc. And finally we can *replace* these negative thoughts with the heart and attitude of Christ, as we ask Him for His truth and receive His Spirit in our hearts. Now, we can start to cultivate the fruit of the Spirit, as we choose to respond with His Spirit in similar situations.

Overcoming a stronghold requires perseverance, as the different branches and roots are dealt with one by one. For example, a 'controlling spirit' may manifest in many ways, and each branch is cut off as the various areas of 'control' are recognised and addressed in turn. Gradually the stronghold will weaken as each branch is addressed. It's as if we are undoing our learnt behaviours and attitudes, as we rewire our minds with the attitude and mind of Christ for each given situation. Each time we react in a negative manner, we can ask the Lord how we are to respond. He will give us His Kingdom perspective and attitude of heart for each situation. As we keep responding with the right attitude of heart, the stronghold becomes weaker until it has little or no influence over us.

Another way of overcoming strongholds is to spend more time soaking in the Presence of God. As we allow our hearts, minds and spirits to marinate in His Presence, He can wash away any negative thoughts and renew our minds with His goodness and truth. As the Psalmist said, we become what we worship (Psalm 135:18). The longer we soak and abide in His Presence, the more our minds and hearts become like Him. (For further reading on strongholds, I recommend reading *Restoring The Foundations* [1]).

John Sandford, in his book *Healing the Nations*, says this about spiritual strongholds: *'By far the most powerful devices by which Satan controls the minds of his victims are* **individual and corporate mental strongholds**. *Every living thing God creates has a life and free will of its own. So do our minds. Once we have shaped them, they have a will of their own and do not submit willingly to the will of God, or even to our own wills.* ***A 'mental stronghold' is a practiced way of thinking that has become ingrained and automatic, with a life and will of its own,'***[2] (Bold print mine). So a mental stronghold is a belief pattern which has become ingrained and until we take it captive by surrendering it to God, we will not perceive or understand the mind of Christ in this area. We are gradually transformed in the way we think and behave by the ongoing renewal of our minds (Romans 12:2).

Battle of the Flesh and Spirit

Most of the battles we fight may seem as if they are of the flesh, but our battles are not of the flesh but the spirit. *'For our struggle is not against flesh and blood, but against the rulers, against the authorities, against the powers of this dark world and against the spiritual forces of evil in the heavenly realms'* (Ephesians 6:12). Instead of us being caught up in the demonic realm, we can choose to see things from God's place of rest in the heavenly realms. God has raised us up with Christ so we may be seated with Him in the heavenly realms, where all things can be placed under our feet (Ephesians 1:2-22, 2:6). We come to the place of inner peace as we rest in His Presence. In doing so, we have authority to overcome the works of the enemy, because it's the God of *peace* that crushes satan under our feet (Romans 16:20).

There is an ongoing war between the flesh and spirit, but the enemy can only attack the areas of our flesh we haven't surrendered to God. Our body, mind, will and emotions may be telling us one thing, but our spirit may be saying another. God's ways and perspectives are always higher and opposite to the way our flesh thinks (Isaiah 55:8). As we daily renew our minds with His revelatory word and Spirit, it will help us to walk in freedom (Romans 12:2).

I remember a vivid time where my flesh was battling with my spirit. I happened to be in Africa when I received a phone call that my sister in England was seriously ill in hospital and wasn't responding to treatment. There was a high chance she might die. My medical friends urged me to go home and be with my parents. My emotions made me feel I should return. However, when I prayed, my spirit sensed I was to stay in Africa and it wasn't the right time to return. In the end, I sensed it was God's will for me to stay and I had an immediate peace along with clarity in my mind and spirit. I knew I had a choice between my emotions and spirit, and chose to trust God with my sister's life. My sister didn't die but made a recovery, and in the meantime, I was able to receive all that God had planned during this significant time in Africa.

Unless our flesh (that is our body and soul), surrenders or comes under the influence of our spirit, then we will be in constant battle with the flesh. Paul said: *'For what I want to do, I do not do, but what I hate I do....For in my inner being, I delight in God's law; but I see another law at work in the members of my body, waging war against the law of my mind and making me a prisoner of the law of sin at work within my members'* (Romans 7:14-24). Paul confessed how he wrestled with his flesh and spirit. His spirit said to do one thing but his flesh opposed. However, he continued by saying this: *'Those who live according to the sinful nature, have their minds set on what that nature desires; but those who live in accordance with the Spirit, have their minds set on what the Spirit desires. The mind of sinful man is death, but the mind controlled by the Spirit is life and peace'* (Romans 8:5-7).

If our spirit is under the influence of the Holy Spirit, then our mind, will and emotions will come under the Lordship of God. Jesus demonstrated this in the desert when He submitted His flesh to His Spirit, and acted from His Spirit at all times. Jesus never responded from His flesh; He always responded from His Spirit. When He heard the distressing news of Lazarus, instead of immediately leaving, He waited. If He had responded from His emotions He would have rushed to the scene, especially when He heard of Mary and Martha's anguish, but He didn't. Instead He waited two more days until Lazarus had died. He listened to His Father first and responded from His Spirit. He saw how His Father had other plans.

Jesus told Peter to watch and pray so that he would not fall into temptation. He said: *'The spirit is willing but the flesh is weak'* (Mark 14:38). As we learn to pursue His Spirit, instead of our flesh, it becomes easier for us to commune with Him and live a Spirit-led life. We were created to be spirit beings where our spirit houses our physical bodies, not the other way round. This happens as we daily surrender our flesh to come under our spirit, and our spirit to come under the rulership of the Holy Spirit.

Each response we make with our flesh comes from the orphan area of our heart. These are areas we haven't yet surrendered to Jesus or overcome with our spirit. The enemy is able to attack the flesh until it is surrendered to Jesus. Only then can we truly say that it is no longer I who live, but Christ who lives in me (Galatians 2:20).

Common Battle Grounds

Here are some of the common battles of the mind we may face. Once we recognize these negative thoughts and belief patterns, we can take each one of them captive by yielding each one to God. *'Take captive every thought and make it obedient to Christ'* (2 Corinthians 10:5).

Judgment & Criticism

One of the common battles of the mind is when we are judgmental and critical towards ourselves and others. So often, we may unknowingly carry a judgmental and critical spirit, especially when we feel hurt, offended, a failure, or rejected. Hurt people will hurt other people. People criticise when they feel misunderstood, rejected, frustrated, a failure, or disappointed. The problem is that every time we think or speak critical words, we open our hearts to the enemy and this quenches God's Spirit.

A critical spirit is based on deceptive enemy language. We are deceived into thinking or feeling we have the right to speak or think such negative words. However, the enemy will use such words to come against us, because the real truth is that when we judge, we too are being be judged (Luke 6:37). The very things we judge others for end up becoming issues for ourselves. This is because when we judge others, we open our hearts to the enemy. Hence, we are encouraged to guard our hearts and minds from entertaining such negative thoughts, about ourselves, God or others.

Instead, we can renounce the spirit of criticism, judgment, and fault-finding, and ask the Lord to renew our minds with His truth as He reveals things through His lens and from His perspective. This is how we learn to discern His ways and thoughts, instead of succumbing to the thoughts of our flesh or the enemy. This may mean daily forgiving others and ourselves, and repenting where we have entertained negative thoughts or spoken word-curses. This includes fault-finding, accusing, gossiping, jealous comments, or resentful thoughts, and saying word-curses using harsh, condemning, or intimidating words.

It is far easier to criticise than to bless, but more powerful to bless than speak negative words. So for each negative word we speak, be it critical, judgmental, or fault-finding, we can reverse its effect by praying a blessing over a person or situation. By doing this, our hearts will feel lighter instead of heavy and oppressed.

A friend was feeling weary and burdened by the ongoing mental struggles with her children. She had allowed negative thoughts and emotions to rule her, and had become critical of others. So I got her to pray a blessing on everyone in her family, and as she did, her spirit rose above her flesh. She became empowered and felt much lighter and had more freedom in her heart. This was a simple exercise for her spirit to rise above the flesh and release blessings instead of negative word-curses.

Anxiety & Fear

Many are held captive or imprisoned by fears and anxious thoughts. This is a daily battle for some until they learn to overcome each fearful thought with faith, trust or His word of truth. Fear is False Evidence Appearing Real. Some may require inner healing from painful traumas and memories, and others simply need to look into Jesus' eyes and hear His words of truth.

Some may have had parents who failed to provide protection, security, provision, acceptance or comfort. This can generate fears and anxious thoughts and each fear or anxious thought produces a lie or false belief. These areas in our heart become healed when we choose to forgive those who failed us, and exchange each fear with His word that carries love and truth.

We were created to be warriors not *worriers*. All anxious thoughts are based on false beliefs or fears, but the good news is that we can exchange these lies for His truth. Jesus will gladly reveal His truth for every anxious thought we surrender to Him, and in exchange give us His peace. He is our source of Truth and you know what the truth does - it sets us free from fears and enemy bondage! (John 14:6).

Our confidence is not to be in man or ourselves but in Him alone. *'You will keep in perfect peace him whose mind is steadfast, because he trusts in You. Trust in the Lord forever, for the Lord, the Lord, is the Rock eternal'* (Isaiah 26:3-4). His ways aren't our ways and His thoughts aren't our thoughts. This is because they are far greater than ours (Isaiah 55:8-12). Sometimes we may have to trust Him with child-like faith, even when we don't know the outcome.

Another way to overcome our anxious thoughts is through prayer and thanksgiving: *'Do not be anxious about anything, but in everything, by prayer and petition, with thanksgiving, present your requests to God. And the peace of God, which transcends all understanding, will guard your hearts and minds in Christ Jesus'* (Philippians 4:6-7). When we give each anxious thought to God and thank Him, He will give us His peace in exchange. The word 'guard' in this scripture is a military word because His peace guards or *protects* our minds and hearts from entertaining anxious thoughts.

Vanity & Pride

God created us to be significant, accepted, valued, loved and to belong. However, as a result of our childhood experiences, some may feel unloved, ignored, not listened to, rejected or insignificant. Consciously or subconsciously, we feel the need in our orphan hearts to be successful, to belong, to be significant, or to achieve. Subsequently, these thoughts may become a source of vanity or pride.

On our own, we can do little in God's Kingdom, but with God we get to do the outrageous, extraordinary and the most amazing things. So it is imperative we guard our hearts if we want to advance in His Kingdom. The Lord knows the motives of our hearts, for nothing is hidden from Him. *'"Let him who boasts **boast in the Lord**." For it is not the one who commends himself who is approved, but the **one whom the Lord commends**'* (2 Corinthians 10:18).

HE WHO OVERCOMES

Many of us, if not all, have probably struggled at some point with being offended by someone or something. Offense is a form of pride and not of God, and it is a choice to resist being offended. For some, being offended is a huge battle of the mind and can even bring division in a church or family.

Each time we allow our hearts to become offended, we are on the slippery slope of judging, fault-finding, and criticising others. We think we have a right to be offended when a person hurts, disappoints, accuses, or disagrees with us in any way. The truth is that this is a trap of the enemy to try and pull us down. We overcome when we choose to forgive those who offended us and pray for them. Then we give all our feelings of hurt and pride to God. We can *agree to disagree*, instead of falling out or causing disunity.

A good friend of mine disagreed with something I firmly believed in, and it was distressing to see that she didn't understand and couldn't see the truth in the matter. However, she said something wise for the sake of the friendship: *'Ange, let's agree to disagree'*. And we did. Friendship is greater than falling out over something we don't agree with.

Distractions & Temptations

Many times, we fail to recognise the distractions and temptations that come from the world, flesh and devil, that are contrary to the Spirit and will of God. It is easy to be distracted with food, pleasures, and things that feed our flesh. John highlights this: *'Do not love the world. For everything in the world- the **cravings of sinful man, the lust of his eyes and the boastings of what he has and does** – comes not from the Father but from the world'*(1 John 2:15-17). Even in ministry, some may crave after success, lust for power, sex, wealth, or to elevate themselves above others. Though we are in the world, we are not of the world.

When the Lord calls us to press in deeper with Him, or to fast and pray, our flesh may try to resist. This is because we easily give in to tiredness or the needs of the flesh, instead of yielding ourselves to Him. When the Lord asked the disciples to stay awake and pray, they gave in to their flesh and tiredness, and fell asleep. In the same way, we are to stay awake so we don't fall into temptation. Jesus said: *'Watch and pray so that you will not fall into temptation. The spirit is willing but the flesh is weak,'* (Matthew 26:40-41).

One of the ways to overcome temptations is to daily surrender our entire being to Him, by offering our body, soul and spirit to Him as a living sacrifice (Romans 12:2). His grace is more than sufficient and enables us to do all that He has called us to do.

What is Deception?

One of the battles of the mind is the area of deception. Deception means being tricked or misled by someone, or made to believe in something when it is false. We are all deceived beings, some more than others. It is easy to fall into deception when we are misguided by other people's thoughts or advice. Most of the time, we are unaware of being deceived until the truth comes to light and exposes the deception or lie. Hence deceptive thoughts can easily lead us into captivity or imprisonment.

John said that if we claim or think we are without sin, then we are *deceived*, and God's *truth* isn't in us (1 John 1:8). One of the enemy's main weapons is deception. He is out to hold back the truth and keep us in bondage as long as he can. Our minds are held captive until the Holy Spirit reveals the truth. Jesus is the Truth and He sent His Spirit of Truth to lead us into freedom (John 14:6+17). It is His Truth that sets us free from bondage (John 8:32). I have seen many people walk in freedom once they see the real truth concerning a situation or belief, and this includes how they think God sees them.

The more we become aware of the enemy's weapons and schemes, the less likely we will be imprisoned by his lies and deception. Self-pity is a good example of where he deceives us. He invites us to throw pity parties when things don't work out the way we want. As we do, we walk into the *pit of self* that turns our hearts away from God. The Lord showed me how self-pity is a sin. The moment I realised this, I repented and renounced the spirit behind it. I don't entertain it anymore, since I know where it comes from.

Another area where we easily fall into deception is thinking life is about striving for success and achievement. This is a worldly concept and not a Kingdom one. It comes from the orphan areas of the heart, that is, our carnal nature that hasn't been transformed by the heart and mind of Christ. As a result, we strive for achievement with our natural abilities, until God speaks His truth. We were created to have intimacy with Him. Our relationship with Him matters more to Him than what we do. He actually wants to crucify our need for success and achievement.

Life is not about how big I can make my ministry or empire, or how successful I become, but about the effect I have to help others grow in their relationship with God. Success is to be measured by God's standards and not man's.

We succeed not by might nor by power but by the power of His Spirit at work in us (Zechariah 4:6). This refers to overcoming the ways of the world through His Spirit of Wisdom, Knowledge, Revelation, Counsel, Power, and Fear of the Lord, as we choose a life of abiding in His Presence (Isaiah 11:2).

Western culture is very work focused. I was brought up to think that life was about achievement and success. However, the Kingdom of God is not work focused but people and relationship focused. The first two commandments are not about work, but about loving others. We are to *love the Lord our God...and love our neighbour* as ourself (Luke 10:27).

When we repeatedly struggle with the same thing again and again, it may be because we have come under an ungodly stronghold. It helps not only to recognise the stronghold but to address it. The enemy tries hard to keep us from knowing the truth. He wants us to believe the lie that 'this is the way we are' or 'this is the way we have to live our lives' or 'we are in the right and others are wrong'. Jesus came to break these lies and set our minds free with His Spirit of truth, for where the Spirit of God is there is freedom (2 Corinthians 3:17).

I saw a woman who was struggling to forgive her best friend who had let her down. The issue was that she had set standards which her friend couldn't live up to. She felt disappointed with this friendship and expected far more than what she got. As we prayed, she was able to forgive her friend and the Lord revealed His truth to her. She realised she had been deceived about friendship. The only person who would never let her down was Jesus. He was to be her best friend. From her relationship with Jesus she could learn how to love others. She learnt the truth that we can't own, possess or control anyone. Friendship is to be based on unconditional love, not what you can get out of it. Many truths were revealed as the Lord began to heal this area of her orphan heart.

One of the reasons we become easily deceived is because we don't seek God's truth or perspective on a matter. We rely too much on the voice of man, soulish beliefs, or the ways of the world including social media. The wisdom of the world is foolish compared to God's Wisdom, and the foolishness of God is wiser than man's wisdom. Jesus is Wisdom personified (1 Corinthians 1:25- 3:18). The more we learn how to hear God, the more we will discover His truth and be set free from different areas of deception. The only one who is without deception is the one who walks one hundred percent with God and is without sin. Jesus is the only one I know who meets this criteria. Until we deal with the various areas of sin in our life, we are living in a greater or lesser degree of deception.

John said: *If we claim to be without sin, we have deceived ourselves and the truth is not in us. If we claim we have not sinned, we make Him out to be a liar and His word has no place in our lives* (1 John 1:8-10). The good news is we discover more of His truth as we follow Him and seek His ways. We are all on a life long journey that leads to healing, wholeness and inner freedom. We can choose which lens to look through. When we look through God's lens, we will be able to see and discern things with more clarity, instead of with blurred vision. Jesus has sent us His Counsellor and Spirit of Truth to help us overcome the battles of the mind (John 15:26).

Paul lived in great deception before he encountered Jesus. After this encounter, he was on the path of discovering the truth as he followed God and learnt to discern His ways.

Dealing with Disappointment

Many, if not all, have probably faced disappointment at some point in life. This can range from minor to major, depending on how quick we can deal with it or get over it. We can be disappointed with ourselves, others or God, especially when things don't turn out the way we want or expect. It is easier to blame God or others for our disappointments, when the truth may be that we simply didn't surrender the situation to Him.

Dis-appointment means not being in 'appointment' or alignment with God. To put it another way, it is when we step out of line with His will. We can ask God to reveal His truth concerning each situation, so we see from His perspective instead of our own or the enemy's perspective. This will bring comfort, healing and freedom from any past or present disappointments.

There was a time I felt hugely disappointed when I failed one of my final medical exams. There was no reason I should have failed, for I had studied hard and I knew He had called me to be a doctor. However, I had to deal with this feeling of disappointment. So I cried out to Him, venting all my frustration and anger, and asked why I had failed. After releasing my negative emotions He replied to my spirit. He said it was because I had allowed pride to enter my heart, and reminded me that I would succeed not by might or by strength but by His Spirit.

When I was convicted by this truth, I instantly repented and humbled myself and His peace flooded my heart again. Six months later I re-sat the exam and walked through it with no problem. It dawned on me that the test I faced was not the medical exam but the test of my heart.

If we give our *dis*-appointments to God, and let go of our negative emotions and frustrations, He will convict our hearts with His truth. When we see things from His perspective and hear His voice, everything falls into place and the disappointment lifts.

I saw a lady who felt disappointed with God after her husband walked out with her children. She cried out to God and asked Him why did He not intervene and stop her husband from leaving? After she released tears from her deep pain I saw in my spirit Jesus standing beside her. So I asked her to look into His eyes. As she gazed into His eyes of suffering love, her tears soon turned into laughter and joy. She felt His warm liquid love flooding through her innermost being. She realised He had never left her and had always been with her. The Lord says: *'Those who hope in Me will not be disappointed'* (Isaiah 49:23). As we trust in God and look to Him, He will never disappoint us.

Renewing of the Mind

One of the ways to overcome the battles of our mind is to *take captive every thought and make it obedient to Christ* (2 Corinthians 10:5). This sounds easy but we have to be aware of our negative thoughts in order to resist them and then take authority over them. Paul said: *'Do not conform any longer to the pattern of this world but be transformed by the renewing of your mind'* (Romans 12:2). The Greek word used here for 'transform' is *'metamorphoo'*, where we get the word 'metamorphosis'.

Metamorphosis means to change form by either natural or supernatural means. The word 'renewing' refers to an ongoing process or a continual renewal of the way we think, until our minds become transformed into the likeness of Christ. Studies have shown it takes around three to four weeks for the brain to form new nerve pathways. New nerve pathways form when we develop new thoughts and new ways of behaviour. Hence, we renew our minds as we learn to think and behave as sons and daughters of the King, and as we do, we gradually take on the mind of Christ.

His word is a light to our path and a lamp to our feet (Psalm 119:105). Something we can pray each day is that our Father would give us His Spirit of Wisdom and Revelation, so that the eyes of our heart may be enlightened to know the hope to which He has called us (Ephesians 1:17-18).

There have been seasons in my life when it has been difficult to see where God was leading me or know what He was doing. Many times I have felt tempted to quit and return to my former things in life. It has been like climbing a spiritual mountain and at various points I have been tempted to turn back instead of continuing up. However, I managed to continue on by holding onto God's words and promises. In hindsight, I realised that it was during these seasons that my heart and spirit were being tested. God was taking me deeper in Him, though at the time it felt like He was miles away.

The different aspects of our soul may be tested. Sometimes, my *mind* may have been tested with regards to my thoughts. Or my *emotions* may have been tested with regards to what I was feeling. And other times my *will* was being tested with regards to my choices. Sometimes, we may need to stand on His truth and declare His word and promises, as we walk through the seasons of uncertainty by faith. When we declare His word, believe His truth and promises, things may begin to stir in the heavenly realms that bring breakthrough in our lives on earth.

Declaring His word, truth and promises is more powerful than rehearsing negative words or doubtful thoughts. As we rise in the Spirit, declare in the Spirit, be led by the Spirit, then we will overcome in the power and authority of God's Spirit, even when everything looks doubtful or impossible. God is God of the impossible and is inviting us to walk by faith instead of by our natural sight, and to hold onto His truth instead of the lies and fears of the enemy. Then we will see God do amazing things in our lives and the lives of others. The choice is ours.

Lord Jesus, I ask You to highlight any strongholds in my carnal nature especially familiar strongholds (eg pride, criticism, fear, control…) and their roots, including any false beliefs and deception. Help me to recognise and overcome the battles in my mind as I give my soulish (or negative) thoughts and emotions to You, in exchange for Your revelatory-truth. Lord renew my mind with Your Word and Your Spirit, and transform the orphan areas of my heart. Help me to follow Your will as I surrender my heart to You, and discern Your heart for Your people.

END NOTES

[1] Kylstra, Chester & Betsy: *Restoring The Foundations: An Integrated Approach to Healing Ministry*, (Proclaiming His Word, Aug 2001)
[2] Sandford John; *Healing the Nations, p 151 (Chosen Books, 2000)*

8

Godly Wisdom & Discernment

*Dear friends, do not believe every spirit, but
test the spirits to see whether they are from God*

1 John 4:1

Kingdom wisdom and discernment are both gifts and fruit of the Spirit. The man without the Spirit doesn't accept the things that come from the Spirit of God, because they are *spiritually discerned* (1 Corinthians 2:14). Only with His Spirit in our innermost being may we *discern in the Spirit* the things that are of God or of the enemy. It is important for us to be able to discern in the Spirit what is taking place in the spiritual realms in the times we live in.

The *discernment of spirits* is seen as one of the nine spiritual gifts that are freely given to all Spirit-filled believers (1 Corinthians 12:10). Some translations refer to this as 'distinguishing between the spirits' (NIV) and others refer to it as the ability to 'discern the source' that is if a word is from the Spirit, the flesh, or a demonic source (TPT).

All thoughts, feelings and words come from a source. The source can either be the flesh (including the world), the devil, or God. Jesus said His sheep know His voice for they have become familiar to hearing Him. In the same way that we become familiar with a close friend's voice or a spouse's voice, so we develop the ability to discern God's voice as we grow and mature in our relationship with Him.

General Discernment

The word *discern* in the Old Testament is the ability to distinguish between good and evil. When God told Solomon he may have whatever he wanted, Solomon asked for a *'discerning heart'* so he may govern God's people and discern right from wrong (1 Kings 3:9). God gave him this gift and he was known as the wisest of all kings.

General discernment comes with experience and maturity: *'Solid food is for the mature,* **who by constant use have trained themselves to distinguish good from evil***'*. The New American Standard version reads: *'Have* **their senses trained to discern good and evil***'* (Hebrews 5:14).

Spiritual discernment comes with maturity as we grow more in our relationship with God. Many may say, 'God is speaking', but we must test this for ourselves. Jesus warned there will be false prophets, false teachers, and anti-Christs, and not to believe everything they say. *'At that time if anyone says to you, "Look, here is the Christ!" or "There he is!" do not believe it. For false Christs and false prophets will appear and perform great signs and miracles to deceive even the elect - if that were possible. See, I have told you ahead of time'* (Mathew 24:23-25).

There will be those who perform miracles, signs and wonders and we are not to assume all miracles are from God, but discern if the source of power is or is not from Him. *'And he (the beast) performed great and miraculous signs, even causing fire to come down from Heaven...***he deceived the inhabitants** *of the earth'* (Revelation 13:13, 2 Thessalonians 2:9).

Sometimes, fellow believers who mean to speak well may not necessarily be speaking from the heart of God but their flesh or the enemy. We are to test what we hear, even from those who have a prophetic anointing for they may not always be speaking from God's heart.

Nehemiah was given 'ungodly wisdom' and intimidating words from a prophet who falsely prophesied he would be killed if he didn't flee and meet him in the temple. He discerned these words were not from the heart of God but fear-based and so rejected them, as these words were drawing him away from his God-given assignment (Nehemiah 6:10-11).

Paul encourages us to *'test everything'* we hear so that we can hold onto the good or that which is from God and discard the evil. There are many believers who quench what the Holy Spirit is doing by rejecting what they see or hear when actually it is from God. We can simply ask God, *'Is this really You, Lord? Is this Your word or will or not?'* Or ask Him, *'What is the truth concerning this?'*

Paul tells us not to quench the Spirit's fire or treat prophecies with contempt (1 Thessalonians 5:19-22). John, on the other hand, encourages us not to believe every spirit we hear but to test the spirits to see whether they are from God or not. Many may give a mixed prophetic word and we are to discern what is from God and what is from the flesh (1 John 4:1-2, 2 Thessalonians 2:9).

I have come to understand that when someone has given me a true prophetic word from God, or speaks under the power of the Holy Spirit, I usually feel a stirring in my spirit that is good and brings life. It is as if my spirit becomes alive or on fire, and I feel the joy, love or peace of the Holy Spirit inside me. This is the same as when Jesus spoke to the disciples on the road to Emmaus, their hearts were burning within (Luke 24:32).

When a word given to me is not from God, I usually notice that my spirit doesn't respond. Instead, it washes over me or I may feel a heaviness and loss of peace. If it washes over me, then it is usually from the flesh, but if my spirit feels heavy or not at peace, then it is usually from the enemy. Jesus said: *'The **Spirit gives life**; the **flesh counts for nothing**. The words I have spoken to you are **Spirit** and they are life'* (John 6:63).

However, I would like to mention that there have been occasions when a word or prophecy has been spoken in my life that has been of God but my spirit hasn't responded. This is because I have not been in the right place with God at that moment in time or my heart didn't want to receive this word. So we mustn't discard the words that don't automatically bring our spirits to life but test them before God, especially if it is a word involving significant change.

I received a prophetic word spoken by a man of God and my spirit didn't respond for the word didn't make sense. However on further discussion with others and testing it before God, my spirit became more open to hear what God was saying to me.

On another occasion there were two pastors, both with a prophetic gifting, who had spoken significant words in my life. One was strongly encouraging me to do one thing and the other was strongly telling me the opposite. In my heart, I naturally wanted to do what was more adventurous but I knew I had to surrender my will to God. So I got before God in prayer and fasting to seek His will on the matter. After a few hours of laying down my desires and waiting on Him, I felt a deep peace about the choice to make. His still quiet voice spoke to my spirit as He made His will clear through a picture and revealed who was speaking from the flesh.

God wants us to bring everything to Him so we can hear and discern His voice. It is wise to test everything we hear by bringing it before God and not assume it is from Him because of the person who spoke the word.

Discerning the Spirit from the Flesh

We are all learning to discern between the flesh (body, soul) and the spirit because there is a constant battle going on between the two. Our body, mind, will and emotions may be telling us one thing but our spirit may be telling us another. The soul feeds from the Tree of Knowledge of Good and Evil, whereas the spirit feeds from the Tree of Life.

As I was praying for some church leaders I had a picture. In the picture I saw one of the pastors on his knees in prayer listening to God with streams flowing in all directions from his heart. As he came before God I saw he was tapping into the Tree of Life. Hence, the River of Life was flowing in all directions from his heart as he focused on God. However, to his left I saw the Tree of Knowledge of Good and Evil. It was trying to distract him by 'good' man-made suggestions and ideas that were not from God. The pastor couldn't afford to agree with these man-made suggestions as they would quench the flow of the Spirit. They were counterfeit to God's Spirit. All thoughts and suggestions were to be 'tested' by offering them to God in prayer.

For example, a person had suggested how 'good' it would be to have stage smoke for a youth church service. This was easy to produce and a copy of something real, but it was man-made and not authentic. The Lord can provide His manifest Presence, His cloud of glory, if we are willing to seek Him and engage in His Presence. Do we settle for what is counterfeit from the Tree of Knowledge of Good and Evil, or pursue what is authentic and real from the Tree of Life?

We are to be led by the Spirit and not our soul, for it is those who are led by the Spirit who are the mature sons of God (Romans 8:14). Jesus demonstrated this in the desert when He submitted His flesh to His Spirit, and acted from His Spirit at all times. It's much easier to respond from the spirit when we engage in His Presence. As we regularly interact with God, our spirit will begin to take rule over our flesh. Let's not forget that we were created to be spiritual beings residing in physical bodies.

Check the Motive

Whenever we receive a prophetic word, or 'good' suggestion or proposal, it is good to check the underlying motive behind the source. Are the motives pure, impartial, and sincere, flowing from the Tree of Life? Or are they contrived with an ulterior motive coming from the Tree of Knowledge of Good and Evil? Here are some thoughts to help us discern.

Tree of Knowledge of Good and Evil

Is the person who is giving the word displaying any greed, selfishness, personal bias, self-reasoning or man-made opinion, jealousy, pride, fear or control? Are they seeking anything for themselves or do they have the individual's best interests at heart? Or does the word puff up your ego, flatter you, or minister to your flesh? Check the motive behind the word, and that will help confirm the source of where it is coming from. People have said God was speaking a certain word to me but when I have sensed fear, control, the flesh, 'good ideas' or ungodly spirits, I have smiled but graciously not accepted it in my heart.

Solomon checked the motive behind two women's testimony when they both claimed that a baby was theirs. He tested their hearts by seeing which one would stop him from cutting the baby in half. Then he knew who was the real mother, for her motives were genuine and loving (1 Kings 3:16-27). The Lord searches our hearts and knows every motive behind our thoughts.

Tree of Life

On the other hand, a word spoken from the Tree of Life comes with unconditional love, selflessness and humility. The word will point to God and not self. The word may come through dreams, visions, or spiritual insights during prayer or worship. The word can be outrageous and something never imagined and is revelatory like a light bulb being turned on. You clearly know it is not your own thought for the idea is God-focused and comes by revelation of the Spirit.

It is usually amazing and it requires radical faith and obedience, since it is 'out of the box' thinking. There is no place for 'self' for it is God's idea because it is revelatory. It causes the spirit to come alive and feel excited. It stirs faith and requires more prayer and leaning on God for strategy, counsel and wisdom. It can't be done by the flesh but requires God's grace and Spirit. And this means we have to trust in Him and allow His Spirit to lead. His peace rests with us when our confidence isn't in self or others, but Him.

Is it possible for the same person to speak a word from God one moment and then a word from the flesh or devil the next moment? Yes! No-one is perfect and we are all prone to sin. This is why we are to weigh up what we hear for ourselves and whether it is from God or not. This was seen with Peter, when Jesus asked Peter, *'Who do you say I am?'* Peter replied He was the Christ, the Son of the living God. Jesus blessed Peter and said this was revealed to him by his Heavenly Father. However, a few verses later when Jesus told His disciples He must suffer and be killed, Peter rebuked Jesus saying: *'This shall never happen to You!'*

Jesus replied: *'Get thee behind Me Satan! You are a stumbling block to Me'* (Mathew 16:15,23).

A similar thing happened when James and John were not welcomed in a Samaritan village. They asked Jesus if they should call fire down from Heaven and destroy the village. Jesus rebuked them and they continued on their travels (Luke 9:51-55). Peter, James and John, whom Jesus rebuked, were His closest disciples.

Discerning in the Spirit is something to pursue, for when we lack discernment, we are at great risk of falling into deception. However, as we seek God by yielding our flesh to His Spirit, we will discern His ways more.

Is it from the Flesh, Devil or God?

Here are some ways to help us discern if the source of what we think, feel, see, or hear is from the flesh (or world), the devil or from God. As we draw closer to God, we will become more familiar with the ways He speaks, for His sheep know His voice (John 10:4).

Source from the Flesh

*'We have not received the spirit of the world, but the Spirit who is from God, that we may understand what God has freely given us. We speak not in words taught us by **human wisdom but in words taught by the Spirit**, expressing **spiritual truths in spiritual words**. The man without the Spirit does not accept the things that come from the Spirit of God, for they are foolishness to him, and he can't understand them for they are spiritually discerned…For the wisdom of this world is foolishness in God's sight'* (1 Corinthians 2:12-14, 3:19).

People who lack the Spirit of God will not accept the things which are from God. The more we recognize this, the less we will be influenced by worldly wisdom or man-made opinions.

'See to it that no-one takes you captive through hollow and deceptive philosophy which depends on human tradition and the basic principles of this world rather than on Christ' (Colossians 2:8). Most of the traditions or cultures of this world are man-made and not God-

made. Jesus told us to seek first the Kingdom of God and what is right in His eyes (Mathew 6:33).

When a word or thought is from the flesh it is usually based on man-made logic, common sense, reasoning and self-opinion. If there is any fear, anxiety, guilt, doubt, anger, criticism, jealousy, pressure or other negative feelings behind it, then it probably is from the flesh or enemy. If there is a sense of any fear or control behind someone's 'wise' words, then they are probably not from God. Human wisdom sees things from God as foolish for it sees things as the world sees, and is very much intellectual or fear-based.

Also, things of the flesh feed our flesh especially in the areas of greed, possessions, wealth, comfort, pride, and the lust for power, fame or status. The flesh is self-focused instead of God-focused and follows traditional beliefs instead of Kingdom culture. Since the flesh opposes the word of God, our spirit will lack a positive response.

Many of us may want to believe something is from God when it isn't because we desperately want this thing. This is when we are to examine our hearts before God and let go of our own desires so we may discern His will and desires.

There was a missionary who felt called by God to serve in Africa but during their stay in Africa they went into financial debt. They came back feeling disappointed with God and questioned why God hadn't provided for them financially. As I was ministering to this person's heart I discerned that they were running away from their responsibilities back home and that God hadn't called them to the mission field. The truth came out that they wanted to flee from the country where they were living. I spoke the truth in love as I questioned their motives for being in Africa. Their finances began to recover as they faced up to their responsibilities back home.

Source from the Devil

The devil is very cunning and deceptive for he never wants us to know that our words or thoughts are from him. That is why it's important we know his schemes and character in order to discern his ways.

One of his traits is accusation for he is the accuser of the brethren (Zechariah 3:1). We are to be careful not to point our finger at others or speak malicious words or gossip (Isaiah 58:9). Any accusation, even if true, is not from God but the devil. This is because God convicts with love but the enemy accuses and condemns. Instead of accusing others we can forgive and point them in the right direction by speaking the truth with love.

A fellow missionary came to see me to tell me *her concerns* regarding another missionary. I listened and agreed with some of the issues she mentioned, but then suggested we pray for this missionary. As we prayed, a heavy oppressive spirit came upon me and I asked the Lord what had happened. He said I had opened my heart to an ungodly spirit by agreeing with this missionary for the spirit behind what she spoke was not from Him. I instantly repented and renounced this spirit, and it left me as quick as it came. I realized that there was an accusing and judging spirit behind her words and I shouldn't have come into agreement with what she said.

The enemy condemns by bringing judgment and making us feel there is no way out. Jesus, on the other hand, convicts by speaking the truth in love and offers us a solution or way out through repentance and forgiveness. *'God didn't send His Son into the world to condemn the world, but to save the world through Him'* (John 3:17). We have only one true Judge and that is God, which means we are not to judge others but allow Him to do it (James 4:12).

A word or thought that comes from the enemy is usually negative, accusing, fearful, or self-focused. It can bring a sense of guilt, shame, hopelessness and despair. Or there may be a sense of failure and disappointment. It releases doubt instead of faith. Ungodly words release a sense of unease or oppression. Satan is the father of lies, so a thought may be either a lie or a twist of the truth. If the source isn't from God then we should simply reject it. The enemy will even deceive us into believing a sin is ok or that no-one will find out (Jude 4). There is no excuse for any sin. Sin is sin.

Sometimes, words or thoughts from the enemy come with a sense of pride of knowledge, self-righteousness, 'my rights', or a sense of superiority to others. The thought is glorifying self instead of glorifying God. We should be careful how we receive a word of flattery or praise from men, especially when it boosts the ego and flesh (John 12:43). This is not to be confused with words of encouragement which we gratefully accept. Sometimes there may be a sense of pressure or manipulation to do something against our personal will. Words spoken in a manipulative or controlling manner are usually from a source of witchcraft.

Thoughts from the enemy are opposite to the character and nature of God. Such thoughts do not bear Kingdom fruit. Hence there will be no peace, joy, love, self-control, gentleness, humility and so on. Or the word may sound good but be coming from an ungodly source. There is usually no peace and something just doesn't feel right. I have met people who know how to speak the 'right words' but recognized they had an underlying spirit of fear, manipulation, people pleasing, or pride behind their words.

Words that are not from God may bring confusion and lack clarity. They may be empty or come with oppression. Sometimes, we may feel a sense of false guilt or false responsibility. This is when we are made to feel guilty or responsible for something which was not our problem in the first place. People usually blame others for something when it is their own fault, and this includes the *spirit of fault-finding* which is not from God. The closer we draw near to God, the more we will come to know His ways and discern what is of the enemy and what is of Him.

Source from God

Sometimes, things may happen in life that seem to be from the enemy but may be from God. Instead of assuming something, we can ask God if He is behind what is happening or if it is an attack from the enemy. However, it may be the enemy has initiated something, but with prayer, God can work through it for the good. Sometimes, God may use a negative experience to simply get our attention or speak to us because we have been too busy to hear Him.

Words from God give life to our spirit because they are Spirit and they are life (John 6:63). His words bring freedom for where the Spirit of the Lord is, there is freedom (2 Corinthians 3:17). His words release faith and encourage us to put our trust in Him. God speaks the truth in love. He brings conviction not condemnation. His word can bring a Godly rebuke because the Father disciplines those He loves (Hebrews 12:5-6). Both a conviction and a rebuke encourage our hearts to repent.

Thoughts and words from God are uplifting and bear witness to His character and nature. They are opposite to our ways of thinking. His words are usually backed by scripture though not always. However, they don't contradict scripture.

A word or thought from God brings revelation and clarity. His word releases unity amongst Spirit-filled believers. There is no shame or failure in the Kingdom. God forgives when we truly repent. There is a sense of peace when we are in His will, or a word is from Him. He can always confirm His word to us in other ways when we ask. Sometimes, there can be a sense of urgency in His word but it is usually a wake-up call to position and prepare His people. We can always ask God to confirm if a word or thought is from Him, and He will.

Specific Discernment

Sometimes, we may require specific discernment especially when ministering to others. Some may have the gift to discern or distinguish between spirits, and this is known as the 'gift of discernment of spirits' (1 Corinthians 12:10). It is one of the revelatory gifts along with the gifts of wisdom and knowledge.

Some may have the ability to discern the presence of angels in a room, either through supernatural sight or a sense of awareness. The angels may be ministering joy, healing, deliverance, breakthrough, prophecy, and so on.

Some may discern the function of a spirit (or spirits) operating in an individual, church, or over a nation, especially when seeking God's strategy for an individual, church or geographical area. Usually the name of a spirit is its function, for example, a spirit of defilement, a spirit of rejection, a spirit of deception, or a spirit of fear. A person may carry the fruit of God's Spirit, such as a spirit of joy, a spirit of boldness, a spirit of discernment, and so on.

Spiritual discernment is an important asset in the healing and deliverance ministry and also when interceding for breakthrough in churches, families, communities and nations. For example, a person may be struggling with a problem but also have an underlying spirit which is to be discerned, so the person may be set free and healed. Or there may be struggles in the churches, work places, communities, or families, and the Holy Spirit can highlight the underlying issues and ungodly spirits at work. Ungodly spirits may be passed down the blood-line or from predecessors, and from having doors in our heart that are still opened to sin.

Sometimes, the issue may be obvious by the demonic fruit that is manifesting in a person's life, but at other times it isn't. This is when we ask the Holy Spirit to reveal the underlying spiritual root. Many times when people have asked me to pray for a specific issue, the Lord has revealed an underlying spiritual root to their problem.

Most times we are not aware of what we are carrying until the Holy Spirit brings it to light. The Lord will shine His light on a situation if we ask Him to reveal which spirit is operating behind a problem. Prophets who are seers are usually good at discerning for they can usually 'see' in the Spirit what is taking place in a given situation.

True versus False Discernment

Something I have learnt when we are 'discerning' something is to be careful we are not holding onto judgment. If we are, then we will be discerning with our flesh instead of the spirit, and this is *false discernment*. If we want true discernment on a matter, then we are to be spiritually immune from judging others.

James says the wisdom that comes from God is first pure, then peace loving, considerate, submissive, full of mercy and good fruit, *impartial* and sincere (James 3: 14-17).

Francis Frangipane said: *'We will never possess true discernment until we crucify our instincts to judge'*[1]. True discernment is rooted in love, whereas false discernment is rooted in criticism. False discernment is slow to hear, quick to speak and quick to anger. It carries judgment, condemnation, disunity, fear, control, gossip and rejection. People may unknowingly carry a spirit of false judgement, false discernment, and fault-finding.

On the other hand, true discernment is quick to listen, slow to speak, slow to become angry (James 1:19) and comes with restoration, redemption, reconciliation and peace. It has no human bias or man-made opinion, for it is impartial.

Paul prayed for the Philippians that **their love** may abound more in knowledge and depth of insight so that they may be able to **discern** what is best (Philippians 1:9). Love releases true discernment. However, let's not forget to be shrewd as snakes and innocent as doves (Matthew 10:16).

Sometimes, people may give advice and say it is from God when their underlying spirit is one of fear and control, or false judgement and false discernment. They may call it wisdom but true wisdom is spoken in love and peace with no fear, control, or other agenda attached. False wisdom (or worldly wisdom) is usually fear-based and based on man's opinion.

The more we get to know someone, the more we will discern their thoughts. Hence, as we listen to God and grow in our relationship with Him, we will come to discern His thoughts, both for ourselves and others. (See Appendix B: Summary of Spiritual Discernment).

Two Wisdoms

Many of us struggle with our flesh and spirit through a lack of wisdom and discernment. There are two kinds of wisdom; the wisdom of the world and the wisdom of God. The wisdom of the Lord brings peace, truth and freedom, whereas the wisdom of the world brings fear and bondage. The wisdom of God comes from the Tree of Life (Proverbs 3:18), whereas the wisdom of this world comes from the Tree of Knowledge of Good and Evil.

HE WHO OVERCOMES

The wisdom of God is Jesus Himself, and points to His ways and His Spirit (1 Corinthians1:30). This is contrary to the wisdom of the world which points to 'self' and the flesh. Therefore, true wisdom focuses on God and His people (Matthew 11:19, Proverbs 8:12-14), but the wisdom of the world focuses on 'self', for it comes from the mindset of man instead of God. The wisdom of the world is deceptive, though it appears to be true. It will stop us fulfilling our call and destiny as it is based on fears, false beliefs, insecurities and man's opinion, instead of God's ways.

I was strongly advised by someone who loved me to not give up my medical career and go to Africa. They couldn't understand because they were viewing it through the eyes of worldly wisdom and not God's Spirit. It was a battle but I knew in my heart that God was calling me to Africa and this meant laying down my career for Him. The enemy was trying to stop me through their 'wise' thoughts.

There is the *gift* of wisdom and the *Spirit* of Wisdom. The gift of wisdom is one of the nine gifts of the Spirit available for everyone (1 Corinthians 12:8). James said: *'If any of you lacks wisdom, he should ask God, who gives generously to all'* (James 1:5). We ask by faith, for God is a generous giver and wants His children to see through His Wisdom instead of the wisdom of the world. However, the Spirit of Wisdom is more than a gift, for it is one of the seven-fold Spirits given by God to His mature sons and daughters: those who carry His Presence, revere Him, and are led by His Spirit (Isaiah 11:2).

We can daily ask for His wisdom and revelation (Ephesians 1:17) and Spirit of discernment. And He will gladly give it to those who earnestly desire it.

Lord Jesus, thank You that I can ask for Your Wisdom and Discernment to guide me though life. Help me to grow in Godly Wisdom and Discernment, so I may discern and overcome the ways of the world, flesh, and devil. May I seek Your Truth at all times, as I follow You.

END NOTES

[1] Frangipane, Francis; *The Three battlegrounds (Arrow Publication, 2006), p73.*

9

Pursuing the Fear of the Lord & Holiness

The fear of the Lord is pure, enduring forever
Psalm 19:9

Our Heavenly Father chose us before the creation of the world to be holy and blameless in His sight (Ephesians 1:4). He predestined us, in love, to be His adopted children through Christ. To be holy is to be set apart and to consecrate our lives for God. It is choosing a sanctified lifestyle where purity flows from our hearts. Jesus prayed that we may be one with Him as He is one with the Father, and this includes choosing a sanctified lifestyle.

The reverential awe of the Lord is known as the *fear of the Lord* and has many rewards for those who posture this attitude of heart. There is a difference between being scared of God and the fear of the Lord. Being scared of God is running away from Him because we are aware of our sins. Those who fear the Lord want to run towards Him and draw closer to Him, and obey Him. David said: '*Let all the earth **fear the Lord**, let all the people of the world **revere Him**'* (Psalm 33:8).

The fear of the Lord goes hand-in-hand with His love: *'Let those who fear the Lord say, "His love endures forever"'* (Psalm 118:4). *'The Lord delights in those who fear Him, who put their hope in His unfailing love'* (Psalm 147:11).

To love God and to fear Him are like the opposite sides of a coin. God is our Father, who is love, but He is also our Judge. David knew what it was to love God with all his heart and seek His face, but he also revered His awesome power and holiness. His relationship with God mattered more to him than anything else. He was so conscious of God's holiness and awesome power that he never wanted to grieve Him, and when he did, he would cry out to God for His mercy and forgiveness so he could be back in a love relationship with Him.

An angel of the Lord said in a loud voice: *'Fear God and give Him glory, because the hour of His judgment has come. Worship Him who made the heavens, earth, sea and springs of water'* (Revelation 14:7). To fear God is to worship Him, giving Him praise, honour and glory, for who He is, what He has done, and what is yet to come. He is omnipresent which means He is everywhere. He is omniscient meaning that He is all knowing, and omnipotent meaning He is all powerful.

There have been times when God's Presence has been so tangible that it has brought me to my knees with such reverence and awe of His Holiness. During such encounters I have taken off my shoes, as if I've been standing on Holy ground (Joshua 5:15, Exodus 3:5).

The fear of the Lord is one of the seven-fold Spirits for those who choose a lifestyle of abiding in God's Presence and is the only one that is mentioned twice. This is because the Spirit of the fear of the Lord is required to receive the seven-fold Spirit. The seven-fold Spirit is described in the book of Isaiah: *'The Spirit of the Lord will rest on him – the Spirit of Wisdom and of Understanding, the Spirit of Counsel and of Power, the Spirit of Knowledge and of the Fear of the Lord – and he will delight in the Fear of the Lord'* (Isaiah 11:2-3). The Book of Psalms and Proverbs repeatedly say that the fear of the Lord is the beginning of wisdom, knowledge, and understanding.

I was worshipping at a conference with my arms horizontally outstretched when I had a vision. In this vision, I saw my body taking the shape of a Menorah. A Menorah is a Jewish lampstand with three branches on either side and one in the centre. The modern version of a Menorah is a candlestick with seven candles, but the original Hebraic Menorah burned with pure olive oil, in the Holy Place of the temple of the Lord (Exodus 25:31). My body (from head to toe) formed the main central part of the Menorah oil lamp, and my arms became like the side branches, with three lights burning on either side. I realized the centre piece of the Menorah was where His Presence rested and this flowed out to the right and left side branches. The branches consisted of the Spirit of Wisdom on one side and the Spirit of Understanding on the other, the Spirit of Counsel on one side and the Spirit of Power on the other, and the Spirit of Knowledge on one side and the Spirit of the Fear of the Lord on the other.

God has created us to become carriers of the oil of His Presence, through yielding our hearts in a life of abandonment to Him. It is as we discover how to abide in the oil of His Presence, that His seven-fold Spirit begins to flow and manifest in our hearts.

Fear God, Not Man or Satan

God created satan, a guardian cherub (Ezekiel 28:14), and unlike man, he was not created in God's image. Satan was a chief worshipper of the Lord until he rebelled and wanted to be powerful 'like' God and get others to worship him. It was pride, control and rebellion that led to his downfall (Isaiah 14:12-15).

Satan imitates and counterfeits everything because he can't create, since he is a created being, and can only be in one place at any moment in time. He was created by God and is not the Creator. He said he would make himself *like* the Most High (Isaiah 14:14). Peter said that satan is *like* a roaring lion, meaning he tries to imitate (1 Peter 5:8). This is why he uses fear as a major stronghold and weapon to imprison us and stop us from listening to or obeying God.

After the Holy Spirit rested on Peter at Pentecost a holy boldness came upon him such that he could stand before men and witness to the power of the Name of Jesus. He was no longer afraid of men, even authorities, or death, because he had encountered the reverential awe of the risen Lord.

The apostle Paul knew the fear of the Lord and encouraged us to work out our salvation with fear and trembling, so God may work in us according to His will and purpose (Philippians 2:12).

Living a Sanctified Lifestyle

There is a difference between justification and sanctification. Justification is what God has done for us through Jesus' death and blood shed for us on the cross. However, sanctification is what God is calling us to do for Him as we choose to live a sanctified life. As we journey along the path of salvation with God, He continues to do a deeper work in our hearts through the process of sanctification and transforming us from the inside out.

The Greek word used for 'sanctify' is *hagiazo* which means *'to make holy, to purify or to consecrate'*. The word 'consecrate' means to be set apart. Jesus said we are in the world but not of the world. We belong to another world and that is the Kingdom of God. He told Pilate that His Kingdom was not of this world but from another place, and that He came to testify to the truth (John 18:36). Though we live *in* the world we are not *of* the world. The moment we accept Jesus as our Lord and Saviour we choose to live and serve Him in His Kingdom. To be set apart doesn't mean to cut ourselves off from the rest of the world, but rather not to agree or live by its standards. Instead, we choose to live in a Kingdom culture under the power and authority of King Jesus, instead of the worldly culture.

*'It is **God's will that you should be sanctified**; that you should avoid sexual immorality; that each of you should learn to control his own body in a way that is holy and honourable, not in passionate lust like the heathen. For **God did not call us to be impure but to live a holy life**'* (1 Thessalonians 4:3-7). Paul then prays: *'May the **God of peace, sanctify you through and through**. May your **whole spirit, soul and body** be kept **blameless at the coming of our Lord Jesus Christ**'* (1 Thessalonians 5:23).

We are encouraged to keep our whole being, body, soul and spirit, pure and cleansed from all sin until Jesus returns. He is coming for

His spotless bride. He will be looking for those who have made themselves ready by choosing to do what is right in His eyes (Revelation 19:7-8). The enemy is out to defile our hearts and minds through lust (for sex, fame, power, money), sexual sin (fornication, adultery, masturbation, pornography, sexual abuse, homosexuality), addictions, occult involvement, unforgiveness, pride, fear, rebellion and lies and so on, to prevent our hearts from living the sanctified life God calls us to.

*'Then I looked and there before me was the Lamb, standing on Mount Zion, and with Him 144,000 who had His Name and His Father's Name written on their foreheads. These are those who **did not defile themselves with women, for they kept themselves pure. They follow the Lamb wherever He goes**. They were purchased from among men and offered as first fruits to God and the Lamb. **No lie was found in their mouths; they are blameless**'* (Revelation 14:1, 4).

Peter said: *'As obedient children, do not conform to the evil desires you had when you lived in ignorance. But just as **He who called you is holy, so be holy** in all you do; for it is written: "**Be holy for I am holy**"'*(1 Peter 1:14-16). This was the same Peter who previously said to Jesus, *'Go away from me Lord, for I am a sinful man!'* (Luke 5:8). The moment God comes into our lives we are aware of the things of this world that are not of Him. They appear dirty and profane. We have the choice to turn our hearts to Jesus and no longer come under their influence. This is the 'Yes' to follow Jesus and choosing a sanctified life, as we set ourselves apart for Him.

David knew what was required to come into God's Presence. *'Who may ascend the hill of the Lord? Who may stand in His holy place? **He who has clean hands and a pure heart**, who does not lift up his soul to an idol or swear by what is false'* (Psalm 24:3-4). Clean hands represent doing what is right in God's eyes. A pure heart refers to what we feel, think or speak being acceptable and pleasing to our Heavenly Father.

After David had committed adultery with Bathsheba, he cried out to God to be made pure and holy once more. *'Cleanse me with hyssop, and I will be clean; wash me, and I will be whiter than snow...create in me a pure heart, O God and renew a steadfast spirit in me'* (Psalm 51:7, 10). A pure heart is whiter than snow for it is both transparent and radiant. God cleanses our hearts with the power of His blood, as we choose to live for Him instead of the ways of this world.

The writer of Hebrews said: *'Without holiness, no-one will see the Lord'* (Hebrews 12:14). Jesus said: *'Blessed are the pure in heart, they will see God'* (Mathew 5:8). So holiness refers to a sanctified lifestyle and this enables us to come into God's Presence and engage with Him. God meets many people when they are deep in their sin, like Joshua the high priest (Zechariah 3) and Peter (Luke 5:8). It is our choice to walk away from sin and choose a sanctified life. It is like being taken off the streets and given new royal clothes in exchange for our filthy rags, as we are invited to live in a new home as adopted children in His royal family. However, it requires a change of heart and lifestyle to become a royal child of God (Matthew 22:13).

Esther was an orphan who was seen as a beautiful woman in the eyes of the king. Before she met him, she received twelve months of beauty treatment which included six months of the oil of myrrh and six months of perfumes and cosmetics (Esther 2:12). She was transformed during this time from having the mindset of an orphan to that of a queen. She learnt how to live a royal lifestyle. One of the greatest qualities that enabled her to become a queen was her humility and desire to please her king. She had no selfish ambition or desires. She was simply focused on serving her king.

I believe God is raising up His 'Davids' and 'Esthers' as He is preparing our hearts to be His beautiful and spotless bride. Man looks at the outward appearance but the Lord looks at our hearts (1 Samuel 16:7). It is our choice to let God sanctify our hearts and minds each day through His Word, His truth (John 17:17), His Spirit and fire (Isaiah 4:4), and His blood that purifies us from all sin (1 John 1:7).

Holiness and the Fear of the Lord

It was a few years ago when Carol Arnott, Co-Founding Pastor of Catch The Fire in Toronto, gave a powerful word she received from God in a dream.

'In the dream, I was standing at the front of our church, down on the floor in front of the stage, worshipping. All of a sudden, I was caught

up in a whirlwind that took me up, up, up to the ceiling. I thought, "God, am I going through the roof?" And then I came down and stood right by the podium. I don't really know what happened; something either came on me or off me. It was like a cloak and it was heavy. I grabbed the microphone from the stand and spoke to the people. I said, "The Lord is saying, **'There's another cloud- a cloud of holiness. It will not be a cloud of outward good behaviour, but it will be a cloud of My holiness- the reverent fear of the Lord, which is the beginning of wisdom'**"[1] (bold print mine).

Carol Arnott was informing the church that the next revival wave of God's Spirit would not be what we were expecting or like the previous revival waves we have seen. Instead, it was going to be one of *Holiness and the Fear of the Lord*.

An international Ugandan pastor, John Mulinde,[2] gave a powerful testimony at Mike Bickle's International House of Prayer in Kansas of a visitation he had with the Lord. This man of God had a sobering encounter with Jesus, where Jesus said that if He was to suddenly return for His bride, John wouldn't be included. He was shocked, until the Lord revealed the reason. It was because of the hidden sin in his heart. Though he had been ministering under the power of the Spirit, healing the sick and bringing the lost into the Kingdom in Northern Uganda, his heart had become defiled. It was a wakeup call for him to get his heart right with God and pursue His way of holiness. As he humbly gave this testimony, I could see he carried such a fear of the Lord and holiness in his heart. Listening to his testimony was a wakeup call for the bride of Christ to get her heart right before the Lord returns.

God unconditionally loves us as our Heavenly Father but He also disciplines us as His children: *'My son, do not make light of the Lord's discipline, and do not lose heart when He rebukes you, because* **the Lord disciplines those He loves and He punishes everyone He accepts as a son.** *For what son is not disciplined by his father?* **If you are not disciplined, then you are illegitimate children and not true sons.** *Moreover, we all had human fathers who disciplined us and we respected them for it. How much more should we submit to the Father of our spirits and live!* **God disciplines us for our good that we may share in His holiness**' (Hebrews 12:5-10). God disciplines our hearts and minds, so we may learn from Him and grow more like Him and share in His holiness.

The fear of the Lord is pure, enduring forever (Psalm 19:9). Again we see the fear of the Lord linked to holiness. We see this with David who passionately loved and feared the Lord. When he was convicted of committing adultery with Bathsheba, he cried out to God to cleanse and purify his heart so his relationship could be restored with God (Psalm 51).

Paul had the revelation that the fear of the Lord went hand in hand with holiness: *'Let us purify ourselves from everything that contaminates body and spirit,* **perfecting holiness out of reverence for God** (2 Corinthians 7:1).

A Bible school student once asked me if it was okay to have sex with his girlfriend and repent, then do it again and repent again. I felt the answer was 'No' because he wasn't truly repenting in his heart and wasn't willing to change. Repentance means turning away from our sin, turning our hearts towards God and following His ways. Yes, there may be times when we truly repent for our sin but then mess things up again or may struggle to be free from a particular thing. God sees our hearts and if He sees we are truly sorry or want to be set free from something, then in His mercy and love He will forgive us and deliver us. However, in the case of this student, I sensed he was not truly repentant in his heart and wanted to continue with a sinful life instead of following Jesus.

John said that no-one who lives in Christ keeps on sinning; if they do then they don't personally know Him (1 John 3:6). I believe the problem with sexual sins and addictions is that we don't hate the sin enough. We must reach a point in our hearts where we hate the sin and see it for what it really is.

A well known man of God testified to committing the same sin again and again and repenting again and again. When he asked God why he was still struggling with the sin, God replied it was because he didn't hate it enough. Deep down in his heart, he was still enjoying it, even though he knew it was wrong. In order to walk free requires us to hate the sin so we may pursue a lifestyle of holiness.

I met a man who told me that it was okay to sin because of the grace of God. He was essentially saying that God's grace gives us a license to sin. Here he was twisting the truth that we have been saved by grace with the lie that we can continue to sin. Jude warned us about such false teachers. He said: *'They are godless men, who change the grace of our God into a license for immorality'* (Jude 1:4).

Manifestations of those who Fear the Lord

One of the outward manifestations of someone who fears the Lord is that they choose to obey Him even if it doesn't make sense or may hurt. And this includes the willingness to obey even if there are no immediate rewards or benefits. They simply obey Him all the way to completion, whatever the cost.

Another manifestation of those who fear the Lord is they hate what the Lord hates and love what the Lord loves. They give attention to what matters to the Lord and they don't give attention to what doesn't matter to Him. They fear the Lord more than people, and choose to follow Him instead of pleasing man (Galatians 1:10).

People who fear the Lord have nothing to cover up or hide from God but choose to live transparent lives, as they pursue holiness and a sanctified lifestyle (Hebrews 4:13).

Abraham is a great example of someone who was a friend of God and feared Him. He demonstrated the fear of the Lord as he obeyed God's will by willingly offering his only son Isaac as a living sacrifice, even though it didn't make any sense and would cost him. As Abraham was about to thrust the knife into his son Isaac, the angel of the Lord appeared and said: *'Do not do anything to him. Now I know that you fear God'* (Genesis 22:12). This radical obedience and friendship with God was a sign that he feared the Lord.

Rewards for those who Fear the Lord

'Blessed is the man who fears the Lord, who finds great delight in His commands' (Psalm 112:1). There are many blessings God gives to those who fear and honour Him. Here are some of them.

Confiding

The Lord confides in those who fear Him, He makes His covenant known to them (Psalm 25:14). The New Living Translation reads: *'Friendship with the Lord is reserved for those who fear Him. With them He shares His secrets'*.

Friendship with the Lord is based on our willingness to obey Him, including laying down our lives for Him (John 15:13-14).

Knowledge & Wisdom

The fear of the Lord is the beginning of wisdom (Proverbs 9:10, Psalm 111:10, Job 28:28). *The fear of the Lord is the beginning of knowledge* (Proverbs 1:7).

He will be the sure foundations for your times, a rich store of salvation and wisdom and knowledge; the fear of the Lord is the key to this treasure (Isaiah 33:6). I was given this verse by a lady who prayed for me when I was young in my faith. It made me pursue the fear of the Lord to receive His salvation, wisdom and knowledge. God releases His wisdom and knowledge to those who fear Him.

Protection

The Angel of the Lord encamps around those who fear Him and He delivers them (Psalm 34:7).

The eyes of the Lord are on those who fear Him, on those whose hope is in His unfailing love, to deliver them from death and keep them alive in famine (Psalm 33:18-19).

*He who fears God has a **secure fortress** and for his children it will **be** a safe refuge* (Proverbs 14:26).

The Lord provides protection and watches over those who fear Him and call on His name.

Covenant of Life and Peace

My covenant was with him, a covenant of life and peace, and I gave them to him; this called for reverence and he revered Me and stood in awe of My Name (Malachi 2:5).

Those who fear the Lord receive His covenant of life and peace.

Instruction & Guidance

Who then is the man who fears the Lord? He will instruct him in the way chosen for him (Psalm 25:12).

God leads us along His path of righteousness, as we fear and obey Him.

Health & Life

The fear of the Lord adds length to life (Proverbs 10:27, Proverbs 19:23).

*The fear of the Lord is a fountain **of life** turning the man from the snares of death* (Proverbs 14:27).

*Fear the Lord and shun evil. This will bring **health** to your body and nourishment to your bones* (Proverbs 3:7).

Humility and the fear of the Lord bring wealth and honour and life (Proverbs 22:4)

'Blessed are all who fear the Lord, who walk in His ways; you will eat the fruit of your labour, blessings and prosperity will be yours' (Psalm 128:1-2).

The fear of the Lord blesses our bodies and health, including our longevity.

Fulfil the Desires of Your Heart

He fulfils the desires of those who fear Him; He hears their cry and saves them (Psalm 145:19).

God hears the prayers of those who fear Him.

Anointing with seven-fold Spirit

The Spirit of the Lord will rest upon him, the Spirit of Wisdom and understanding, the Spirit of Counsel and of Power, the Spirit of Knowledge and of the Fear of the Lord- and he will delight in the Fear of the Lord (Isaiah 11:2-3).

The Lord reveals His seven-fold Spirit to those who fear Him and abide in His Presence.

These are some of the blessings for those who revere the Lord.

Mercy Triumphs over Judgement

God is a God of mercy and judgment. He is our loving Father and righteous Judge. However, God is rich in mercy and would rather release mercy instead of His righteous judgment.

Mary knew what it was to fear the Lord and said: *'His mercy extends to those who fear Him'* (Luke 1:50). God releases mercy to those who love and fear Him.

The criminal who hung on the cross next to Jesus rebuked the other criminal who hurled insults at Jesus, and said: *'Don't you fear God? We are punished justly for we are getting what our deeds deserve. But this man has done nothing wrong'*. He then asked Jesus to remember him in His Kingdom. Jesus could see that this man's heart was full of sorrow before God, and His heart of mercy extended to this criminal. Jesus not only forgave him, but said: *'Today you will be with Me in Paradise'* (Luke 23:40-43).

On earth there are judges who consider the evidence and the facts before making a verdict. They judge according to the evidence given and the laws made by man. However, God is our One true Judge who knows everything in a person's life and sees from every angle, knowing the real truth behind why we do what we do. He is the only Lawgiver and Judge who is able to save and destroy (James 4:12).

Jesus said: *'I did not come to judge the world but to save it. There is a Judge for the one who rejects Me and doesn't accept My words'* (John 12:47-49). Paul said: *'It is the Lord who judges me. Therefore judge nothing before the appointed time; wait until the Lord comes. He will* **bring to light what is hidden in darkness** *and will* **reveal the motives of men's heart**' (1 Corinthians 4:4-5). God rewards each of us according to what is in our hearts and our obedience to His will.

Though God is our Judge, He also abounds in grace and mercy and longs to give it to those who ask. Mercy is given when we don't receive the punishment we deserve for our sin and have been granted forgiveness. God, in His love and mercy, is looking for people to stand in the gap to repent for the sins of His people, so He may release mercy instead of judgment.

Where there is *no* repentance then *no* mercy can be released and this means judgment will be passed instead. Satan is constantly looking for someone to accuse before the throne of God. If there is no-one to stand in the gap to plead God's mercy and forgiveness for our sins, then a judgment is issued.

Abraham pleaded for God's mercy on the people of Sodom, asking for Him not to destroy it, and God was ready and willing to grant mercy if Abraham could find ten righteous men (Genesis 18:16-32).

Moses would stand in the gap pleading for God's mercy for the sins of his people, and in the majority of cases, God would respond to Moses' cry by withholding the punishment the Israelites would have otherwise received (Numbers 11:1-2, Numbers 14:11-20, Exodus 34:9).

God is looking for someone to stand in the gap and repent for the sins of an individual, a group, or a nation. When He finds no-one, then He has to decree His judgment instead (Ezekiel 22:30).

It is God's mercy that triumphs over judgment when we cry out to Him with sorrowful hearts (James 2:13). We see this throughout the scriptures. Only when there is no repentance for sin (be it for an individual or group or a nation) then He will execute His judgment, for He is a God of righteousness and justice.

I have heard amazing testimonies of people who have been waiting for their prison sentence but as a result of God having overruled their case with forgiveness and mercy, they were released from jail. One man was in the illegal drug business which led to his arrest. He was waiting to be heavily sentenced for using Class A drugs when his Mum got the church to pray for him. They cried out for God's mercy and forgiveness and prayed the man would end up serving God in His Kingdom. After the man realized what he had done, he repented and recommitted his life to Jesus while in prison. He was miraculously released and the judge said he didn't know why he was giving him a community sentence instead of a prison sentence. Years later I met this man who is faithfully serving God as a pastor of a church.

God is our Judge and is the One who will have the last say. We can approach the throne of grace, pleading our sinful cases to be forgiven through the precious blood of Jesus, and see miracles take place as a result of God extending His mercy. This is mercy triumphing over judgement.

'Since we have a great high priest who has gone through the heavens, Jesus, the Son of God, let us then approach the **throne of grace** *with confidence, so that we may* **receive mercy and find grace** *to help us in our time of need'* (Hebrews 4:15-16).

Let us pursue the reverential awe of the Lord and a sanctified lifestyle, as we choose to set ourselves apart for Him.

(For more reading I recommend the newly released book by John Bevere, 'The Awe of God' [3]*).*

Heavenly Father, I ask for Your forgiveness for the times I have not pursued a lifestyle that was pleasing to You. Create in me a pure heart O God and renew a steadfast spirit in me. Teach me Your ways and truth, and give me a revelation in my spirit and heart of the awe of the Lord, and what it means to live a sanctified life for You, in Jesus' mighty Name!

END-NOTES

[1] Arnott, John & Carol: *'Preparing for the Glory'*; Chapter 9 p132 (Destiny Image, 2018)
[2] Mulinde, John: *'Set Apart For God: The call to a surrendered life'* (Sovereign World 2005) www.worldtrumpetmission.com
[3] Bevere, John: *'The Awe of God'* (Thomas Nelson Publishing Group, 2023)

10

Accessing the Courts of Heaven

The court was seated and the books were open
Daniel 7:10

There is a powerful way to overcome the schemes of the enemy without coming directly against him and for seeking divine breakthrough, healing, or justice, especially when dealing with high-ranking demonic entities and principalities. This is accessing the *Courts of Heaven* and is a valuable tool in ministry and prophetic intercession. It may be used for ourselves or when ministering to others, and when praying for our churches, neighbourhoods or nations.

Sometimes, when prayers are bouncing back or things don't seem to be shifting in our favour, we may come before the Courts of Heaven to present our issue or 'case' before our Heavenly Father and Judge. The Lord has given us authority to heal the sick, cast out demons, set the captives and prisoners free, cleanse the lepers, and raise the dead. However, when dealing with high-ranking demonic spirits (such as, involvement with the occult, freemasonry, satanic ritual abuse, principalities, or those involved in witchcraft) then we can approach the Courts of Heaven to receive healing, breakthrough and freedom.

God always acts with righteousness and justice, for righteousness and justice are the foundation of His throne. No power or principality can come against God our Judge. What He declares and decrees in the Courts of Heaven will over-rule the demonic influences and spiritual entities concerning the issues we are encountering on earth.

After a case has been presented before God and a verdict has been made in the Courts of Heaven, then changes will begin to take place on earth as has been decreed in the Courts of Heaven. Hence, Jesus taught us to pray: *'Your Kingdom come,* **Your will be done**, *on earth as in heaven.'* Or perhaps we could pray: *'On earth as has been decreed in the Courts of Heaven'*.

Praying to the Father and Judge

When Jesus first showed His disciples how to pray, He taught them to pray to the Father and this has become known as the 'Our Father' prayer (Matthew 6:9). However, when Jesus taught His disciples to *persevere* in prayer and not give up hope, He spoke about the parable of the 'Widow and the Judge' (Luke 18:1-8). Here, He was referring to bringing our prayers or cases before God our Judge. So, we can pray to God our Father or bring our cases before God our Judge.

Throughout the scriptures the Heavenly Courts are revealed to those who pursue righteousness and justice. These were His sons and daughters who were relatively mature in their faith and looked to Him for divine wisdom and revelation. He revealed the Heavenly Courts to His servants like Job (Job 13:18-19), Daniel (Daniel 7:9-11), David (Psalm 89:7 + 50:4) and probably most of the Old Testament prophets. Also, He revealed the Courts of Heaven to Paul (Colossians 2:13-14, Hebrews 12:22-24) and His beloved disciple John (Revelation 19:11 + 20:12).

In the Old Testament there were the royal courts and temple courts. The king or queen would act as ruler and judge in the royal courts, whereas the priest would act as judge in the temple courts. Though we have one English word for 'court', there are different Hebraic words used when referring to the 'temple court' (*Chatser*[1]) and 'legal court' (*Diyn*[2]).

After Joshua the high priest was accused by satan, he was forgiven and cleansed of his sins, and then given this charge by the Lord: **'If you will walk in My ways and keep My requirements**, *then you will* **govern My house** *and* **have charge** *of* **My courts'** (Zechariah 3:7). Interestingly, the Hebrew word used for 'govern' is *'diyn'*, the same word that is used for 'judge' in a legal court. And the Hebrew word for courts is *'chatser'*, the same used for temple courts. So this charge refers to Joshua, the high priest, as governing God's house and temple courts in His Kingdom.

The original church or Ekklesia was a legislative governmental authority where legal decisions were made for a city. Jesus said to Peter: *'I give you the name Peter, a stone. And this truth of who I am will be the bedrock foundation on which I will build My church- My legislative assembly, and the power of death will not be able to overpower it'* (Matthew 16:18 TPT). When Jesus used the Greek word 'Ekklesia', He was referring to a legislative assembly of people who would govern the affairs of a city. In other words, He was giving Kingdom authority to His 'church'.

To access the Courts of Heaven requires faith, knowing it exists and is as real as the courts on earth. It also helps if we have an understanding of the purpose of the Courts and how they operate. The Courts of Heaven may operate in a similar way to courts on earth. There is the Judge, the Prosecutor, and the Defence Attorney. Jesus is our Defence Attorney or Advocate. *'If anybody does sin, we have one who* **speaks to the Father in our defence- Jesus Christ, the Righteous One.** *He is the atoning sacrifice for our sins.'* This same verse in the NLT says: *'But if anyone does sin, we have an* **advocate who pleads our case before the Father.** *He is Jesus Christ, the One who is truly righteous. He Himself is the sacrifice that atones for our sins'* (1 John 2:1).

It was John the beloved who referred to Jesus as being our Advocate. There is only one accuser and prosecutor of the brethren, and that is satan (Zechariah 3:1, Revelations 12:10). In the Courts there may be witnesses, a scribe, and angels attending the legal cases. People who are prophetic seers may witness or see in the Spirit realm what is taking place in the Heavenly Courts. However, others may not see, but rather hear or sense in the Spirit the things that are taking place in the Courts.

God is our Father and also our Judge. James said: *'There is only one Lawgiver and Judge, the One who is able to save and destroy'* (James 4:12). Since God is a just Judge and the Judge of all judges, He will act in our favour when we come to Him with repentant hearts. He will grant mercy and forgiveness where there is true repentance, and release justice where needed.

It is God's desire to over-rule the accuser of the brethren who is constantly looking for legitimate reasons to accuse us before His throne. However, once we have dealt with any 'outstanding sin', we can ask God to release His favour on a case. Once God has over-ruled satan's accusations we can receive His favour and blessings. Then we will start to see changes on earth as has been decreed in the Courts of Heaven.

The writer of Hebrews appears to be describing the Heavenly Courts in these verses: *'You have come to thousands and thousands **of angels in joyful assembly**, to the church of the firstborn whose names are written in heaven. You have come to God, the **Judge of all men**, to the **spirits of righteous men made perfect**, to **Jesus the Mediator** of a new covenant, and to the **sprinkled blood** that speaks a better word than the blood of Abel'* (Hebrews 12: 22-24).

These verses describe thousands of angels assembling before God the Judge, and Jesus our Mediator or Advocate, along with righteous men made perfect. Here, he is probably referring to the cloud of witnesses previously mentioned in Hebrews 12:1. The writer also refers to the blood of Jesus that 'speaks a better word' on our behalf than the blood of Abel. This is because it is through Jesus' blood that we are forgiven when He declares to God our Judge, 'Forgiven by My blood!'

The words 'justice' and 'mercy' are frequently mentioned in the scriptures because God is a lover of justice who is right in all His ways. It is by the grace of God that we can come before His throne and make our petitions, either for mercy or justice. *'Let us then approach the throne of grace with confidence, so that we may receive mercy and find grace to help us in our time of need'* (Hebrews 4:16).

So, as we bring our cases before Jesus our Advocate and God our Judge, He can decree a victory in our favour, as long as our hearts are right and pleasing to Him (Daniel 7:21-22).

When we come before God with clean hands and pure hearts, we can ask for His judgement on a matter. *'Who can ascend the hill of the Lord? He who has clean hands and a pure heart'* (Psalm 24: 3-4). The enemy can no longer accuse us on a matter once we have come clean before God. When we are forgiven through the blood of Jesus, the enemy has no more legal-hold on us. Hence, the case can now be turned in our favour, and victory seen on earth.

Satan the Accuser & Thief

The enemy is known as the *accuser of the brethren* because he accuses us of our sins before the throne of God day and night (Zechariah 3:1, Revelation 12:10). Sin gives the enemy a legal foothold to accuse us before the throne of God and prevent God's favour or blessings from flowing.

Paul referred to this when he said: *'Do not let the sun go down while you are still angry, and **do not give the devil a foothold'*** (Ephesians 4:26-27). Where there is unresolved sin, such as anger or generational sins, then this can prevent us from receiving God's blessings.

Since God is a God of righteousness and justice, He is waiting for us to come to Him or present our case, so He may over-rule any legal accusations made by the enemy. God is on our side, but we still have to receive cleansing and forgiveness of any outstanding sins before He may grant us His favour and blessings. Jesus is our Advocate who is waiting to forgive our sins by the sanctifying power of His blood. However, this usually doesn't automatically happen until we pray or present our cases to Him.

Likewise, God is looking for people who will stand in the gap and repent for the sins of His people. By repenting of the sins, God can lift the punishment and release His mercy and blessings. God said to Ezekiel: *'I looked for a man among them who would build a wall and stand before Me in the gap on behalf of the land so I would not have to destroy it, but I found none'* (Ezekiel 22:30).

The enemy is a thief. He will steal finances, health, businesses, relationships, and ministries. Therefore, we can take such cases to the Courts of Heaven and ask God our Judge for justice, so we may receive pay back for what has been stolen or the years the locusts have eaten. God said to Joel: *'I will repay you for the years the locusts have eaten'* (Joel 2:25).

However, in all cases, our hearts have to be willing to forgive our enemies before we can ask God for His mercy or justice. James warns us that judgement *without mercy* will be shown to those who have *not been merciful* (James 2:13). It is when we are willing to show mercy and forgiveness instead of judging our enemies, that God can grant us His mercy and forgiveness, instead of judgement. Hence, Jesus said: *'Do not judge and you will not be judged. Forgive, and you will be forgiven'* (Luke 6:37). And He taught us to pray in the Our Father's prayer: *'Forgive us our sins **as we forgive** those who have sinned against us'* (Matthew 6:12).

Courtroom Cases in Scripture

There are various passages in the Bible that refer to issues or cases being brought before the Courts of Heaven. Here are some of the cases where God's people approached the Heavenly Courts for breakthrough, healing, deliverance, and justice.

Job

Job was a man who did what was right in the eyes of the Lord, so satan asked God's permission to sift him. As a result, Job faced many tests and trials with regards to his health, finances, and loss of reputation, as well as loss of loved ones and family. Then Job decided to stand before God and present his case so he could be vindicated from the enemy.

*'I desire to speak to **the Almighty** and to **argue my case** with God...Indeed this will turn out **for my deliverance**, for no godless man would dare come before Him! Now that I have **prepared my case**, I know I **will be vindicated**. Can anyone **bring charges against me**? Only grant me these two things O God, and then I will not hide from*

*You: withdraw Your hand from me and stop frightening me with your terrors. Then **summon me** and I will answer or let me speak and You reply'* (Job 13:3-18).

Job uses words that describe a legal courtroom. He brought his *case* before God so that he could be *delivered*. He was willing to face any sin, so that he may be *vindicated* from the *charges brought against him*. He waited for God to *summon* him and reply.

God replied by revealing His Almighty power, wisdom, knowledge and counsel before Job, such that Job was convicted of his prideful attitude and humbled. *'Job replied to the Lord: "I know that You can do all things; no plan of Yours can be thwarted. You asked, 'Who is this that obscures My Counsel without knowledge?' Surely I spoke of things I didn't understand, things too wonderful for me to know. My ears had heard of You but now my eyes have seen You. Therefore **I despise myself and repent in dust and ashes**'* (Job 42:1-6).

After Job repented of the attitude of his heart, everything was lifted and turned around in his favour, and God was able to release blessings instead. Finally, he was given double the portion of what he had lost and the enemy had stolen (Job 42:10).

Daniel

Daniel was a devout man who feared the Lord more than he feared man. Nothing would stop him praying to God. The enemy was prowling around looking for a reason to accuse him to block his position of power and influence, and even to destroy him. Daniel, knowing he could lose his life, still chose to pray to the Lord each day. God saw in Daniel's heart faithfulness, obedience, and the fear of the Lord, and protected him from the lions' den. Daniel received great visions and revelations concerning the End-Times, because the Lord could trust him.

In one of Daniel's great visions, he saw the Ancient of Days seated in the Courtroom of Heaven. The books were opened where the accuser was attacking the saints of the Most High. *'As I looked, thrones were set in place and the **Ancient of Days took His seat...** **Thousands upon thousands attended Him.... The court was seated, and the books were open**'* (Daniel 7:9-10).

The Hebraic word used here for 'court' means 'judgment', and refers to the legal courts.[2] As Daniel continued with the vision he saw the Son of Man approach the Ancient of Days on behalf of the saints of the Most High. The moment the Ancient of Days pronounced judgement in favour of the saints, the enemy was defeated. *'As I watched, this horn was waging war against the saints and defeating them, until the **Ancient of Days came and pronounced judgement in favour of the saints of the Most High**, and the time came when **they possessed the Kingdom**,'* (Daniel 7:21-22). Once the Ancient of Days pronounced judgement in favour of the saints, the battle was finally won on earth (Daniel 7:9-27).

When God grants us justice or mercy, the case is acquitted and the enemy has no more legal grounds to come against us. Then we will see the battles being won on earth, as in heaven. Once the final decree or verdict has been issued, the war can finally be won on the battlefields on earth. *'With justice He judges and makes war'* (Revelation 19:11).

Persistent Widow

Some may disagree, but I believe Jesus was teaching on the Courts of Heaven when He spoke about the widow and the judge. The story concerns a widow who kept bringing her case before an ungodly judge, until she got the justice she deserved. It was a case for justice and protection against her accuser. She requested: *'Grant me justice and protect me against my oppressor'* (TPT Luke 18:3). She pleaded with the judge until he finally granted her justice.

Jesus was teaching on coming to God our Judge when seeking justice or breakthrough, persisting until this has been granted. This may be in regards to a breakthrough in relationships, finances, ministry, or healing. Instead of giving up hope and prayer, we can bring our 'case' before God our Judge.

Note that she didn't come against her accuser but brought the issue directly to the judge. She didn't have the power or authority to overthrow her accuser and humbly knew this. However, she knew someone who did have the power and authority, and persisted until she got it. The best place to seek justice is to go directly to our Judge. The enemy can no longer attack, steal or destroy when he is overthrown by God's decree on a matter.

Spiritual battles may be seen as legal cases taking place in the heavenly realms. Jesus' final comment about the widow and the judge was this: *'And will not God bring about **justice** to His chosen ones who cry out to Him day and night? Will He keep putting them off? I tell you, He will see that **they get justice**, and **quickly**'* (Luke 18:1-7).

Peter Sifted

Like Job, God allowed Peter to be sifted by the enemy. Jesus said: *'Peter, My dear friend, listen to what I am about to tell you. Satan has **demanded to** come and sift you like wheat and test your faith'* (TPT Luke 22:31). When Jesus told Simon Peter he would be sifted like wheat, He was implying that his faith would be tested or 'put on trial.' The Greek word here for 'demanded to'[3] is the same used when meaning to demand for trial. Satan wanted to put Peter on trial to try to prevent Peter becoming a history maker.

Approach His Courtroom for Mercy and Forgiveness

The enemy has legal access to accuse us before God our Judge when we have sin in our camp (Zechariah 3:1). We can oppose this legal foothold by coming before God our Judge. Here, we can plead our case by humbly coming before the holy council of God. *'In the **council of the holy ones** God is greatly feared'* (Psalm 89:5-8).

Once we have dealt with the relevant areas of 'outstanding' sin including forgiveness towards others and generational sins, then the enemy no longer has a legal foothold to prosecute us before God our Judge. We can be freed from the effects of sin, as we ask God for His mercy and forgiveness concerning each case.

God is loving and generous and will grant us His mercy and favour once we have dealt with any outstanding sin. Once the case has been acquitted, the accuser of the brethren no longer has any legal hold over us and we will see victory come forth on earth, as is declared in the Courts of Heaven. Paul writes: *'He forgave us all our sins having cancelled the written code, with its regulations, that was against us and that stood opposed to us; He took it away, nailing it to the cross'* (Colossians 2:14).

Satan looks for every opportunity to accuse us before the judgment seat of God. In the Courts, books are opened and read before our heavenly Judge (Revelation 20:12). He will reveal the sin in our life (or in the person or nation for whom we are interceding). There may be generational sins or some other sins that need to be overturned through repentance and forgiveness, before God's favour and blessings are released. Sin may have been passed down the bloodline or through predecessors in our work or ministries. We can break off any effects this may be having as we confess the sins of our forefathers or predecessors, and ask God for His forgiveness.

David sought the Lord after there had been a famine for three years. God revealed it was the result of Saul's sin passed down the royal bloodline. Once David dealt with the sin through repentance and forgiveness, the famine ceased (2 Samuel 21:1).

In the Courts on earth when the judge gives the final verdict, then the case is acquitted. Likewise, when we ask God for a final verdict and the case is *acquitted,* then the enemy has no more legal ground on which to accuse us and we can now fight from a place of victory.

The accuser of the brethren accused the saints day and night. However, they overcame by the *blood of the Lamb* and by the *word of their testimony* (Revelation 12:11). Some translations say, 'the word of *His* testimony'. Both may apply and be true. The actual word *testimony* is used in the courtroom settings and the verb to *testify* is derived from this. People have to testify or 'bear witness' to the truth when they are in legal courtrooms.

The Greek word used here for testimony is *marturia* [4] and refers to the 'witness' or 'evidence' that is given by a person in a court. *Marturia* can also refer to 'martyr', hence the saints overcame not only by the blood of the Lamb and the word of testimony, but also by being willing to lay down their lives, even unto death. Many apostles and followers of Christ were martyred for their faith, and I believe we will see more of this in the years to come.

So, as we approach God our Judge and present our case, we can overcome by the blood of the Lamb. Also, we can overcome by the word of *His* testimony as we declare His spoken or written word, as well as His promises for us. This is because the testimony of Jesus is the Spirit of prophecy (Revelation 19:10). Here, we can declare what is written in the Scriptures or the prophetic words we have received that are yet to be fulfilled. Likewise, the word of *our* testimony bears witness to His truth and power, and renders the accuser powerless. Giving testimonies about what God has promised and done is powerful, and no-one can argue against them.

Approach the Courtroom for Justice

Another reason we may want to approach the Courts of Heaven is when seeking justice for something that appears to be unfair or unjust. Whenever the enemy tries to steal, kill or destroy, we can approach the Courtrooms of Heaven to ask for justice or 'pay back', instead of allowing the enemy to get away with it.

Jesus said the enemy comes to kill, steal and destroy (John 10:10). He is the father of lies and thief of all thieves. He tries to steal our rightful inheritance and all God has given us, until we declare 'Give it back!' or 'Grant me (us) justice!' Whenever we are falsely accused or robbed, whether in the natural or spiritual realm, we can come before God our Judge and ask for justice, and this includes paying back what the locusts have eaten. This is what the Lord instructs us to do:

'Present your case', says the Lord, 'set forth your argument', says Jacob's King (Isaiah 41:21).

'Review the past for me, let us argue the matter together; state the case for your innocence' (Isaiah 43:26).
'No weapon forged against you will prevail, and you will refute every tongue that accuses you' (Isaiah 54:17).
'For I the Lord, love justice; I hate robbery and iniquity' (Isaiah 61:8).
'With justice He judges and makes war' (Revelation 19:11).
'Yet if he (the enemy) is caught, he must pay seven fold' (Proverbs 6:31)

Whenever we have been robbed maybe concerning our ministry, relationships, or finances, then we can demand a payback for what the enemy has stolen. Scripture says we can ask for a seven-fold payback (Proverbs 6:31), or humbly demand justice like the widow did with the judge (Luke 18:3).

David was familiar with the Courts of Heaven. In one case where he appealed to God for justice, he said: *'Awake, My God;* **decree justice**. *Let the* **assembled peoples** *gather around You. Rule over them from on high; let the* **Lord judge the peoples**. **Judge me**, *O Lord according to my righteousness, according to my integrity, O* **Most High**' (Psalm 7:6-8).

David came before God with holy reverence, acknowledging God as his Judge. In his heart he didn't think he had done wrong but was willing for God to judge him in case he had. He was willing to confess any sin he had committed, knowing God will decree justice once we are found not guilty or our sins are forgiven.

We can come directly before our Heavenly Father and Judge, asking for justice because He said: **'For I the Lord, love justice; I hate robbery and iniquity'** (Isaiah 61:8). Justice may be needed where there have been false accusations or the enemy has robbed us of homes, businesses, relationships, ministries or anything else. As we ask God for justice, we can claim back in the Spirit that which has been taken from us. We're not to let the enemy get away and for us to suffer defeat or loss, but to declare, 'Give it back!' as we seek His justice and wait for the results.

However, when doing this, we must be careful not to fall into the enemy's trap of pointing the accusing finger at the enemy (or our enemies). Instead, we are to forgive those who have opposed or offended us, before we ask God for His justice. *'If you do away with the yoke of oppression,* **with the pointing finger and malicious talk,** *and if you spend yourselves on behalf of the hungry and satisfy the needs of the oppressed, then your light will rise in the darkness, and your night become like the noonday'* (Isaiah 58:9-10).

There was a case where a person had lost a significant amount of money that they had invested in a company. The company hadn't been faithful to their promises and refused to give the person the money they had invested. However, the person sensed that God was telling them to bring it before the Courts of Heaven. As they did, they forgave the company owners or directors who misused their money, and asked God for a rightful pay back of what was theirs. Shortly after this they received an email saying that the money was going to be paid back into their account. Justice in the Courts of Heaven released justice on earth.

Approach the Courtroom for Breakthrough

Sometimes the reason prayers aren't answered is because there are legal blockages. There may be things that are legally binding that can be annulled in the Courts of Heaven before we see a breakthrough in our finances, health or ministries. Also, there may be more than one issue or layer that needs addressing until the final one is reached and breakthrough can occur.

It may be that someone was involved in making illegal trade deals or ungodly covenants, and these can be annulled in the Heavenly Courts. Just as we see things annulled in earthly courts, so things may be annulled in the Courts of Heaven. When the people had entered into a covenant with death, God made justice the measuring line and said: *'Your covenant with death will be annulled'* (Isaiah 28:18).

Other times we may be seeking a breakthrough in God's promises and purposes. What has been written in the books of Heaven concerning God's will and purpose for us? What are the prophecies we have received or words God has spoken regarding our callings and His purposes that are yet to be fulfilled? Robert Henderson who teaches on the Courts of heaven[5][6] refers to the 'Bill of Rights'. This is where we ask for our God-given rights, according to what is written in His word and His promises. We can say, 'Lord, Your word says...' or 'Lord, Your word promises...' or 'Lord, I was given the prophetic word by 'X', that You will...' or 'Lord, You told me that You have called me to...' and so on.

We can ask God to release what is written in the books of Heaven concerning our present or future, so it may come to pass. Or we can ask for God to reveal what is blocking His purposes being fulfilled, and then deal with it accordingly. Likewise we can pray this for others so God's word or promise may come to pass, based on His calling and purpose for each one of us.

Ask the Judge for a Restraining Order

Another amazing thing we can do in the Courts of Heaven is to ask for a restraining order. Restraining orders are protective orders that can be released by a court when someone is seeking protection from assault, harassment, stalking, or violence. Just as we have natural restraining orders, so we can ask God our Judge for a divine restraining order.

A divine restraining order is a protective order issued by the Judge to protect God's people from attacks by their 'adversary'.[7] Hence, we can ask God for a restraining order to stop or block demonic entities from coming against us or other people. This may be extremely powerful when dealing with high-ranking demonic entities, especially during a ministry session or prophetic intercession.

Rev Andrew Miller, Founder of Heartsync Ministries[8], teaches on making an appeal to the Heavenly Courts when coming up against high-level celestial (demonic) beings, especially when ministering to victims of satanic ritual abuse. He makes special reference to Dr Tom Hawkin's inner healing ministry and his teaching on *'An Appeal to the Heavenly Court'*[9].

I was ministering to a man who required deliverance from a spirit of deep seated anger and unforgiveness. During the session, he started to choke and struggled to breathe as a demonic spirit began to manifest around his airways. I took authority over the spirit in the name of Jesus, but nothing happened. At this point, I sensed it was a high-ranking demonic spirit that had been given legal access by a door opened to anger and hatred. So I instantly asked Jesus for a restraining order to be released against the demonic spirit(s). Within thirty seconds, he started to breathe normally again. Then we were able to continue with the session, and once the emotional and spiritual roots of anger and hatred had been addressed, he was completely set free (physically, emotionally and spiritually) with no further demonic manifestations.

How to Enter His Courts

Here is a summary guide to approaching the Courts of Heaven. Sometimes, it can be helpful to have a seer or prophetic person to assist us in the matter because they can see and hear in the Spirit with greater clarity. Or we can ask God to cleanse our spiritual senses, so we may see, hear and sense in the Spirit what He is saying. If we struggle to hear Him, then we can always approach by faith.

By Faith

For any matter where the Holy Spirit may prompt us to take a certain case or issue to the Courts, we can approach God our Judge by faith. This is with the knowledge that our Father God is a just Judge and will gladly bring to our attention any 'accusations' or outstanding sin the enemy is holding against us. Remember, God is for us and not against us, though we are to plead our case and deal with any outstanding sin, in order to see things changed and overturned.

With Reverence & Humility

As already mentioned, our hearts are to come with an attitude of humility and reverence, knowing we are coming before God our Judge. We can approach His throne of grace with confidence, as we ask for His mercy in our time of need (Hebrews 4:16). In doing this, we acknowledge God as our righteous and just Judge, and Jesus as our Advocate who can speak to the Father and Judge on our behalf.

Covered by His Blood

A safe way of approaching the Courts and the accuser is to come under the covering of the blood of Jesus. Through His blood we receive grace, forgiveness, cleansing, deliverance and protection from the accuser. It is good to get our hearts right before we ask Him for justice or mercy.

'You have come to God, the Judge of all men, to the spirits of righteous men made perfect, to Jesus the mediator of a new covenant, and to the

sprinkled blood that speaks a better word than the blood of Abel,' (Hebrews 12:23-24).

Present Your Case

God wants to know the case we are presenting to Him. This means we are to come prepared, knowing God's purposes for us and the opposition we face to seeing this being granted or fulfilled. We may be aware of the spiritual opposition, but if not, we can ask God to reveal if the enemy is holding anything against us. *'Present your case'*, says the Lord, *'set forth your argument'*, says Jacob's King (Isaiah 41:21).

Deal with any Outstanding Sin

As we present our case, we are willing to be judged ourselves. This means we are willing to deal with our own sin first and repent of our faults or what we have said or done wrong, and also forgive those who have come against us, for what they have said or done. This is essential in order to be released from any judgement the enemy is holding against us and also to receive forgiveness from God. Sometimes we may not be aware of what we have said or done. In such a case we can ask the Lord to review our documents or scrolls, and show us what is being held against us or the spiritual accusations that have been made and we can repent accordingly. It is through the blood of Jesus that our sins can be forgiven. Jesus says, 'Forgiven by My blood!'

Remember, it is God's desire to forgive us and release His mercy and blessings, rather than His judgment. He will make it easy for us to follow as we are guided by His Spirit. There is no place for pride and we don't have to confront the accuser. As we humbly come before God we let Him deal with the accuser.

Declare His Word & Promises

Once the outstanding sin has been dealt with, we can declare the written or spoken promises of God through His word and prophecies. We can remind the Lord of what He has promised or spoken to us. 'Lord you promised this...Lord you declared... Lord Your word says...' The Lord delights when we rest on His word and promises and call them forth into being. Jesus declared the word at all times when He was opposed by satan in the wilderness. He said, 'It is written...!' In the same way that we agree or accept what is written in the laws, so God will agree with what is written in His Word. Hence, we can declare His Word and promises.

We can also ask what is written in the scrolls or Books in Heaven concerning a particular case or God's will for us. Then we can present our case, not from a basis of need but a basis of God's will and written purpose for us

The Final Decree & Verdict

At the end we can ask God for a decree or verdict to be released concerning the case and what blessings God wants to give in exchange? Some may receive words from the Spirit or words from scripture, or that a sense of breakthrough has occurred. Finally, we can stand on these words decreed by God and declare them into being, on earth as in Heaven.

Nehemiah knew he would face opposition by the Trans-Euphrates governors on his way to Jerusalem, so he requested an official document from the king. This document gave him legal access to enter into Jerusalem and accomplish his assignment to rebuild the walls. This meant he could fight the battle and oppose his enemies once he had obtained a place of victory in the legal court. The king's royal stamp gave Nehemiah the legal approval he needed. The same applies to us after we have received God's legal approval and we can decree His word that has been released in the Courts.

Understanding the Courts of Heaven is a priceless tool when it comes to walking in freedom and healing. Once we've received justice and mercy from our Judge, we then have authority to defeat the enemy on the battlefield, and witness victory on earth as has been declared in the Courts of Heaven.

Heavenly Father, give me a fresh understanding of the Courts of Heaven and how they work, especially with regards to seeking Justice, Healing and Freedom. Prompt my spirit when to bring a situation before Your Heavenly Courts or to ask for a restraining order to prevent demonic

spirits from manifesting in someone else's or my life. Thank You that You will guide me what to do and how to pray, for You are for me and not against me. In Your Name I pray.

END-NOTES

[1] Chatser (Hebrew 2691): Strong's Expanded Exhausted Concordance, Red Letter Edition
[2] Diyn (Hebrew 1780): Strong's Expanded Exhaustive Concordance, Red Letter Edition
[3] Exaiteomai (Greek 1809): Strong's Expanded Exhaustive Concordance, Red Letter Edition
[4] Marturia (Greek 3141); Strong's Expanded Exhaustive Concordance, Red Letter Edition
[5] Henderson, Robert: *Operating in the Courts of Heaven*; 2014
[6] Henderson, Robert: *Receiving Healing from the Courts of Heaven*; p138; *(Destiny Image 2018)*
[7] Dr Myles, Francis: *Issuing Divine Restraining Orders from the Courts of Heaven* *(Destiny Image 2019)*
[8] Rev Miller, Andrew: *www.heartsyncministries.org*
[9] Dr Hawkins, Tom: *An Appeal to Heavenly Court*; Restoration in Christ Ministries: *www.rcm-usa.org*

11

PROMOTION IN THE WILDERNESS

Jesus, full of the Holy Spirit, was led by the Spirit in the desert...
He returned to Galilee in the power of the Spirit

Luke 4:1-2,14

There may be seasons in life when we feel like we are going through a wilderness or desert. These are times when we may feel spiritually dry or distant from God. There can be various reasons for this and one is that God is drawing our hearts closer to Him.

I believe we all encounter wilderness seasons where it feels like God has withdrawn His tangible Presence. Some people may call this the *dark night of the soul*. However, there can be beauty in the wilderness especially when the bride comes out of the desert leaning on her lover (Song of Songs 8:5).

For some, a spiritual wilderness may occur during a time of grief, such as the loss of a job or a loved one. For others it may occur during a sickness or life-changing illness. One tool I have found to be valuable when journeying through a spiritual wilderness is the tool known as 'journalling' (or prophetic writing). This is a way of hearing God, where the Holy Spirit bypasses our intellect and speaks to our spirit as we write down the words that flow through our heart and spirit.[1]

One of the key reasons the Lord leads us through wilderness seasons is to draw our hearts closer to Him: *'Therefore, I am now going to allure her into the desert and speak tenderly to her'* (Hosea 2:14). During such times, He usually tests or reveals the orphan areas in our hearts, and in doing so, He strengthens our faith and trust in Him. Going through the wilderness is a time to hold onto His word and seek His Spirit: *'Your word is a lamp to my feet and a light for my path'* (Psalm 119:105).

I believe His passion and desire is for us to walk intimately with Him where our hearts become a habitation for His Presence. Needless to say, this usually involves dying to our flesh and carnal nature, as He transforms the orphan areas in our hearts.

I believe that mighty men and women of God have all experienced wilderness seasons and encountered the cross, where they have chosen to lay down their lives for the Lord. This was the case of Moses, David, Joseph, Esther, Paul, John the beloved, and Jesus Himself. They encountered a wilderness whether in a desert, prison, palace, or somewhere else, where God spoke tenderly to them and ministered to their hearts.

Each significant season in my journey with the Lord has usually involved a wilderness, where I have entered into a deeper place of communion with Him. I believe the full measure of spiritual sonship is given to those who have been through wilderness seasons and encountered the cross. This will be unique for each one of us in our personal walk with God. It is an opportunity for us to hear His still quiet voice, like Elijah did, as we depend more on Him and put our trust in Him.

Wilderness seasons are meant to be temporary and transitional, and not permanent. They are opportunities to overcome any weaknesses or temptations, and to mature as God's royal sons and daughters, becoming His princes and princesses.

For each spiritual wilderness we encounter, our response to God's Spirit will determine how long we stay there. I believe each wilderness addresses an orphan area of the heart and is where we willingly die to our flesh, and in exchange receive a part of His resurrection life.

Reasons we Encounter a Wilderness Season

There are three main reasons why we may encounter a spiritual wilderness. The first is self-inflicted. This may be the result of choosing to walk away from God by disobeying His will and doing what we want. It could simply be that we have allowed things to come between us and God and have drifted apart.

The second reason is when God may withdraw His tangible Presence to test and see what is in our hearts. This is an opportunity for us to press deeper into Him and not give up. It is a time to discover more about ourselves and God's character. And it is a time to walk by faith instead of by our feelings.

The third reason may be that God is calling us to lay down our lives for Him. He may be lovingly removing the things that matter most to us, especially if these things have come in the way of our relationship with Him.

Self-inflicted by Disobedience & Sin

My first experience of a spiritual wilderness was when I took a year out before University. I had planned to go on a kibbutz in Israel but things didn't turn out quite the way I had expected and for different reasons I didn't go. I ended up turning away from God as I thought He had let me down, and decided to get on with life by myself. However, during these months of rebellion I felt spiritually empty and depressed inside. I even questioned what the point of life was? I felt like I was in a desert, lost and alone, with nothing around me and nothing to see ahead.

Some friends who were aware of my situation prayed for me. One of them suggested doing a Discipleship Training School with Youth With A Mission (YWAM). Miraculously, God opened a door making it possible for me to attend a Discipleship Training School (D.T.S). During the D.T.S a pastor sensed a block in my relationship with God and encouraged me to be open with God about how I felt. Tears welled up as I walked outside to have it out with God in private. I vented my feelings and asked why He had deserted me and let me down? After letting out my emotions, I laid flat on my back in a field of long grass and shut my eyes.

Suddenly, a brilliant white light, brighter than the natural sun, came and overshadowed me. I didn't open my eyes for fear I would go blind. God's awesome Presence then descended on me and I heard these loving words, *'Ange, I didn't leave you. You left Me!'* I felt an instant conviction in my spirit along with His truth. I repented for going my own way and realized it was never God's will for me to go on the kibbutz. His reason for my year out was to do this D.T.S all along. However, if I had known this, I probably wouldn't have taken a whole year out since the D.T.S was just three months long. But what I gained in those three months was well worth the whole year out as it transformed my life and relationship with God.

My wilderness season had been self-inflicted. I had walked away from God under the misunderstanding that He had let me down because things didn't work out as I hoped they would. The moment I repented, I turned back to Him and found myself back on the path where I had left Him. My depression instantly lifted as His joy and love filled my heart. Psalm 23 flowed out of my heart. God had brought me to His quiet waters; He restored my soul.

It is easy to fall away from God, especially if we do our own thing or fall into enemy deception that He has left us. One thing I learnt was this truth - He never leaves or deserts us (Joshua 1:5), we are the ones who leave Him. Our disappointment is the result of our *dis*-appointment with God, especially when our thoughts haven't been in appointment with His will. Thankfully, He waits for us to return to Him just like the father who eagerly waited for his prodigal son to return home (Luke 15:11-32).

There may be times when we have allowed anxiety, fear or stress to distance us from God. He wants to be included in every part of our lives. He knows what is going to happen before we do, but He usually won't do anything until we ask Him or call on His name, or until others pray for us. It is then we feel peace when He is with us. It is not that God isn't with us during these situations but we shut Him out by allowing our fears and stresses to get in the way.

As we let go of our negative thoughts and feelings and give them to Him, we receive His peace in exchange. We are not to be overcome by our circumstances but rather allow God to reign in our hearts and minds, so we can rise above our circumstances. It is then we experience His peace in the midst of the storm. For it is in this place of inner peace and rest where we overcome whatever is going on around us!

Sometimes, we may drift from God because we have neglected our relationship with Him. Instead we have allowed the success of our ministries, successes in life, or influences of this world to get in the way. Success in the world is all about achievement in the eyes of man, whereas success in God's Kingdom is about intimacy with Him and being obedient to His will.

An idol in life is anything we have allowed to come between ourselves and God. It may be a friend or relationship, our work, possessions, money, the television, social media, or whatever we 'worship'. Jesus said we are in the world but not of this world, for we belong to Him (John 15:19). We simply repent for letting things come in the way of our relationship with God, as we turn our eyes and hearts back to Him. He is waiting for us to do this.

When the Israelites were in the wilderness, the next generation became dependant on God to show them the way through. And with Joshua's help, they entered the Promised Land. However, the problem re-occurred when they soon forgot all God had done for them and became self-sufficient and self-reliant, to the point where they focused more on their work and livelihoods than the Lord their God (Deuteronomy 8: 1-20). This is a common mistake we can all make, where we allow our self-sufficiency or pride to get in the way when things are going well, instead of keeping our hearts yielded to God and pursuing a Spirit-led life.

One of the things the Lord spoke to the church in Ephesus was that they had abandoned their first love. This was because their hearts had turned from Him and become more focused on work, achievement, and success. If they were unwilling to repent and turn their hearts back to Him, then He would remove their lampstand, figuratively meaning the church (Revelation 2:4).

Testing of our Faith & Character

The second reason we may enter a wilderness, especially if we haven't rebelled or disobeyed God, may be because God is testing our hearts. I have discovered that God is as close to us in the valleys or wilderness seasons as He is with us on the mountain tops. It is just that we don't *feel* His Presence so much in the valleys because He is testing our hearts. It may be He is seeing how much we trust Him and choose to walk by faith and not by sight. In some cases, He may convict our hearts of stumbling blocks, such as pride, as he invites us to humble our hearts.

The Lord sees how much we trust Him as we are tested with the various trials of the heart. Tests reveal our character as they expose the orphan areas of our heart. The Lord may take us through His refiner's fire again and again, as we die to our flesh and He refines our hearts. However, the more we die to our flesh, the more we will encounter His resurrection glory in our hearts.

Over the years I have learnt to ask God two questions when I find myself in a wilderness: Have I done anything to grieve Him where I need to repent? And if not, then what is He testing in my heart? David prayed something similar: *'Search me God and know my heart. Test me and know my anxious thoughts. See if there is any offensive way in me and lead me in the way everlasting'* (Psalm139: 23-24).

I have come to realise that just because we don't feel His Presence doesn't mean He can't still speak to us! He still speaks to us through His Word and Spirit, as we fine tune our ears to hear Him. Even if we don't feel His Presence, we can still give Him thanks and praise. Thanks and praise draws us into His Presence. God can't resist reaching out to us when we are constantly giving Him thanks and praise. David never failed to worship God. He gave Him thanks and praise, especially in the midst of his enemies or when experiencing the dark night of his soul.

Paul encourages us to pray in the Spirit *at all times* (Ephesians 6:18). One way of praying in the Spirit is through the gift of speaking in tongues freely available for all Spirit-filled believers. So if we don't know what to say or pray, we can always pray in our spiritual language. If you haven't received this gift, then ask God for it, for this is a gift which is free for everyone. Paul says that *when* we speak in tongues we are speaking to God, spirit to Spirit, and this is to build up and encourage ourselves in the Spirit (1 Corinthians 14:2-4). Praying in tongues helps to overcome whatever we are contending with or coming up against at that moment in time.

During these desert seasons, God is right with us even though we can't feel His Presence. He is testing what is in our hearts, as well as our attitude and motives. The moment I came to realise this, I would ask Him what He was testing in my heart. I could then work through that area and it wouldn't be long before I came back into His tangible Presence.

These dry seasons are opportunities for spiritual growth. He wants us to pursue Him until we find Him. He said: *'You will seek Me and find Me **when you seek Me** with **all your heart**'* (Deuteronomy 4:29, Jeremiah 29:13).

What I learnt one day while serving in Africa I will never forget. For a few months, I had been seeking Him each morning in prayer and worship, but not feeling His tangible Presence. I had continued in faith reading His word but felt He was somehow holding Himself back from me. Then a friend came to my house for coffee. My friend was someone who was sensitive to the Spirit of God and could easily sense things in the spiritual realm.

The moment she stepped in through my front door she said, 'Wow!' She instantly stopped talking to me and was in awe of something she could sense all around her. Her eyes lit up as she looked around. She said, 'You have been praying much!' I asked her what she meant and how she knew. She said the first thing that hit her as she placed her foot in my room was the tangible Presence of God. I couldn't believe what she was saying. How could she so feel His Presence and I couldn't? I then understood the truth, that He was right there in my room with me but was withholding His Presence a millimetre or so from me.

He had been testing my faith and obedience to seek Him, seeing if I would continue to worship Him even when I didn't 'feel' anything. Without my knowledge He had enjoyed me hanging out with Him. It was such an eye opener for me when she shared this. I felt God was winking at me saying He had been there all the time, just seeing how much I would press on into Him and how hungry I really was for Him. I realised again how true it is that He never leaves us or forsakes us. So even if I don't feel His amazing

Presence, as long as I haven't strayed from His path, I know He is right there with me.

During such times of testing, God is further deepening our faith in Him. He does this because He wants to see if we really do love Him. Do we want to know His will? Do we trust Him? Will we wait for Him? He is actually right with us even if we can't feel Him. This is a time to persevere in faith and keep pressing on into Him. Faith doesn't rely on our feelings but is a choice we make in our spirit. I believe God will take us into a deeper relationship with Him if we are willing to press on further into Him and not give up.

He so wants us to seek His Presence but this requires a hunger in our hearts for more of Him. We must believe the truth that He is always with us and will never leave us or desert us. So if we haven't left Him, then that means He is with us even though we may not feel it. This is when we welcome Christ to *dwell in our hearts through faith* (Ephesians 3:17).

Transformed Hearts

There are times when God calls His bride to come and be alone with Him in the wilderness so He can reveal more of Himself to her. This is when He takes us to another level of revelatory knowledge in our walk with Him. He wants our full attention for what He has next, and draws us aside to be alone with Him, so we may be taken to a deeper place in our intimacy with Him.

There was a season when God led me in the wilderness to be alone with Him. I had just completed an assignment in Africa and sensed He had something new for me to step into. I was in a season of transition and expected doors to open for my next mission assignment, but that didn't happen. Instead, a friend offered me to stay at her flat somewhere on the coast by the sea. Initially I said 'thank-you but no thank-you' for I thought I wouldn't need it. How wrong I was. Finally, realising God had provided her flat as a place to stay, I gratefully took up her offer.

At first, it felt like being alone on a desert island as He took away the things that mattered in my life. These were the things that I belonged to. He was withdrawing me from the mission organisation that I had been working with and also from my home church that I had been a part of for seventeen years.

During my first week away, I felt rather alone and asked God why this was happening to me. I desperately wanted to be somewhere where I felt I belonged. Then the question came, *'Where is my belonging and what do I belong to?'* I was looking to belong to things, like a church or mission organisation or family, but finally God popped the answer in my head. He said, *'Ange, I don't want you to belong to anything else but Me!'* What a surprise. He then gave me a picture in which I saw myself with a cord around my waist, being yoked to the things I belonged to. Then I saw myself with a cord attached to God. I saw that the yoke had been more attached to other things (like church or mission work) than it had been to Him. God wanted to shift this so that I was more bonded to Him than any other influence in my life. Hence He had removed me from the things I had become so attached to. In all of this, He was showing me that He wanted me first and foremost to be bonded to Him. He is to be my belonging. I am to belong to Him. Then I can be attached to the other things like church or other organisations.

This is not to say that we are to isolate ourselves from the body of Christ, on the contrary, for we are part of the body of Christ. Rather, our hearts are to be more bonded to God than we are to anyone or anything else.

This was a challenging time for me as God stripped me of things that mattered in my life, and then asked, *'Ange, am I enough?'* This was not easy to answer. I had been relying on others to meet my needs instead of God to be enough for all my needs. I saw myself holding on to other things, but God wanted me to hold Him not with one but with both of my hands. This meant I had to let go of what I had been holding onto in order to hold onto Him.

For God to be enough means we are willing to hold onto Him and nothing or no-one else. If we hold onto other stuff or depend more on others, then we are only in part, if at all, holding onto God. This made me realise how I had been seeking others to meet my needs. This included the needs for approval, affirmation, recognition, to be loved, to be valued and listened to. God wanted me to have all my needs met in Him. He wanted me to come to

Him for approval, recognition, affirmation, love, or to be listened to. Was He enough? Did He meet all my needs?

I was crying out to God to encounter His Presence and decided to fast until He turned up. On the third day of the fast, His Presence came crashing into my room and overshadowed me. He made it clear that I was in His will and right where He wanted me to be, alone with Him. I found myself spontaneously thanking and praising Him before going to bed and on awakening each morning. It no longer bothered me that I was alone in an unfamiliar place away from everyone. I started to enjoy my time just being with Him and no-one else. This was His doing. It then didn't bother me what I did next. I just wanted to be with Him. He had simply pulled me aside to get me away from everything that mattered to me, so that He could be the only thing that now mattered. It felt like I was on honeymoon with Him, just the two of us together.

This wilderness experience of feeling alone and isolated with no doors opening soon blossomed into a garden of flowers. It was just to be me and Him, enjoying time with each other. I said one day, *'Lord, all I want now is You!'* He was waiting for me to come to this point in my relationship with Him. No longer was I bothered about what I did next. This time was God's doing simply to be more yoked to Him.

During the barren seasons, God exposes what is in our hearts so that the old branches may be pruned back, or even uprooted, and new branches and fruit may come forth. Pruning is never a pleasant season as we let God expose the orphan areas of our heart that He wants to prune or even crucify. It is in the hidden place when He pulls us aside from the things of this world that He can minister to our hearts, so we may bear more fruit in His Kingdom. We are to welcome such seasons as opportunities to go deeper in our love relationship with Him. One thing He revealed during my time in the wilderness was that unless I let Him do the deeper work in my heart, I would not be able to step into what He had next for me.

These desert seasons can be seen as training for reigning. Esther had to undergo a year of preparation before she was made queen.

During this time she developed a mindset and heart that was pleasing to her king. She laid aside all her dreams and plans and became willing to do that which pleased him.

God has great plans for each one of us, but this may require a time of preparation in the wilderness in order for us to grow deeper in our relationship with Him.

Israelites in the Wilderness

In Deuteronomy, we read the reasons why God led His people through the desert: *'Remember how the Lord your God led you all the way into the desert these forty years, to **humble you** and to **test you** in order to **know what was in your heart**, whether or not you would keep His commands. He humbled you, causing you **to hunger** and then feeding you on manna, to teach you that man doesn't live on bread alone but on **every word that comes from the mouth of the Lord**'* (Deuteronomy 8:2-3).

Let's look at these reasons.

To be humbled

The first was to **humble them** so that they would depend more on Him and realise they couldn't do anything without Him. God may lead us to a place of brokenness in our hearts where we know that we can't do anything without Him, and so discover our need for Him. One of the areas to surrender is that of our abilities. For many years I was under the false belief that my abilities were my own doing, as a result of my studying, training or hard work. That was until one day God revealed that *all* my abilities were from Him. With this realization, I knew I could take no praise for myself since it was His doing all along and not mine.

God reminded the Israelites that when all went well for them in the Promised Land, they were not to let their hearts become proud and forget what God had done. *'You may say to yourself, "My power and the strength of my hands have produced this wealth for me". But remember the Lord your God,* **for it is He who gives you the ability to produce wealth**' (Deuteronomy 8:14, 17-18).

In relation to this, the Lord gave me a vision of His harvest fields where I saw His children co-labouring with Him. They were at different stages of spiritual growth hence some were little and others more mature, and each had a different tool to harvest the land. Some had hand tools like sickles, and others had tractors or heavy powerful machinery. Each had been given a tool according to their faithfulness and obedience in their use of the previous tools they were given (see Mathew 25:14-30 on the parable of the talents). The main thing I noticed in this vision was that the children were not harvesting His fields for self-gain or self-glory. Instead they were doing it out of sheer love and devotion to their Heavenly Father. It wasn't about 'look at me and my talents or ministry', but about having humble servant hearts willing to harvest the fields that had been assigned to each one of them - doing it for God's glory not man's. The tools were His and being loaned to His children, and were to be used with humility and honour.

He will reward those who serve Him faithfully. Jesus told His disciples not to rejoice that the demons submitted to them, but to rejoice that their names were written in Heaven (Luke 10:17-20). *'Whatever you do, work at it with all your heart, **as working for the Lord, not for men,** since you know you will receive an inheritance from the Lord as a reward. **It is the Lord Christ you are serving**'* (Colossians 3:23-24).

To test what was in their hearts

The second reason the Israelites spent time in the wilderness was to **test what was in their hearts**. What were their real motives and intentions in life? Were they really after God's heart? Would they still obey Him and keep His commands or rebel and do what they wanted? Would they hunger for Him and His Word or focus on their flesh and the things of this world?

The Israelites repeatedly failed this test of their hearts. They moaned, complained and focused on their flesh and selfish needs more than God. Hence they died in the wilderness and didn't set foot in the Promised Land. It was the next generation who obeyed God and received His promise to enter the Promised Land.

To see how Hungry they were for God's Word

The third reason was to see if they were **hungry to know Him more.** Did they hunger for His Word more than their flesh hungered for food? The Israelites moaned about what they were eating and complained that the manna from Heaven wasn't sufficient. God was waiting for them to cry out for more of His bread, His living Word. He was trying to teach them that man doesn't live on bread alone but on every word which comes from the mouth of God, that is, breathed by the Holy Spirit (Deuteronomy 8:3).

The reason the Israelites didn't make it out of the desert and into the Promised Land was because they kept failing to obey God and remained rebellious in their hearts. They didn't hunger for Him. So God waited forty years until the next generation were of age to make it into the Promised Land. *'Today if you hear His voice, do not harden your hearts as you did in the* ***rebellion,*** *during the* ***time of testing in the desert,*** *where your fathers tested and tried Me and for forty years saw what I did. That is why I was angry with that generation, and I said,* ***"Their hearts are always going astray, and they have not known My ways".*** *So I declared on oath in My anger, they shall never enter My rest'* (Hebrews 3:7-19, Psalm 95:7-11).

The Israelites failed to know God's ways for their hearts were always following their own will and desires. As a result, their stubborn hearts were hardened and they failed to enter His resting place.

It requires faith on our part for God to dwell in our hearts. Faith isn't a feeling but a choice in our spirit. By faith we connect our spirit to God's Spirit. Sometimes we may feel His amazing love and Presence and other times we may be aware of His peace. God chooses how much of His Spirit to release to us, as we engage our spirit with His through faith!

Jesus in the Desert

Jesus, full of the Holy Spirit, returned from the Jordan and ***was led by the Spirit into the desert, where for forty days He was tempted by the Devil.*** *He ate nothing during those days and at the end of them He was hungry'* (Luke 4:1-2). The Lord had to undergo a season in the desert. He was probably alone; most likely no-one knew where He was or what He was doing except His Father and the Holy Spirit.

Jesus was *led* by the Spirit into the desert, for this was God's will and didn't eat for forty days. Though He was alone, God was with Him. He was tested with His flesh, mind, will, emotions, and identity. Jesus experienced the same tests that the Israelites faced while in the desert. In doing so, He demonstrated it was possible to overcome all trials and temptations of the flesh.

Test of Identity

Jesus' identity was tested first. This came after God had just said: *'You are My Son, whom I love; with You I am well pleased'* (Luke 3:22). The devil challenged Him and said, '**If** you are the **Son of God**....' He knew full well who Jesus was but wanted to take the opportunity to test Him with His identity. Jesus didn't have to prove who He was to anyone. He knew who He was and that was all that mattered. So He didn't respond to this temptation but instead chose to ignore it. As a result, He passed the test.

Usually after God has taught us things He will test us, to see if our hearts and minds have changed. And we will be tested again and again, until we pass.

Test of Spirit versus the Flesh

Secondly, Jesus was tempted with His flesh. Satan knew He was hungry so he tempted Him to change a stone into bread and break His fast. The weapon Jesus used to retaliate was the Word of God. He said, *'It is written: Man does not live on bread alone, but on every word that comes from the mouth of God'* (Mathew 4:4). The Greek word used here for 'word' was *rhema* which referred to the breath of God or Spirit-breathed word. Hence, the words He spoke came from the mouth of God.

Jesus was referring to the passage in Deuteronomy regarding God's response to when the Israelites were tested in the desert. The Israelites failed this test, but Jesus gave the right response and passed. He overcame the desires of His flesh by spiritually feeding on the breathed word of God and His spirit took mastery over His flesh.

Test of Obedience to God

Next, satan tempted Jesus by showing Him all the kingdoms of the world and saying: *'I will give You all their authority and splendour, for it has been given to me. So if You worship me it will all be Yours'*. Jesus' response was again to use the sword of the Spirit, the Word of God. He replied: *'It is written...'* and went on to quote the scripture, *'Worship the Lord your God and serve Him alone'* (another quote from Deuteronomy 6:13). Jesus overcame the temptation by declaring the truth through the Word of God and by worshipping God alone. He allowed nothing to get between Him and His Father, not even hunger, wealth, splendour, power or fame. He was totally devoted to His Father.

Test of God-Given Power & Authority

Jesus was tempted again on His identity and also on His authority and power. Satan set Jesus on the pinnacle of the temple and cunningly quoted the scripture from Psalm 91: *"If you are the Son of God",* he said, *"throw yourself down. For it is written: 'He will command His angels concerning you, and they will lift you up in their hands, so that you will not strike your foot against a stone"'* (Mathew 4:6). This was a demonstration of how satan twists the truth to tempt us to sin, like he did with Adam and Eve. However, Jesus replied again with the Word of God: *'It also says, "Do not put the Lord your God to the test"'*.

He overcame all tests and temptations with the sword of the Spirit, the *rhema* word of God (Ephesians 6:17). He was tested with His flesh, pride, identity, status, power, authority, obedience and surrender to God's will. After He had passed all the tests and God was very pleased with His heart, He left the desert.

Jesus was tempted in every way, just as we are, yet was without sin (Hebrews 4:15). God will not let us be tempted unless He knows we can overcome that temptation. God doesn't tempt us, but He does allow our hearts to be tested. *'God is faithful; He will not let you be tempted beyond what you can bear. But when you are tempted He will also provide a way out so that you can stand up under it'* (1 Corinthians 10:13). God has given us free will to say 'no' to sin and temptation and to walk away from it.

After overcoming the tests and trials, Jesus returned to Galilee in the *power of the Spirit* (Luke 4:14). When He left the desert, He had the power of the Spirit resting on Him and was ready to step into the work God had called and prepared Him to do. He had been promoted in the wilderness!

Promotion in the Wilderness

During the Spirit-led wilderness seasons, our character is being both challenged and refined in this time of transformation. Even the friends of Solomon didn't recognise his bride when she came out of the wilderness: *'Who is this coming up from the desert leaning on her lover?'* (Song of Songs 8:5).

Joseph, Moses, David, Esther, John the Baptist and Paul, all had seasons lasting years in the desert. These were times when they were being shaped and refined, as their hearts were being prepared by God for their higher callings.

Joseph's desert was in a prison where he was tested and transformed, as his heart was being spiritually prepared for the work God had in store for him.

Moses was forty years in the desert when God appeared to him in a burning bush and commissioned him to lead His people out of Egypt into the Promised Land (Exodus 3:1-4).

David had been fleeing Saul and hiding in the caves and strongholds in the desert. He underwent thirteen years of training for reigning as he faced many trials and challenges where his heart was constantly being tested. After a time of preparation in the wilderness, he was promoted to be the next king (1 Samuel 23:13).

Esther's wilderness season was twelve months in the palace. During the first six months she received the oil of myrrh as it was rubbed into her skin. Myrrh represents suffering love and during this time, Esther was probably undergoing a death to her flesh and self, as she willingly laid down her life for the king.

John the Baptist lived in the wilderness eating locusts and honey. He was the voice of one calling in the desert to prepare the way for the Lord (Mark 1:3).

After Paul's conversion experience on the road to Damascus, he withdrew and spent the next three years in Arabia (Galatians 1:17-18). This was training ground for Paul where he spent time alone in the desert with God. Paul was learning from God as God was transforming him and preparing his heart for his future calling and ministry.

Each of these amazing men and women of God had a significant season alone with God, where they withdrew from the things of this world and God transformed their hearts. God was preparing their hearts to carry the weight of authority and responsibility that went with the call He had for them. And in doing so, this would help them not to fall into the temptations of the flesh.

The wilderness is not just a time of testing but also a time of spiritual promotion. What we overcome takes us to a new and deeper level in our walk and relationship with God.

James encourages us to count it joy when we face different trials for it is a testing of our faith. *'Blessed is the man who perseveres under trial, because when he has stood the test, he will receive the crown of life that God has promised to those that love Him'* (James 1:2-12).

Wilderness seasons can be short when we find out what God is testing in our hearts and respond with the right attitude of heart. Then we can walk straight across the desert and out of the other side instead of wandering around in circles having to face the same test again and again until we finally pass. Once we have addressed the orphan area in our hearts that God wants us to overcome, He can take us further in our journey with Him.

In the natural we may have to pass tests or take exams before we are promoted at work or given a higher grade of responsibility. The same applies to us in God's Kingdom. Only when we pass the test of our *hearts* does God lead us or open doors to take on greater responsibilities in His Kingdom. His love for us never changes, but we discover more of His love as we choose to obey His will and allow Him to transform the areas in our hearts.

Our flesh (body and soul) is what is being tested in the wilderness. He crucifies our flesh in order to purify our hearts. We overcome by surrendering our thoughts (mind), choices (will), and feelings (emotions) to Him. We can help others overcome in the areas where we have had victory, as God releases more of His authority and anointing to us.

Wilderness seasons can actually be times of preparation as God prepares our hearts for what is next, but this requires pressing on deeper into Him and not being influenced by the distractions or temptations of the enemy. As we continue to press on deeper into Him, He will humble our hearts and crucify our flesh, as we discover the true fullness of a resurrected life in Him. (For more on wilderness seasons I encourage you to read *'Fire In The Desert'*[2]).

Lord Jesus, thank you there is beauty in the wilderness. Forgive me if I have drifted away or allowed things to get in the way of my relationship with You. I welcome You back in my heart and to be Lord of my life. Thank You for what You are doing in my heart and the call You have on my life. May I not resist You but yield every part of my heart and life to You. Thank You that wilderness seasons are opportunities to grow deeper with You. Lord show me what You are testing or refining in my heart. As David prayed, "Search me, O God, and know my heart; test me and know my anxious thoughts. See if there is any offensive way in me, and lead me in the way everlasting". Lord complete what You have been dealing with in my heart, so I may enter the fullness of a resurrected life in You.

END-NOTES

[1] Dr Angela Walker; *Foundation For Healing*, p 66-68 (2020)
[2] Dr Angela Walker; *Fire In The Desert* (2021)

12

He Who Overcomes

*To him who overcomes and does My will to the end,
I will give authority over the nations.*

Revelation 2:26

The Greek word in the New Testament for 'overcome' is *nike*[1] and comes from the verb *nikao*[2] meaning *'to carry off the victory, to conquer'* and refers to winning the battle. Interestingly, of all the writers in the New Testament, John the beloved disciple uses the word *nikeo* the most especially in the Book of Revelation. Each message to the seven churches in the Book of Revelation ends with Jesus' words: *'To him who overcomes...'*. To the church in Ephesus, Jesus said: *'To **him who overcomes I will give the right to eat from the tree of life**, which is in the paradise of God'* (Revelation 2:7).

Jesus said: *'In this world you will have trouble. **But take heart! I have overcome the world**'* (John 16:33). In John's first letter he writes: *'I write to you young men because you are strong and **the Word of God lives in you and you have overcome the evil one**'* (1 John 2:14). And then a few chapters later, he says this: *'You dear children are from God and **have overcome them, because the One who is in you is greater than the one in the world**'* (1 John 4:4).

Part of our calling as God's children is to overcome the works of the enemy. As warriors of the Lord, we all go through boot-camp training in order to build up our spiritual muscles, the fruit of the Spirit, as well as growing in Godly wisdom and discernment. To those who become faithful and obedient even unto death, God will lavish great rewards in His Kingdom. During our boot-camp training, our mind, will and emotions are tested, and this is an opportunity for our flesh to yield to our spirit, as our spirit surrenders to the power and authority of His Spirit.

The higher the calling involves the greater the training and therefore the greater the sacrifice. This may mean laying down our reputation, pride, selfish-ambition, need to be in control, fears, and the desires of the flesh. Jesus has paid the full price by laying down His life for you and me, and is inviting you and me to sacrifice our lives for Him. In order to go higher, there must be a willingness to go lower, as we yield every part of our carnal nature and 'self' to Him.

Overcome by Yielding

God is after our hearts and is looking for those who will yield their hearts to Him. Once, the Lord gave me a picture of a wild horse or stallion, and this strong horse was raising its head and front legs as if it was fighting back. I was surprised when He said I was the horse. I thought I had surrendered my life to God, until He revealed there was an orphan area in my heart I hadn't yet yielded to Him. It was the area of fighting back in self-defence. He reminded me of times when I had come up against opposition and felt threatened and my natural response was to self-defend or fight back. I mistakenly thought this was a strength in my character, until the Lord revealed it was time to yield this orphan area of my heart to Him. Then I saw the horse yield with its head bowed down before the Lord. I was no longer to fight in retaliation or self-defence, but simply yield my flesh to Him. '*His pleasure is not in the strength of a horse nor His delight in the legs of man; the Lord delights in those who fear Him, who put their hope in His unfailing love*' (Psalm 147:10-11).

Peter fought back with his flesh when he cut off the ear of the servant in the Garden of Gethsemane. Jesus rebuked him and told him to put away his sword, for it was His Father's will to be arrested and not to fight (Mathew 26:52-54).

True meekness is a yielding to God's will in the midst of our enemies. It is being aware of our strength but choosing not to misuse it, but to depend on God to protect us and be our strength. This was demonstrated throughout the life of Jesus.

I have learnt that one of the most powerful weapons we have is the weapon of humility. I was with a colleague driving though a town in South Sudan when we were stopped by the local police. They asked for proof of our vehicle documents which my colleague couldn't find. There was a choice. We could argue back that we had them, or submit in humility. The Lord gave us His grace to submit. As we did, we spoke in peaceful, amicable terms, and they waived any charges. After they had left, we found the documents lying there in the car. I believe God was testing our hearts to yield to those in authority, even though they appeared corrupt. Humility quenches enemy activity.

One of the ways to overcome is to yield our stubbornness, our self-defence mechanisms, our judgements, or our need to retaliate. Instead, we respond as the Lord leads us in any given situation, from a place of inner peace and confidence in Him. It will be different on each occasion. Sometimes it may be right to say nothing and be quiet. Other times it may be right to respond with grace and humility. And on other occasions it may be right to take authority or rebuke what we hear, in the Name of Jesus. Instead of reacting with our flesh, we can respond with our spirit. That is, with a righteous spirit instead of a spirit of self-righteousness.

God is looking for sons and daughters to overcome the enemy, as they yield to Him and take up their position in His army. He doesn't want us to step out of line and fight battles by ourselves. Rather, He is looking for surrendered hearts and minds, who willingly obey Him, whatever the cost or outcome.

We can ask the Lord to reveal any areas in our heart or mind that we haven't yet yielded to Him. And He will show us as He did to the seven churches (Revelation 2-3).

One of satan's main weapons is fear. If we have laid down our lives for God, then our lives are no longer our own, so what do we have to fear? In the same way He laid down His life for us, He is inviting you and me to lay down our lives for Him.

The biggest battle Jesus had to face was the cross. He prayed the same prayer three times asking His Father to take the cup of suffering away from Him. Yet, each time He surrendered by saying, *'Not My will but Yours be done'*. He knew the cross was the final chapter and He overcame by yielding to His Father's will. After Jesus was arrested He chose not to defend Himself. He didn't reply to any false accusations or lies, but acknowledged who He was, the Son of God.

The disciple Stephen was a man full of grace, wisdom, and power. Though he was arrested, his face shone like the face of an angel, being full of the Holy Spirit, as he testified before the Sanhedrin. As he was about to be stoned, he looked up to heaven and saw the glory of God and Jesus standing at the right hand of the Father. His final words were these: *'"Lord Jesus, receive my spirit". Then he fell on his knees and cried out, "Lord, do not hold this sin against them!"'* (Acts 6:8 -7:59).

Whenever we face false accusations or persecutions for our faith, we don't have to defend ourselves. Our Heavenly Father will defend us. We simply surrender our lives into His hands, forgive our enemies, pray for them and declare His Kingdom come and will be done. Jesus said: **'Blessed are those who are persecuted because of righteousness, for theirs is the Kingdom of Heaven.** *Blessed are you when people insult you, persecute you and falsely say all kinds of evil against you because of Me. Rejoice and be glad, for* **great is your reward in Heaven'** (Mathew 5:11-12).

Whenever we have to face suffering as a result of our faith, be it betrayal of friendship, false accusations, loss of a loved one or persecution, don't forget Jesus has already gone before us. As we turn to Him, He will give us His divine grace to encounter such suffering, that is, His supernatural power to help us overcome our weakness in our times of need.

Peter who denied Jesus three times was the same Peter who rejoiced that he was counted worthy of suffering disgrace for

Jesus' name (Acts 5:41). *'In this you greatly rejoice, though now for a little while, you may **have had to suffer grief in all kinds of trials**. This has come so that your faith - of greater worth than gold, which perishes even though refined by fire - may be proved genuine, and may result in praise, honour and glory, when Jesus Christ is revealed'* (1 Peter 1:3-7). And a few verses later, Peter said: *'It is better, if it's God's will, to suffer for doing good than for doing evil'* (1 Peter 3:17).

Choose Your Battles

In my earlier days, I naively believed I was to fight every battle or opposition I encountered. Since then, my thinking has changed as I have come to understand the ways of the Lord and the importance of listening to Him before engaging in warfare.

Enquire of the Lord

Ahab, King of Israel, asked Jehoshaphat, King of Judah, if he would fight the city of Ramoth Gilead with him. Jehoshaphat's reply was to *first seek the counsel of the Lord* (2 Chronicles 18:4). The Lord revealed this battle would bring Ahab's death for God wasn't with him. Knowing this, Jehoshaphat still decided to go to battle for Ahab's sake. As a result Jehoshaphat nearly lost his life too until he cried out to God to save him. For every battle it is wise to seek the counsel of the Lord and discern if He is calling us to fight in it or not.

Sometimes we may think we are to fight other people's battles when it may not be His will. I believe the Lord assigns us to the battles He wants us to take part in. These are usually the ones He brings in our midst or to our attention, but I believe we are not to go looking for them or get caught up in someone else's battle, unless the Lord is stirring our heart to do so. I used to take authority over any opposition I encountered until I realised Jesus didn't always act this way. He probably encountered spiritual opposition most of the time but acted with wisdom and discernment. Even when His enemies were about to push Him off the cliff, He suddenly slipped away through the crowd (Luke 4:28-30).

After Jesus had healed a man on the Sabbath, He knew this had provoked the Pharisees to kill Him, so He withdrew from the place (Matthew 12:14-15). One of His responses to satan was to ignore him. He wasn't ignorant of what the enemy was doing but chose not to respond to some of his tactics. Jesus knew when He was arrested that He could call on His Father to dispose more than twelve legions of angels to come to His rescue but He chose not to (Mathew 26:53). There will be times when we too are to ignore the enemy or not be caught up in his schemes.

A fortune-telling slave girl followed Paul declaring he and his men were servants of the Most High God. At first Paul rightly ignored her, until it got to the point where Paul became troubled by what she was doing. So he commanded the spirit to leave the girl. It did and as a result, he and Silas were stripped, beaten, and thrown into prison (Acts 16:16-26). It is important to discern in the Spirit when to ignore enemy distractions or threats, and when to take action, knowing there may be consequences for our actions.

David only fought in the battles if God was with him. He didn't allow any assumption or presumption to get in the way but would fight if God said 'Yes', for that meant God would give him victory. It is wise to seek the Lord and ask if He wants us to engage in certain battles or not. If it is His will, He will be with us and we will see victory, whether on earth or in Heaven. However, if it isn't His will, then we are at risk of having no protection or divine covering.

This is what happened to the Israelites whenever they decided to attack their enemy without first seeking the counsel of the Lord. Many times their presumption ended in defeat for God wasn't with them. They had gone to battle of their own will so God let them suffer defeat. Battles were lost and many were killed when the kings entered into battles without enquiring of the Lord first. However, victory was seen if they sought the Lord and obeyed His orders.

As we follow His strategy, we will overcome the battles He assigns us to. However, if we step out of line and take on giants He hasn't called us to slay, then we shouldn't be surprised if we get hit. We are to obey Him at all times. The safest place is being in the will of the Lord, whether we are called to engage in a battle or not.

King Amaziah of Judah paid for extra troops from Israel to join his men in battle. Though it was God's will he went to battle, a prophet said he was not to take these extra troops, or he would suffer defeat. He was told: *'Even if you go and fight courageously in battle, God will overthrow you before the enemy, for **God has the power to help or to overthrow**'* (2 Chronicles 25:8). He obeyed the Lord, discharged the extra troops and the Lord gave him victory!

Likewise, the Lord may ask us to engage in a battle when we don't want to. King David decided not to go and fight with his men when the Lord was calling him to battle. As a result, he was in a position to be tempted to commit adultery with Bathsheba (2 Samuel 11). The enemy can tempt us in various ways when we choose to do what we want instead of doing God's will. Hence, it is safer to be in the will of the Lord than to separate ourselves from Him.

There was a time while on mission when I was due a period of rest, but the Lord said, 'Not yet' for He had another battle for me to engage in. I resisted at first saying I was tired and needed a rest, but God knew how the enemy was advancing and ordered me to take my position in this particular battle.

It was a certain time of the year when spiritual warfare broke out as a result of the pagan activities taking place around our camp. We couldn't ignore it and God told us to gather together and pray. Interestingly, we were a minority of less than ten (for most missionaries were on leave) compared to the large gathering there was of witchdoctors outside our base. We could sense the oppression building up in the atmosphere so we started to pray around the base, as the Lord instructed. It wasn't a pleasant time but the Lord protected our base and victory was won. We must never forget that the battle belongs to the Lord! This means we are to take our positions under His leadership and give Him full control. He is in charge of every battle we are to fight, and we will have victory if we take our orders from Him and obey Him.

The Battle is the Lord's

During a time of worship, I had a vision of Jesus on His white horse preparing for battle. He was in the front with His back turned to His army of warriors and there were lines of warriors on horses behind Him. They were focused on Him and awaiting His orders. Each one had a sword and a shield and was wearing his armour. Then I heard the words, *'Take up your position, for the battle is the Lord's'*.

Immediately the verse of scripture that came to mind was the battle of King Jehoshaphat. When he saw the vast army that was attacking them, he turned to the Lord for help. The Lord replied: *'Do not be afraid or discouraged because of this vast army.* **For the battle is not yours but God's.** *Tomorrow* **march down against them.** *They will be climbing up by the Pass of Ziz and you will find them at the end of the gorge in the Desert of Jeruel. You will not have to fight this battle.* **Take up your positions; stand firm and see the deliverance the Lord will give you. Do not be afraid, do not be discouraged. Go out and face them tomorrow and the Lord will be with you'** (2 Chronicles 20:15-17).

God gave Jehoshaphat a strategy. First, it wasn't his battle but the Lord's. Many Christians misinterpret this phrase thinking they don't have to take responsibility or do anything. God wasn't saying that. He was actually meaning He was in charge and everyone was to take orders from Him.

Next, God instructed Jehoshaphat on how to act: *'Tomorrow march down against them'*. This was not a 'do nothing' command, but a 'GO' command. He instructed Jehoshaphat to *'take up your positions; stand firm and see the deliverance the Lord will give you'*. This is a battle command.

The king obeyed and as he did, God was faithful. God sent His army of angels to warfare and delivered them from the enemy's hand.

When David faced Goliath, he came against him with his spiritual weapon, the sword of the Spirit. He said: *'"I come against you in the Name of the Lord Almighty...all those gathered here will know that it is not by sword or spear that the Lord saves; for* **the battle is the Lord's and He will give all of you into our hands"'**.

David knew that the battle belonged to the Lord as he took his place in God's army to overcome the enemy.

Different Strategies

Each battle we fight is different, even though it may seem the same, because God may have a different strategy. We should be careful not to assume that what gave us victory in one battle will give us victory in another. David enquired of the Lord for strategy. He didn't just take control and advance, but he took orders from God and obeyed.

When the Philistines advanced on David, he enquired of the Lord what to do. The Lord said, *'"Do not go straight up but circle around behind them and attack them in front of the balsam trees. As soon as you hear the sound of marching in the tops of the balsam trees, move quickly, because that will mean that the Lord has gone out in front of you to strike the Philistine army". So David did as the Lord commanded him'* (2 Samuel 5:23-25). David had clear instructions from the Lord. He obeyed and won the battle, as the Lord's army of angels went before him and attacked the Philistine army.

When I was ministering to the sick in the remote villages in Mozambique, the Lord wanted me to tell them about Him and pray for them. As I did, many encountered Jesus and were healed from the effects of witchcraft and curses. However, when I ministered to a group of another faith, the Lord showed me to minister to them in a different way. He had a different strategy for a different group of people and it worked. There is victory when we seek God's strategy and obey.

Stay Focused on Jesus

To win a battle means keeping our eyes focused on Jesus, until the end. If God tells us to wait, we wait. If He says to take our position, we take our position. And if He says to give thanks and praise, we give thanks and praise.

When Peter stepped out in faith to walk on water, his eyes were on Jesus. However, the moment the waves became turbulent, he took his eyes off Jesus and focused on the storm. Fear entered his heart and he started to drown. Faith requires our eyes to focus on

Jesus, regardless of whatever is going on around us. And as we do, we will walk through the storms.

King Saul failed miserably with his army when he was given orders by Samuel to wait for further instructions. Instead, of waiting, he feared the anxious response from his men and acted irresponsibly. Samuel instructed Saul to go down to Gilgal and wait seven days for him to arrive, then he would instruct him what to do next (1 Samuel 10:8). *'Saul remained at Gilgal and all the troops with him were quaking with fear. He waited seven days, the time set by Samuel; but Samuel didn't come to Gilgal, and Saul's men began to scatter. So he said, "Bring me the burnt offerings and fellowship offerings". And Saul offered up the burnt offering. Just as he finished making the offering, Samuel arrived. "What have you done?" asked Samuel. Saul replied, "When I saw that the men were scattering and that you did not come at the set time, and that the Philistines were assembling at Micmash, I thought 'Now the Philistines will come down against me at Gilgal and I have not sought the Lord's favour'. So I felt compelled to offer the burnt offering". "You acted foolishly", Samuel said. "You have not kept the command the Lord your God gave you; if you had, He would have established your kingdom over Israel for all time"'* (1 Samuel 13:7-13).

Saul feared man more than God and acted under false assumption instead of waiting patiently for Samuel. When God tells us to wait, we are to wait. We are not to advance from a place of fear or control, or it may lead to consequences that we will later regret. We are to wait because God's timing is perfect. *'Those who wait on the Lord shall renew their strength; they shall mount up with wings like eagles. They shall run and not be weary; they shall walk and not faint'* (Isaiah 40:31, NKJV). Instead of reacting from the flesh, we are to wait for the prompting of His Spirit.

Preparation & Team Unity

Joshua told his people to *consecrate themselves* before they crossed the Jordan and went into the Promised Land (Joshua 3:5). All was well until Joshua fought the people of Ai. His men lost the battle because there was sin in the camp (Joshua 7:13). Whenever there is sin in the camp it creates an opportunity for the enemy to attack. Joshua's men would see victory once the sin was removed from their camp.

An opportunity arose for me to take a team to a war-torn nation. However, the Lord made it clear to me that the team were to be spiritually prepared before entering this nation. So over a period of four weeks, we met regularly to pray, worship and get our hearts right before God. During this time, the Lord did some personal refining and healing of hearts and united the team by His Spirit. He released visions and pictures as He spoke to the team using a spiritual military language. At the end of the four weeks, the team was spiritually prepared to enter this war-torn nation. As a result of such preparation, our team was protected from any attack and we reaped a harvest. Much fruit was seen as a result of us being spiritually prepared.

On a different occasion, I joined another team on a two-week mission. We had little spiritual preparation and there was a lack of unity in the Spirit. The result was we ended up doing little outreach because God was more concerned with our hearts and attitudes. For most of the time, He dealt with the sin in the camp which included pride, selfishness and a critical spirit. It was after we repented of our attitude, ministered to one another, washed each other's feet, and took communion, that there was a spirit of unity in the team. God was more concerned about our hearts and about dealing with our issues, before releasing us to reach out to others, especially when we were entering enemy territory.

It matters most to God that a team can work together in the unity of His Spirit before they engage in ministering to others. Where there is unity, there is His anointing and protection (Psalm 133).

I saw something extraordinary when I was walking across fields on a retreat. As I came to the top of a hill, I noticed there was a group of about seven horses sitting or lying down in a circle. This was amazing to see, so I crouched down to observe what they were doing. Three horses were sat upright keeping watch in different directions, while the others were lying down asleep. Then, about ten minutes later, those that were asleep woke up and sat up to let the others that had been keeping watch go to sleep. I noted that the horses were surrounded by a hedge that had some gaps in it and each gap was large enough for a horse to walk through.

I pondered on what the Lord was showing me and could see there was a powerful unity in this team of horses as they lay together in a circle. And as they kept watch over each other, they were protected. I realised that if one of them decided to go astray through the gap in the hedge, then they could fall prey to the enemy. As they remained united, the enemy couldn't touch them. These horses were like warriors who watched each other's backs and knew their authority in God's army.

The Lord loves it when we work together in unity. He knows what lies ahead and will guide us by His Spirit where to go or not go. He knows the enemy's strongholds operating in certain people groups or areas, and His Spirit will show us how to tackle each opposition.

We overcome by advancing in the opposite spirit to the enemy and this means we are not to have any open doors to the same issues in our hearts. The Lord will prepare us for whatever assignment He calls us to, and where there is unity there is divine protection, as we advance His Kingdom.

Prayer Cover

It is good to have prayer cover from fellow prophetic intercessors or prayer warriors whenever we are advancing in God's Kingdom. Paul knew when God had opened a door for him to do effective work, there would be many who would oppose him (1 Corinthians 16:9). Prophetic prayer warriors are like the spiritual air force, for as we are advancing on foot our intercessors are doing battle in the Heavenly realms.

At times when I have been on mission, I have felt a tangible difference when people have been covering me in prayer. For the three years I worked in Mozambique, I never came down with malaria. A lady back in England said she committed herself to praying each day for my protection from malaria and her prayers worked.

It is wise when doing an assignment not to work alone unless the Lord has called us to do so, but instead work alongside others so we can guard each other's backs. Many times I have prayed for my colleagues when they have fallen sick or come under spiritual attack and they have soon recovered. Likewise, when they have prayed for me it has made all the difference. God loves us to work together in unity and pours His Spirit in greater measure on each one of us as we do. Even Jonathan took his armour bearer to fight with him and the two of them defeated the Philistines (1 Samuel 14:7).

We shouldn't forget to cover our families and loved ones in prayer when we are engaged in spiritual battles. If the enemy can't get to us, then he will try and attack those close to us.

Prayer cover is vital for those doing frontline Kingdom work so we can see His Kingdom advance and battles won, on earth as in Heaven.

Heart of a Warrior-Bride

Both David and John the beloved passionately pursued the Lord and were warriors in His Kingdom, such that they displayed the heart of a warrior-bride. Let us look at the characteristics of a warrior-bride.

David

David from a young age carried the heart of a worshipping warrior. He simply loved being in the Presence of the Lord and somehow knew how to connect his heart with God. He was a faithful shepherd who protected his sheep and fought off anything that tried to attack them, whether a lion or a bear. This was boot-camp training in the secret place before he was to overcome Goliath in the public arena.

God's favour was with him: *'I have seen a son of Jesse, who knows* **how to play the harp**. *He is a* **brave man and a warrior**. *He speaks well and is fine looking. And the* **Lord is with him'** (1 Samuel 16:18). As David played the harp and worshipped in the Spirit, the tormenting spirits inside Saul were silenced. David continually demonstrated a humble, servant heart to the King. Even when his men had the opportunity to kill Saul, David rebuked them. With such fear of the Lord he replied: *'Don't destroy him! Who can lay a hand on the Lord's anointed and be guiltless?'* (1 Samuel 26:9). He was a man who feared the Lord and honoured God's anointed.

David knew his position and ranking in the army of the Lord and that the battle was the Lord's. He only fought giants if God was with him. When he fought Goliath, he spoke with holy boldness: *'I come against you, in the Name of the Lord Almighty!'* He knew that true power and authority was in the Name of Yahweh. As long as God was with him, there would be victory (1 Samuel 17:45-47).

God was training David for future reigning. He said: *'I have found David, son of Jesse, a **man after My own heart; he will do everything I want him to do**'* (Acts 13:22, 1 Samuel 13:14). When the enemy heard about David's anointing to be next king, he did everything to stop this. He tempted Saul to kill David through jealousy and anger. David overcame Saul's attacks by choosing to respond in the opposite spirit. With humility and honour he resisted every temptation and waited for God's appointed time to make him king. He never looked for status or power and resisted self-promotion, even when tempted by his own men.

Whereas Saul feared his men, David feared the Lord. David rebuked his men and stopped them committing sin, and at the Lord's appointed time, David became king. Since he had been faithful and obedient to the Lord, God trusted him with much (2 Samuel 5:2).

It is interesting that most of David's life was spent fighting battles and claiming back God's territory, as God called him to claim back His land and unite His tribe of Israel back with Judah.

He didn't care what others thought about him, especially when he was worshipping the Lord, for he was dancing before the Lord and not man (2 Samuel 6:21-22). Unlike Saul, David didn't care what others thought about him. All that mattered was his relationship with the Lord.

In one of David's most beautiful Psalms, we see the heart of a warrior followed by the heart of a bride. *'The Lord is my light and my salvation- whom shall I fear? The Lord is the stronghold of my life - of whom shall I be afraid? Though an army besiege me, my heart will not fear, though war break out against me, even then will I be confident'*. We next see emerging the heart of a bride, a heart that longs to dwell in the Presence of the Lord. *'One thing I ask of the*

Lord, this is what I seek: that I may dwell in the house of the Lord all the days of my life, to gaze upon the beauty of the Lord and to seek Him in His temple. For in the day of trouble, He will keep me safe in His dwelling, and He will hide me in the shelter of His tabernacle...My heart says of you "Seek His face!" Your face Lord, I will seek...wait for the Lord; be strong and take heart and wait for the Lord' (Psalm 27:1-14).

David was a warrior who clearly knew his identity and authority as a son of God. His desire was to gaze upon the beauty of the Lord and dwell in His Presence. He knew the safest place was to rest in His Presence, abiding under the shadow of His wing. David was an amazing Old Testament prototype of the warrior-bride.

Apostle John

John was known as the beloved disciple because of his close relationship with Jesus (John 13:23).

'Dear friends, let us love one another for love comes from God. Everyone who loves has been born of God and knows God. Whoever does not love doesn't know God, because God is love. This is how God showed His love among us: He sent His one and only Son into the world that we might live through Him. This is love: not that we loved God but that He loved us and sent His Son as an atoning sacrifice for our sins' (1 John 4:7-10).

John carried the heart of a bride but also had the heart of a warrior. He spoke specifically on overcoming the enemy as he reminded us that He who is in us is greater than he who is in the world. Also, there is no fear in love, because perfect love casts out fear (1 John 4:4,18). John knew that the reason the Son of God came was to destroy the works of the devil and to draw us back to the Father (1 John 3:8).

While John was in prison on the island of Patmos, he had an amazing encounter with the risen Lord. *'His head and hair were white as snow and His eyes like blazing fire. His feet were like bronze glowing in a furnace and His voice was like the sound of rushing waters. And out of His mouth came a sharp double-edged sword. His face was like the sun shining in all its brilliance'* (Revelation 1:14-16).

HE WHO OVERCOMES

John was caught up to Heaven and given the privilege of writing down what he saw taking place in the Heavenly realms. The Lord told him to write to the seven churches with words of encouragement and also warnings. At the end of each letter he wrote, *'To him who overcomes...'*. I believe the messages given to the seven churches apply to the body of Christ today, and God will reward His faithful ones who persevere in the midst of trials, by standing firm to the end.

One of the most awesome revelations was when John saw Jesus as the Captain of the armies of Heaven: *'I saw Heaven standing open and there before me was a white horse, whose rider is called Faithful and True. With justice He judges and makes war. His eyes are like blazing fire and on His head are many crowns. He is dressed in a robe dipped in blood, and His Name is the Word of God. The armies of Heaven were following Him, riding on white horses and dressed in fine linen, white and clean. Out of His mouth comes a sharp sword with which to strike down the nations. On His robe and on His thigh He has this name written: King of kings and Lord of lords'* (Revelation 19:7-8 +11-16).

Jesus will be returning with His army for His bride. She will be radiant, shining with His glory. One of the seven angels said to John: *'"Come, I will show you the bride, the wife of the Lamb". And he carried me away in the spirit to a mountain great and high, and showed me the Holy City, Jerusalem, coming down out of Heaven from God. It shone with the glory of God, and its brilliance was like that of a very precious jewel'* (Revelation 21:9-11).

John was a New Testament prototype of the warrior bride: one who overcomes, and a bride who has made herself ready for the Wedding of the Lamb (Revelation 19:7-9).

Both David and John loved the Lord with all their heart, such that they yielded their lives to Him. They were willing to fight and suffer for His Name, as they pursued His Presence in the midst of their enemies.

The saints will overcome by the blood of the Lamb and the powerful word of His (and their) Testimony, as they yield their lives to Him, even unto death.

Lord, I choose to yield every part of my life to You. Come and circumcise my heart, so I may overflow with the oil of Your Presence. Make my life no longer be my own but Yours. I belong to You. Lord, I choose to serve in Your army. So teach me, train me, transform my heart and mind, so I may overflow with Your love. Send me out with the fire of Your Spirit, to overcome the works of the enemy and to help prepare Your glorious bride for Your return. Come Lord Jesus, come!

END-NOTES

[1] *Nike* (Greek 3529): Strong's Exhaustive Bible Concordance : Red Letter Edition
[2] *Nikao* (Greek 3528); Strong's Exhaustive Bible Concordance: Red Letter Edition

Conclusion

God is raising up an army of laid-down lovers, an army of people who are utterly devoted to Him and to seeing His Kingdom come and His will be done; an army of worshipping warriors who passionately seek His face; an army who fear Him as they fervently pursue His holiness and hunger for His Presence. Each has chosen to lay down their lives and follow Him. They will go where He goes because they know the safest place is in His will and Presence.

I believe we are in the end-time battles and will see more natural disasters, attacks by militia groups, famines, wars, and biological weapons causing pandemics, than ever before. There has been an increase in fear and deception, false teaching, the spirit of anti-Christ and religious spirit across the nations. Our lives on earth are like a drop in the ocean compared to eternity. All that matters is that our hearts are ready for Jesus' return and in the meantime we do God's will and accomplish all He assigns us to do here on earth, as is written in our books in Heaven.

He has so much in store for us that is beyond our wildest dreams, and He is looking for those who will be His Bride. Who is willing to lay down their life, including their ambitions and plans, even their ministries, to co-labour with Him? He is looking for those who will follow the Lamb wherever He goes. Our life is no longer our own but His, as we choose to no longer come under the influences of this world but the influence of His Spirit.

The Book of Revelation is a mind-blowing wake-up call for God's people to get themselves ready for Jesus' return.

Forerunners to Prepare His Bride

The Lord is raising up forerunners, like John the Baptist, who will carry the spirit and anointing of Elijah. Elijah was called to oppose the enemy and turn the hearts of God's people back to Him. After he testified on Mount Carmel that the God of Abraham, Isaac and Jacob would consume his sacrifice with fire, he prayed, *'Answer me O Lord, answer me, so these people will know that You, O Lord, are God, and that **You are turning their hearts back again**'* (1 Kings 18:37).

The prophet Malachi confirmed over four hundred years later that the same spirit of Elijah would be sent to turn the hearts of God's people back to Him: *'See, I will send you the prophet Elijah before the great and dreadful Day of the Lord comes. He will **turn the hearts of the fathers to their children, and the hearts of the children to their fathers**'* (Malachi 4:5-6).

When the angel Gabriel spoke to Zechariah, he prophesied that his son would be a forerunner for the Lord. *'And he (John the Baptist) **will go on before the Lord, in the spirit and power of Elijah, to turn the hearts of the fathers to their children- to make ready a people prepared for the Lord**'* (Luke 1:17). The Lord is preparing people who will be forerunners and carry the spirit and power of Elijah. They will go ahead and prepare the hearts of God's people for the return of the Bridegroom King.

*'They will make war against the Lamb, **but the Lamb will overcome them, because He is King of kings and Lord of lords and with Him will be His called, chosen and faithful followers**'* (Revelation 17:14).

*'I saw the Holy City, the New Jerusalem, coming down out of Heaven from God, **prepared as a bride beautifully dressed for her Husband.** And I heard a loud voice from the throne saying, "**Now the dwelling of God is with men and He will live with them. They will be His people, and God Himself will be with them and be their God**"'*(Revelation 21:2-4).

The choice is ours. Let us be the bride who overcomes!

Appendix A: Prayer

Here is a prayer which when said on a regular basis can help to align our spirit to come under God, sanctify and protect our whole being, filter what we allow in and out, open our five senses to be influenced by the Holy Spirit and welcome God's seven-fold Spirit to teach, counsel and guide us. I have given sub-titles to highlight each area.

Aligning ourselves with the Spirit of God

Lord, I surrender my body, soul and spirit to You, as a living sacrifice on your altar of fire (Romans 12:1). Consume anything in me that is not of You. I command my flesh (body and soul) to come under my spirit, and my spirit to come under the influence of Your Holy Spirit. Holy Spirit, guide me in all my thoughts, choices and actions (mind, will and emotions), so they are pleasing in Your sight.

Sanctify the Mind

Lord, cleanse and sanctify my mind, will and emotions, including my thoughts and imagination, through the cleansing power of Your blood. I command any negative or unclean spirit(s) to leave in Jesus' Name. By faith I receive cleansing through the sanctifying power of Your blood. I bind and renounce any fears, lies or deceptive thoughts, and I ask for Your Spirit of truth, revelatory-wisdom and Spirit of discernment. (1 John 1:7 & 1 Thessalonians 5:23).

Divine Filters

Lord, filter what I allow in (hear, see, sense/feel, and smell/discern) and what I release out (think, speak and do) and prevent me from receiving or saying things not of You. Cover and protect my eye gate, ear gate and heart gate with the power of Your blood and convict me of sin where needed. (Ezekiel 44:5 guard what we let in and out of our inner sanctuary).

Welcome Seven-fold Spirit of God

I welcome Your Presence, including Your Spirit of Wisdom and, Understanding (including Truth & Revelation), Spirit of Counsel and Power, Spirit of Knowledge and the Fear of Lord, to guide me in all I see, think and do. Help me to see things from Your perspective and not my own opinion. Thank you Lord. I can do nothing without Your grace, so I lean on Your grace and supernatural strength to empower, teach and guide me, as well as meet my needs (Is 11:2-3, Ephesians 1)

Open Eyes, Ears and Senses

Lord, cleanse and sharpen my senses to see, hear, and feel more in the Spirit. Increase my hunger to know You more. Transform my heart and mind through the revelation of Your Word, Spirit and Truth (Hebrews 5:14). Help me to see things through Your lenses and from Your perspective at all times. Increase my spiritual awareness and discernment wherever I go.

Appendix B - Spiritual Discernment

Here is a list of things to help us discern if a word or thought is from God, the flesh, or devil.

GOD	FLESH/WORLD	DEVIL
Truth spoken in love & truth sets free	Man's opinion & fear-based, Or worldly facts	Lies/ twist in truth
Convicts with love		Condemns (no way out)
Unbiased / neutral	Biased	Underlying motive
Builds up the spirit	Builds up pride/ego/ feeds flesh (flattery)	Quenches the spirit
Wisdom of God (revealed by His Spirit)	Wisdom of man / worldly wisdom	False Judgement, fear-based & fault-finding
Revelation (God thoughts)	Logic/ common-sense/rational	Bribery/ tempts/ seeks power
God-focused (bears witness to God)	Self-focused / worldly focused	Draws away from God/ worship other things (idolatry)
Releases faith (not fear)	Anxious thoughts/ doubt	Pressure/ fear/ unbelief
Clarity/ understanding	Man's opinion	Confusion
Unity in the Spirit	Do it myself/ my way	Disunity/ break-ups
Releases peace/ freedom	Unease/ stress	Bondage/ oppression
See Fruit of Spirit: forgiveness, humility, love, servant heart, selfless, joy, peace, encourages, faith, glorifies God...	See Carnal nature: Jealousy, competition, pride, lust greed, hate, anger, bitterness, resentment, judges, critical, selfish, fear...	See Demonic spirits: Spirit of hate, lust, pride, unforgiveness, jealousy, fear, deception, fault-finding, false judgement...
Kingdom mindset	Traditional/ worldly beliefs	Demonic realm
God's Word	Opposes God's word	Twists/distorts God's word
Forgives	Guilt/shame/self-hate	Accuse/ blame/ point finger

1. Is it a man-made fact or TRUTH?
2. Does it glorify self or God?
3. Does it bring clarity or confusion?
4. Does it release faith or fear?
5. Does it bring life to your spirit or quench your spirit?
6. Does it build up your spirit? Does it pull you down & oppress you?
7. Does it convict or condemn?
8. Does it point to God's truth and Word?
9. Does it release freedom or bondage?
10. Does it bring peace or stress/ unease?
11. Is it Holy Spirit revelation or man's good opinion?
12. Does it reflect God's character & nature? (fruit of Spirit)
13. Does it draw you closer to God or away from Him?

HE WHO OVERCOMES

Appendix C

BY THE AUTHOR

Foundation For Healing is Volume 1 in the Kingdom Medicine series and provides a foundation for both the beginner and experienced in the healing ministry. It discusses the possible spiritual and emotional roots behind symptoms, how to take a spiritual history, as well as the ways to hear God and deal with the blockages to healing.

Healing Tools is Volume 2 in the Kingdom Medicine series and looks at the various keys to unlock areas in the heart to release healing and freedom. These tools will help identify the underlying issues as well as provide healing and include: *Forgiving from the Heart, Connecting to the Heart of the Father, Breaking Vows & Covenants, Cleansing the Blood-line, Blessing the Body, Spiritual Discernment* and more.

By the Author

Divine Heart Surgery is the third book in the Kingdom Medicine Series and is a more advanced way for ministering to deeper areas of the heart. It requires coming into God's Presence to assist the Great Surgeon, Jesus, operate on people's hearts. As we minister in His Presence, we have the privilege of seeing what He does, as He delicately heals the wounded and traumatized areas of the heart. Additional tools include *Accessing the Courts of Heaven, Synchronizing Wounded areas of the Heart back together, and Healing & Freedom from Abuse.*

Into His Chambers invites you to come deeper into the heart of God by encountering His chambers of *Belonging, Identity, Suffering Heart of Christ* and *Anointing.* It is full of revelatory insight to help you engage in a deeper level of son-ship, revealing the power of His grace and the cross. It invites you to encounter His Glory-Presence in the Holy of Holies, and become one who carries the heart of a prophet, priest, servant and king.

By the Author

Many may experience desert or wilderness seasons at some point in life, where God seems distant and we feel alone, confused, or don't know where we are going. Some may refer to it as the 'dark night of the soul'. *Fire in the Desert* reveals the reasons we may find ourselves in the spiritual desert and the various ways through. God never leaves us or deserts us. Instead, He longs for us to pursue Him. The desert is the perfect place for us to seek Him, hear His Spirit and encounter His Presence.

At the peak of her medical career, Angela had a call on her life to work amongst the poor in Africa. What she didn't know was that God was going to derail her and take her down an unfamiliar path. As she obeyed God's call, she discovered another realm to sickness and disease; a realm that wasn't found in medical textbooks. Instead she received "on the job training" from the Great Physician Himself. This book combines faith with medicine, the supernatural with the natural and the physical with the emotional and spiritual, as you read the powerful testimonies and teachings on how to heal the sick, God's way!

Appendix D

ABOUT THE AUTHOR

Angela Walker qualified as a doctor at Liverpool Medical School in 1991 and went on to pursue a career in Paediatrics and Child Health at the London teaching hospitals. She furthered her studies by taking a master's degree in Clinical Paediatrics, followed by a diploma in Tropical Medicine and Hygiene. After this she served with Voluntary Services Oversees as a Paediatric lecturer for eighteen months in Uganda.

After becoming a consultant in 2004 she went on to study at All Nations Bible College in Hertfordshire. Following this, she served with Iris Global for seven years on the mission field in Africa, where she practiced Kingdom Medicine. During this time she discovered there could be spiritual and emotional roots to sickness and disease which prompted her to write her first book, 'Healing God's Way'.

She is an inspirational teacher, trainer and pioneer with a passion to see hearts restored, people set free, lives transformed and God's Kingdom advance across the nations. She is the founder and director of THEO Ministries.

For copies of her books, retreats, training & ministry courses, or other enquiries please visit the web or email:

www.theoministries.com
www.amazon.com/author/drangelawalker
info@theoministries.com

Printed in Great Britain
by Amazon